Microsoft®

Internet Explorer 5
Step by Step

PUBLISHED BY
Microsoft Press
A Division of Microsoft Corporation
One Microsoft Way
Redmond, Washington 98052-6399

Library of Congress Cataloging-in-Publication Data
Microsoft Internet Explorer 5 Step by Step / ActiveEducation, Inc.
      p.   cm.
     Includes index.
     ISBN 1-57231-968-2
     1. Microsoft Internet Explorer. 2. Internet (Computer network) 3. World Wide Web (Information retrieval
system)
    I. ActiveEducation (Firm)
  TK5105.883.M53M5356 1999
  005.7'13769--dc21   98-48191
                                            CIP
Printed and bound in the United States of America.

1 2 3 4 5 6 7 8 9 WCWC 4 3 2 1 0 9

Distributed in Canada by ITP Nelson, a division of Thomson Canada Limited.

A CIP catalogue record for this book is available from the British Library.

Microsoft Press books are available through booksellers and distributors worldwide. For further information about
international editions, contact your local Microsoft Corporation office. Or contact Microsoft Press International directly
at fax (425) 936-7329. Visit our Web site at mspress.microsoft.com.

For ActiveEducation, Inc.
Managing Editor: Ron Pronk
Project Editor: Holly Freeman
Writer: Mary Millhollon
Production/Layout: Kate Dawson
Technical Editors: Kate Dawson, Rebecca Van Esselstine
Indexer: Lisa Probasco
Proofreader: Noel Carlson

For Microsoft Press
Acquisitions Editor: Susanne M. Forderer
Project Editor: Jenny Moss Benson

Contents

*Quick*Look Guide vii

Finding Your Best Starting Point xiii

Finding Your Best Starting Point in This Book xiii • New Features in
Internet Explorer 5 xv • Corrections, Comments, and
Help xvi • Visit Our World Wide Web Site xvi

Using the Microsoft Internet Explorer 5 Step by Step CD-ROM xvii

Installing Microsoft Internet Explorer 5 xviii • Installing the Practice
Files xviii • Using the Practice Files xix • Using the Multimedia
Files xx • Uninstalling the Practice Files xx • Need Help with the
Practice Files? xxi

Conventions and Features in This Book xxiii

Conventions xxiii • Other Features of This Book xxiv

PART 1 **Using Internet Explorer 5: The Basics**   **1**

Lesson 1 **Exploring the Web** 3

Starting Microsoft Internet Explorer 4 • Browsing a Web
Site 6 • Creating a Desktop Shortcut to a Web Page 14 • Printing
Web Page Information 15 • One Step Further: Saving Web
Pages 21 • Lesson 1 Quick Reference 25

Lesson 2 **Finding and Managing Information** 27

Searching for Information on the Web 28 • Creating a Favorites List
34 • Using Favorites 37 • Managing Your Favorites List 38 • Using
the History Folder 43 • One Step Further: Managing Your Temporary
Internet Files 46 • Lesson 2 Quick Reference 49

Lesson 3   **Customizing Your Work Space** **51**

Specifying Your Home Page 52 • Using the Status
Bar 53 • Customizing Your View 54 • Customizing the Toolbar 60
• Working with the Links Toolbar 64 • One Step Further: Specifying
How Links Appear 65 • Lesson 3 Quick Reference 69

Part 1   **Review & Practice** **71**

PART 2   Optimizing Internet Explorer 5 Features   77

Lesson 4   **Activating Security and Personal Information Settings** **79**

Customizing Internet Explorer's Security Settings 80 • Setting Content Rating Preferences 86 • Adding Personal Information to
Microsoft Wallet 92 • One Step Further: Adding Components
98 • Lesson 4 Quick Reference 100

Lesson 5   **Working Offline** **103**

Marking Web Sites for Offline Viewing 104 • Synchronizing Offline
Web Pages 107 • Automating Offline Web Page
Synchronization 110 • Viewing Offline Web Pages 115 • One Step
Further: Managing Offline Web Pages 118 • Lesson 5 Quick Refer-
ence 120

Lesson 6   **Enjoying Multimedia on the Web** **123**

Recognizing Graphics File Formats 124 • Using Windows Media
Player 129 • Configuring Multimedia Options 133 • One Step Further: Using Shockwave 137 • Lesson 6 Quick Reference 138

Part 2   **Review & Practice** **139**

PART 3   Communicating on the Internet   143

Lesson 7   **Managing Your Electronic Mail** **145**

Starting Outlook Express 146 • Creating and Sending
Messages 148 • Receiving Messages 156 • Forwarding and
Responding to Messages 163 • Printing Messages 165 • Managing
Your Address Book 166 • Using Electronic Business Cards 172
• Finding E-mail Addresses on the Internet 173 • One Step Further:
Using Digital IDs 175 • Lesson 7 Quick Reference 179

Lesson 8   **Participating in Newsgroups** **183**

Getting Acquainted with Newsgroups 184 • Viewing Newsgroup
Messages 191 • Accessing Newsgroups Offline 196 • Posting
Messages 199 • Printing Messages 203 • One Step Further: Cleaning Up Your Outlook Express Folders 204 • Lesson 8 Quick Reference 208

Lesson 9   **Collaborating on the Internet with NetMeeting** **211**

Starting NetMeeting 212 • Calling Meeting
Participants 214 • Using Audio and Video Capabilities 221 • Using
the Chat Window 226 • Drawing on the Whiteboard 228 • Sharing
Files and Applications 235 • One Step Further: Using Microsoft's
Online Support 241 • Lesson 9 Quick Reference 244

Part 3   **Review & Practice** **247**

Appendix A   **Installation and Setup Procedures** **251**

Installing Internet Explorer 252 • Connecting to the
Internet 255 • Setting Up Your E-mail and News Accounts 259
• Specifying Default E-mail and Newsreader
Applications 263 • Configuring NetMeeting 264 • Using a Con-
figuration Script 267

Appendix B   **If You're New to Windows** **269**

If You're New to Windows 269 • Using the Mouse 270 • Using
Window Controls 271 • Using Dialog Boxes 275 • Getting Help
with Windows 276 • Viewing Help Contents 277 • Finding Help
About Specific Topics 278

Index **285**

*Quick*Look Guide

Stopping a page from downloading, see Lesson 1, page 12

Refreshing a Web page, see Lesson 1, page 13

Printing Web pages, see Lesson 1, page 18

Using the Address bar, see Lesson 2, page 33

Using the Search Assistant, see Lesson 2, page 30

Finding text on a Web page, see Lesson 1, page 14

Viewing your history, see Lesson 2, page 44

Adding a Web page to your Favorites list, see Lesson 2, page 34

Configuring your history settings, see Lesson 2, page 45

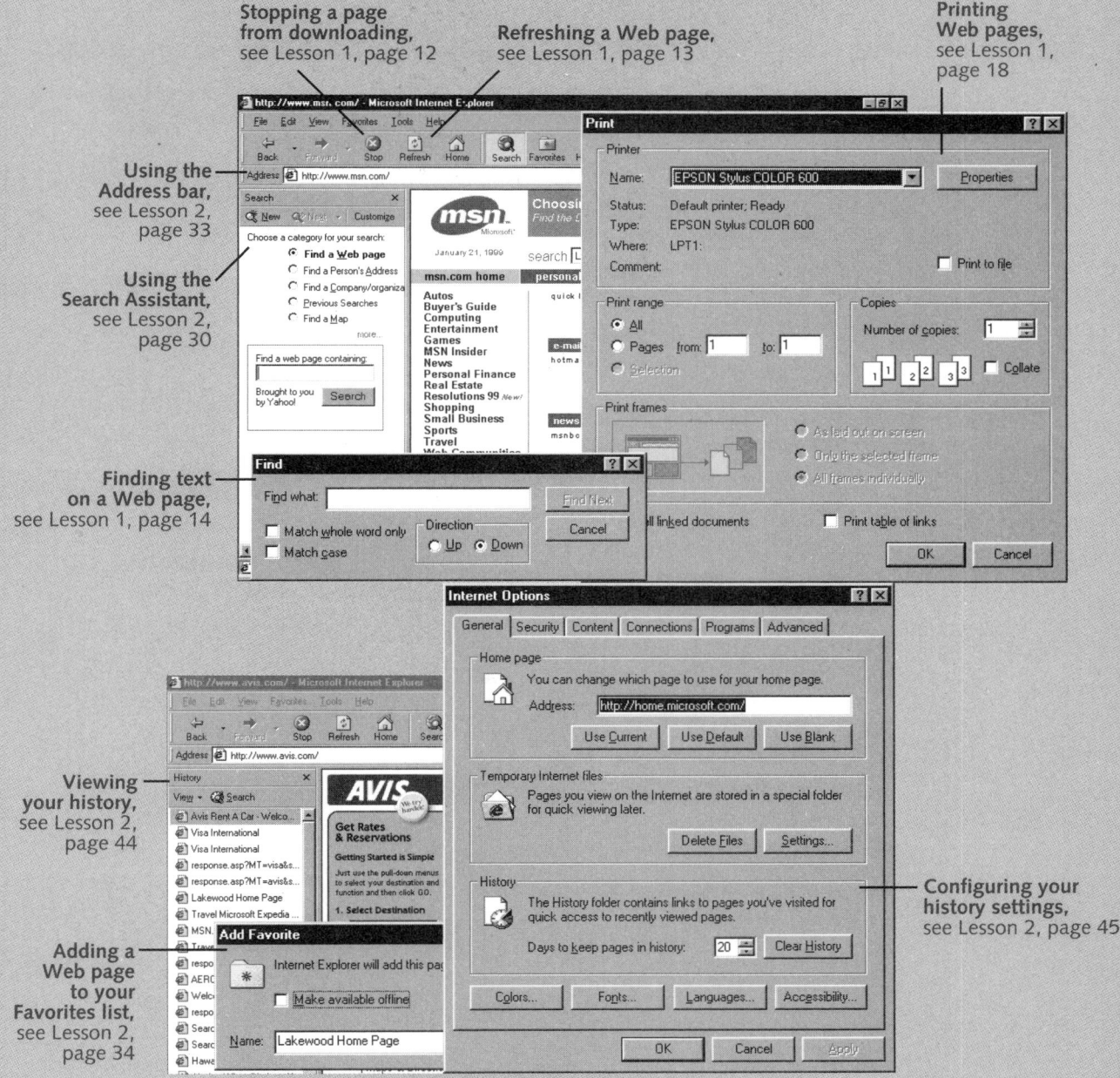

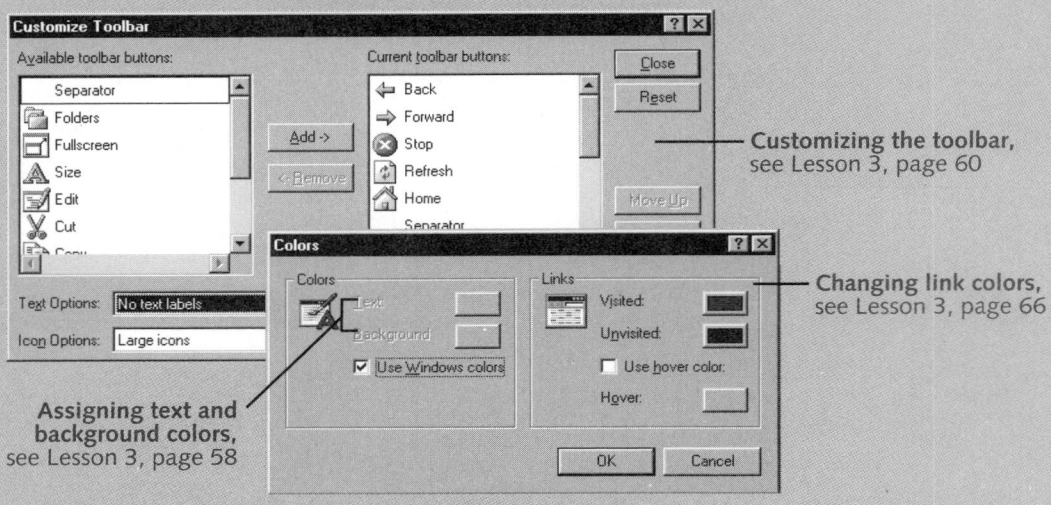

Customizing the toolbar,
see Lesson 3, page 60

Changing link colors,
see Lesson 3, page 66

**Assigning text and
background colors,**
see Lesson 3, page 58

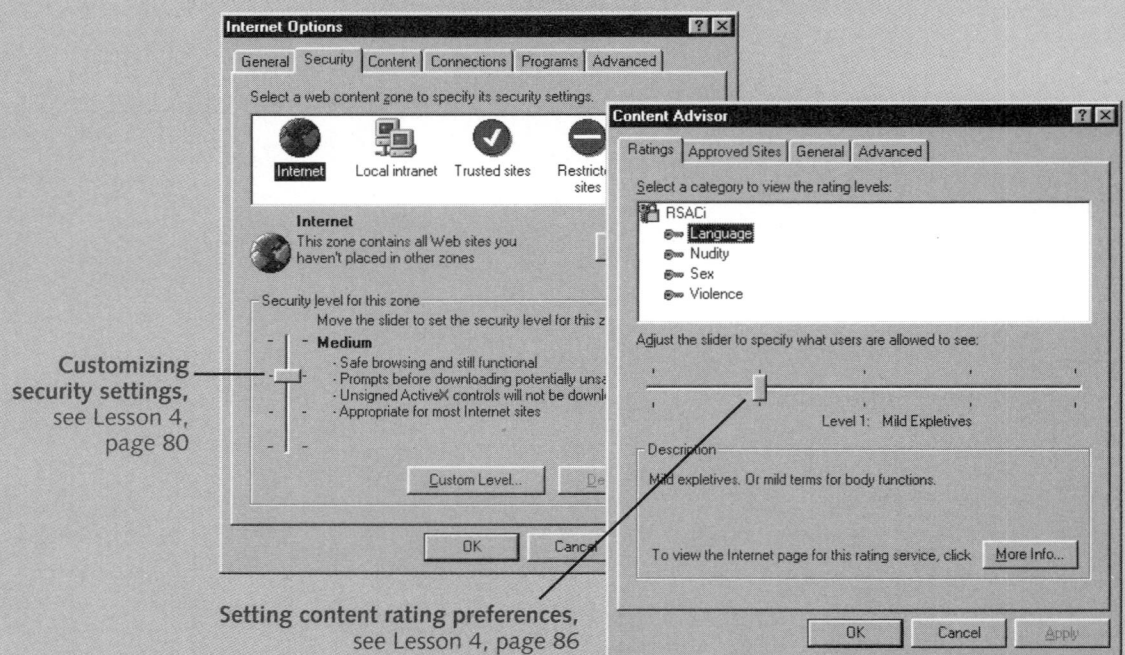

**Customizing
security settings,**
see Lesson 4,
page 80

Setting content rating preferences,
see Lesson 4, page 86

**Marking Web sites
for offline viewing,**
see Lesson 5, page 104

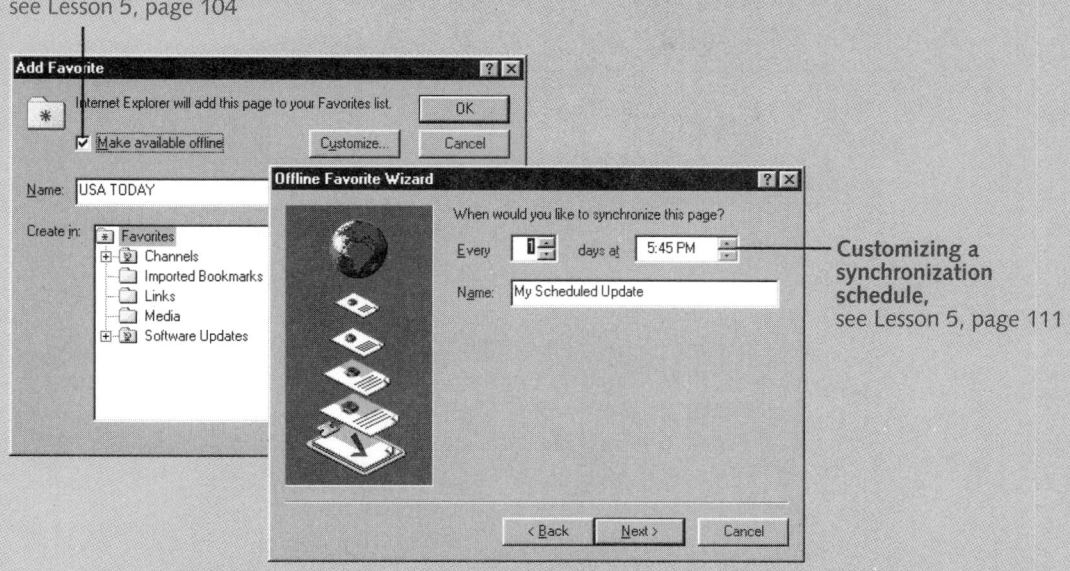

**Customizing a
synchronization
schedule,**
see Lesson 5, page 111

**Creating
and sending
e-mail messages,**
see Lesson 7, page 148

**Creating e-mail
messages using
stationery,**
see Lesson 7, page 153

**Configuring
multimedia options,**
see Lesson 6, page 133

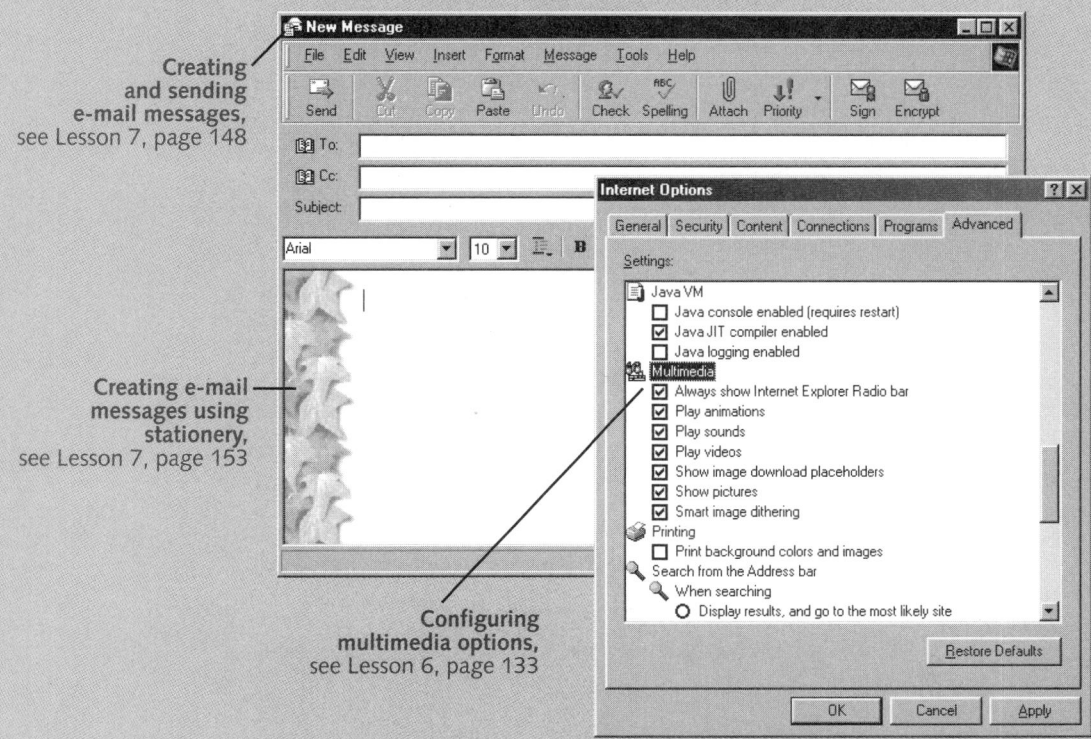

Creating a group to send multiple e-mail messages, see Lesson 7, page 169

Using your Address Book, see Lesson 7, page 168

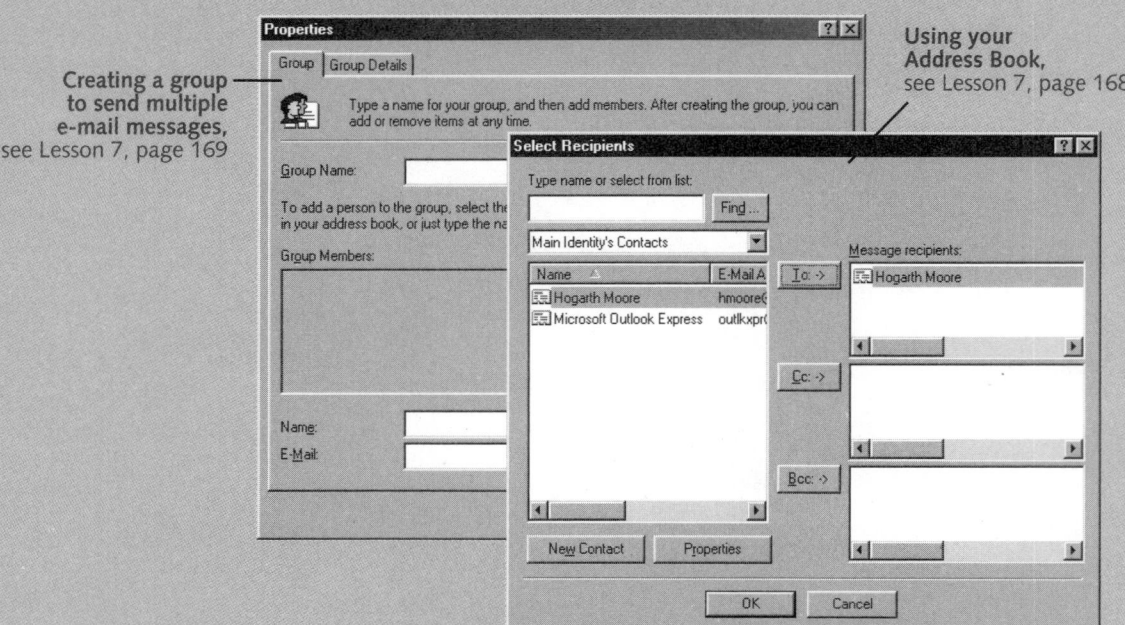

Posting messages to a newsgroup, see Lesson 8, page 199

Finding a newsgroup, see Lesson 8, page 187

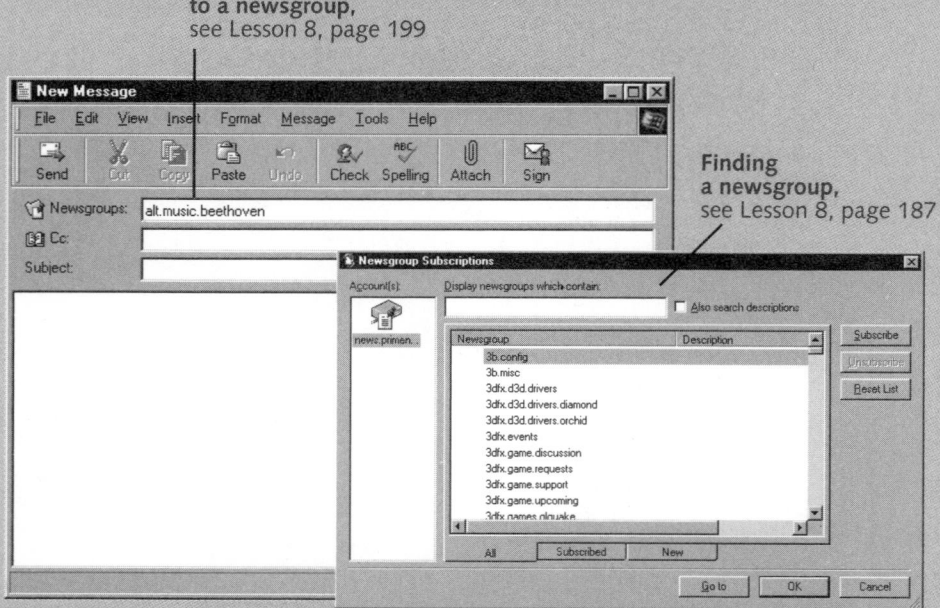

Using audio and video,
see Lesson 9, page 221

**Using the
Whiteboard,**
see Lesson 9,
page 231

**Calling meeting
participants,**
see Lesson 9,
page 214

Using the Chat window,
see Lesson 9, page 226

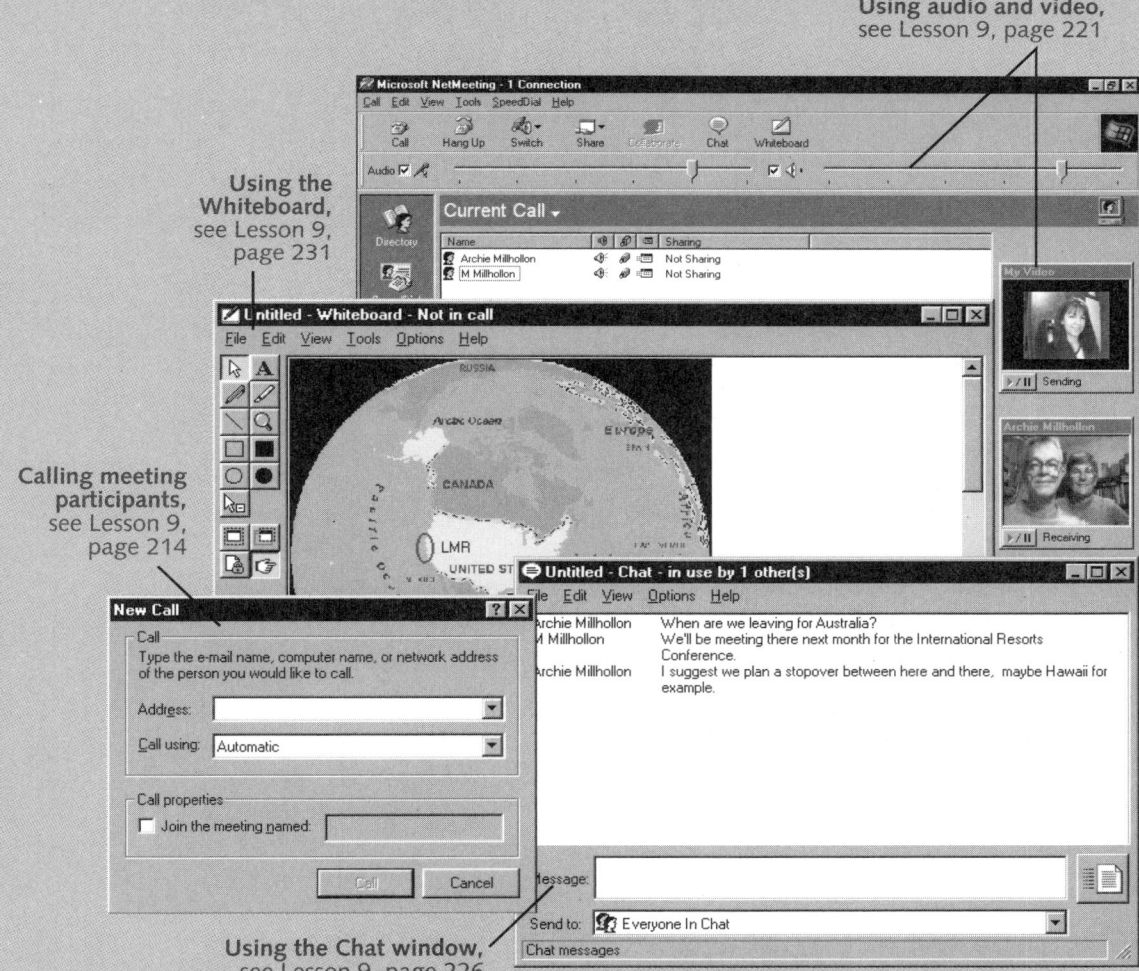

Finding Your Best Starting Point

Microsoft Internet Explorer 5 is the newest Microsoft browser for personal computers. Internet Explorer 5 expands the foundation of Internet Explorer 4 to allow you to take full advantage of the latest developments in browser technology. Whether you use a browser for your job, for your personal interests, or for both, you will find that Internet Explorer 5 is efficient, fast, and reliable. With *Internet Explorer 5 Step by Step,* you will quickly and easily learn how to use Internet Explorer 5.

Finding Your Best Starting Point in This Book

This book is organized for beginning users of browsers, as well as readers who have had experience with these types of programs and are switching or upgrading their current browser to Internet Explorer 5. Use the following tables to find your best starting point in this book.

If you are		Follow these steps
New		
To computers, Windows, or Microsoft Internet Explorer	**1**	Install the practice files as described in "Using the Microsoft Internet Explorer 5 Step by Step CD-ROM."
	2	Become aquainted with the Windows operating system and how to use the online Help system by working through Appendix B, "If You're New to Windows."
	3	Learn basic skills for using Microsoft Internet Explorer 5 by working through Lessons 1 through 3.

If you are	Follow these steps
New	
To browsers	❶ Work through Appendix A.
	❷ Work through Lessons 1 through 3 in sequence.
	❸ Work through Lessons 4 through 9 as needed.

If you are	Follow these steps
Switching	
From a different browser	❶ Work through Appendix A.
	❷ Skim through Lessons 1 and 2 to review basic browsing concepts.
	❸ Work through Lessons 3 through 9 in sequence to learn the Internet Explorer approach to browsing.

If you are	Follow these steps
Upgrading	
From Internet Explorer 4	❶ Work through Appendix A.
	❷ Skim through Lessons 1 and 2 to review basic browsing concepts and learn about some of the new features in Internet Explorer.
	❸ Work through the section "One Step Further: Adding Components" in Lesson 4 to learn how to add and upgrade Internet Explorer's components.
	❹ Work through the other lessons as needed to review Internet Explorer and learn about other new features.

If you are	Follow these steps
Referencing	
This book after working through the lessons	❶ Use the index to locate information about specific topics, and use the Table of Contents to locate information about general topics.
	❷ Read the Quick Reference at the end of each lesson for a brief review of the major topics in the lesson. The Quick Reference topics are presented in the same order as the topics are presented in the lesson.

New Features in Internet Explorer 5

The following table lists the major new features of Internet Explorer 5 covered in this book and the lesson in which you can learn how to use each feature. You can also use the index to find specific information about a feature or about a task you want to perform.

The New! icon appears in the margin throughout this book to indicate these new features of Internet Explorer 5.

To learn how to	See
Save Web Pages	Lesson 1
Search with the Search Assistant	Lesson 2
Add and organize Web pages with the Favorites bar	Lesson 2
Customize icons on the toolbar	Lesson 3
Use Microsoft Wallet	Lesson 4
View multimedia on the Windows Media Player	Lesson 6
Find additional stationery for e-mail messages	Lesson 7
Create a block senders list	Lesson 7
Use the preview pane to view an attachment	Lesson 7
Use electronic business cards	Lesson 7
Clean up Outlook Express folders using the Maintenance tab	Lesson 8
Upload files via FTP	Lesson 9

Corrections, Comments, and Help

Every effort has been made to ensure the accuracy of this book and the contents of the Microsoft Internet Explorer 5 Step by Step CD-ROM. Microsoft Press provides corrections and additional content for its books through the World Wide Web at *mspress.microsoft.com/support*

If you have comments, questions, or ideas regarding this book or the CD-ROM, please send them to us.

Send e-mail to:

mspinput@microsoft.com

Or send postal mail to:

Microsoft Press

Attn: Step by Step Editor

One Microsoft Way

Redmond, WA 98052-6399

Please note that support for the Internet Explorer software product itself is not offered through the above addresses. For help using Internet Explorer 5, you can call Internet Explorer 5 Technical Support at (425) 635-7070 on weekdays between 6 A.M. and 6 P.M. Pacific Time.

Visit Our World Wide Web Site

We invite you to visit the Microsoft Press World Wide Web site. You can visit us at the following location:

mspress.microsoft.com

You'll find descriptions of all of our books, information about ordering titles, notices of special features and events, additional content for Microsoft Press books, and much more.

You can also find out the latest in software developments and news from Microsoft Corporation by visiting the following World Wide Web site:

microsoft.com

We look forward to your visit on the Web!

Using the Microsoft Internet Explorer 5 Step by Step CD-ROM

The CD-ROM inside the back cover of this book contains Microsoft Internet Explorer 5, the practice files that you'll use as you perform the exercises in the book, and multimedia files that demonstrate nine of the exercises. When you use the practice files, you won't waste time creating the samples used in the lessons, and you can concentrate on learning how to use Microsoft Internet Explorer 5. With the files and the step-by-step instructions in the lessons, you'll also learn by doing, which is an easy and effective way to acquire and remember new skills.

important

Before you break the seal on the Microsoft Internet Explorer 5 Step by Step CD-ROM package, be sure that this book matches the version of Internet Explorer that you want to use. If you have an earlier version of Internet Explorer installed on your computer, you can upgrade to Microsoft Internet Explorer 5 by using the Microsoft Internet Explorer Step by Step CD-ROM in the package inside the back cover of this book. If you don't want to install Microsoft Internet Explorer 5, a Step by Step book matching your software is probably available. Please visit our World Wide Web site at *mspress.microsoft.com* or call 1-800-MSPRESS (1-800-677-7377) for more information.

Installing Microsoft Internet Explorer 5

You can install Microsoft Internet Explorer 5 from the CD-ROM included with this book.

1. If your computer isn't on, turn it on now.
2. If you're connected to a network, you will see a dialog box asking for your user name and password.
3. Type your user name and password in the appropriate boxes, and click OK. If you see the Welcome dialog box, click the Close button.

Close

4. Remove the CD-ROM from the package inside the back cover of this book.
5. Insert the CD-ROM in the CD-ROM drive of your computer.
6. On the Windows taskbar, click the Start button, and click Run.
7. In the Run dialog box, click Browse.
8. In the Browse dialog box, navigate to the CD contents, double-click the msie5 folder, and double-click the file named Setup.
9. In the Run dialog box, click OK.
10. Click Install Internet Explorer 5 And Internet Tools.
11. Read the End User License Agreement, click the I Accept The Agreement option, and then click Next.
12. In the Windows Update dialog box, make sure the Install Now – Typical Set Of Components option is selected, and click Next.
13. After the installation and optimization processes are complete, save and close all other open files, and then click Finish in the Windows Update dialog box.

Installing the Practice Files

Follow these steps to install the practice files on your computer's hard disk so that you can use them with the exercises in this book.

1. Remove the CD-ROM from the package inside the back cover of this book.
2. Insert the CD-ROM in the CD-ROM drive of your computer. In My Computer, double-click your CD-ROM drive.
3. Double-click the Setup file, and then follow the instructions on the screen.

   The setup program window appears with recommended options preselected for you. For best results in using the practice files for this book, accept these preselected settings.

④ When the files have been installed, remove the CD-ROM from your CD-ROM drive and replace it in the package inside the back cover of the book.

A folder called Internet Explorer 5 SBS Practice has been created on your hard disk, and the practice files have been placed in that folder.

If your computer is set up to connect to the Internet, you can double-click the Microsoft Press Welcome shortcut to visit the Microsoft Press Web site. You can also connect to this Web site directly at *mspress.microsoft.com*.

Using the Practice Files

The lessons in this book explain when and how to use any practice files for that lesson. The lessons are built around scenarios that simulate a real work environment, so you can easily apply the skills you learn to your own work. For the scenario in this book, imagine you are an executive in the small public relations firm, Impact Public Relations. The firm specializes in designing multimedia campaigns including print, radio, and television ads for mid-sized companies.

For those of you who like to know all the details, here's a list of the practice files used in the lessons.

Filename	Description
Lesson 1 - folder	Folder used in Lesson 1
Archived Web Page.mht	File used in Lesson 1
Complete Web Page.htm	File used in Lesson 1
Html Only.htm	File used in Lesson 1
Text File.txt	File used in Lesson 1
Lesson 1 - Complete Web page files - folder	Folder used in Lesson 1
Bac315.TMP	File used in Lesson 1
Default2.htm_cmp_expeditn110_bnr	File used in Lesson 1
exphorsa.gif	File used in Lesson 1
exptextb.jpg	File used in Lesson 1
FrontPageLogo.gif	File used in Lesson 1
Main_building.jpg	File used in Lesson 1
Lesson 7 - folder	Folder used in Lesson 7
Letter.doc	File used in Lesson 7
Lesson 9 - folder	Folder used in Lesson 9
Facts.txt	File used in Lesson 9
World.doc	File used in Lesson 9

Using the Multimedia Files

Throughout this book, you will see icons for movie files for particular exercises. Use the following steps to play the multimedia files.

1 Insert the Microsoft Internet Explorer 5 Step by Step CD-ROM in your CD-ROM drive.

2 On the Windows taskbar, click the Start button, point to Programs, and then click Windows Explorer.

3 In the All Folders area, click the drive D icon (or the appropriate CD-ROM drive letter).

The contents of the CD-ROM are displayed.

4 In the Contents Of area, double-click the Multimedia folder.

The Multimedia folder opens.

5 Double-click the multimedia file that you want to view.

Windows Media Player runs the video of the exercise.

Close

6 After the video is finished, click the Close button in the top-right corner of the Media Player window.

Media Player closes and you return to Windows Explorer.

7 Close Windows Explorer, and return to the exercise in the book.

Uninstalling the Practice Files

Use the following steps when you want to delete the practice files added to your hard disk by the Step by Step setup program.

1 On the Windows taskbar, click the Start button, point to Settings, and then click Control Panel.

2 Double-click the Add/Remove icon.

The Add/Remove Programs Properties dialog box appears.

3 Click Microsoft Internet Explorer 5 Step by Step Practice from the list, and then click Add/Remove.

A confirmation message is displayed.

4 Click Yes.

The practice files are uninstalled.

5 Click OK to close the Add/Remove Programs Properties dialog box.

6 Close the Control Panel window.

Need Help with the Practice Files?

Every effort has been made to ensure the accuracy of this book and the contents of the Microsoft Internet Explorer 5 Step by Step CD-ROM. If you do run into a problem, Microsoft Press provides corrections for its books through the World Wide Web at:

mspress.microsoft.com/support/

We invite you to visit our main Web page at:

mspress.microsoft.com

You'll find descriptions of all of our books, information about ordering titles, notices of special features and events, additional content for Microsoft Press books, and much more.

Conventions and Features in This Book

You can save time when you use this book by understanding, before you start the lessons, how instructions, keys to press, and so on are shown in the book. Please take a moment to read the following list, which also points out helpful features of the book that you might want to use.

Conventions

- Hands-on exercises for you to follow are given in numbered lists of steps (1, 2, and so on). A round bullet (●) indicates an exercise that has only one step.

- Text that you are to type appears in **bold**.

- A plus sign (+) between two key names means that you must press those keys at the same time. For example, "Press Alt+Tab" means that you hold down the Alt key while you press Tab.

- The icons on the following page are used to identify certain types of exercise features.

Icon	Alerts you to
	Skills that are demonstrated in multimedia files available on the Microsoft Internet Explorer 5 Step by Step CD-ROM.
	New features in Internet Explorer 5.

Other Features of This Book

■ You can get a quick reminder of how to perform the tasks you learned by reading the Quick Reference at the end of a lesson.

■ You can practice the major skills presented in the lessons by working through the Review & Practice section at the end of each part.

■ You can see a multimedia demonstration of some of the exercises in the book by following the instructions in the "Using the Multimedia Files" exercise in the "Using the Microsoft Internet Explorer 5 Step by Step CD-ROM" section of this book.

PART 1

Using Internet Explorer 5: The Basics

1

Exploring the Web

**ESTIMATED
TIME
30 min.**

In this lesson you will learn how to:

✔ *Start Microsoft Internet Explorer.*

✔ *Browse a Web site.*

✔ *Create a desktop shortcut to a Web page.*

✔ *Print Web page information.*

✔ *Save Web pages.*

Almost everyone has heard of the Internet, and most people know that *www* and *dotcom* have something to do with Web pages. But the Internet is much more than just Web page addresses. With the Internet, you can read up-to-the-minute news reports, reserve plane tickets, listen to music, send and receive electronic messages, get weather reports, shop, conduct research, and much more.

Microsoft Internet Explorer 5 helps you "get on the Net," and *Microsoft Internet Explorer 5 Step by Step* allows you to learn about the Internet at your own pace. By learning how to use Internet Explorer, you'll be able to take advantage of the Internet and its generous supply of information.

If you want an introduction to the Internet and the World Wide Web, if you need to learn just the latest features of Internet Explorer 5, or if you're switching to Internet Explorer from another product, this book is for you. You can work through this book from cover to cover, or you can skip around—turning to sections that help you most as you browse the Web.

In this lesson, you'll master techniques for using Internet Explorer and learn some Internet basics along the way. Whether your learning curve is a gentle slope or a near-vertical incline, this lesson gets you started on a sure-footed path toward using Internet Explorer.

Before heading too far down the path, though, a fundamental concept needs to be addressed—the difference between the Internet and the World Wide Web. The *Internet* is a network of computers, cables, routers, and other hardware and software that interconnect and run on a network. The *World Wide Web* consists of documents that are transmitted across the Internet's hardware. The Web is made up of *Web pages* and *Web sites*. A Web page is a specially formatted document that can include text, graphics, hyperlinks, audio, animation, and video. A *Web site* is a collection of Web pages. Here's where Internet Explorer steps in—before you can view Web pages, you need a *browser* such as Internet Explorer.

Internet Explorer incorporates Microsoft's most advanced techniques for finding, viewing, and managing information on the Internet. The Internet stores millions of Web pages, and your browser is your key to displaying and finding the information you want. The Internet can tell you exactly what you need to know, and it can provide information you didn't even know you wanted. It can also waste hours of your time if you don't know how to manage the data, or if you're using an outdated browser. By using Internet Explorer, you can ensure that you're getting the best return for your Internet time.

Setting the Scene

To demonstrate how the exercises in this book can apply to your day-to-day tasks, a scenario is carried throughout the text. Imagine you are the main contact for a public relations firm, Impact Public Relations, and you're promoting Lakewood Mountains Resort, a luxury resort. You're using Microsoft Internet Explorer to gather information for your work.

important

The exercises in this book assume that your desktop has the Web Style feature enabled, including the single-click feature. To turn on the Web Style feature, click Start on the Windows taskbar, point to Settings, and then click Folder Options. In the Folder Options dialog box, select Web Style, and click the OK button. If the Single-click dialog box appears, click OK.

Starting Microsoft Internet Explorer

The best way to learn about the Internet is to jump right in. Of course, you must get to the water before you can dive in, so make sure you've configured a connection before starting Internet Explorer.

You can connect to the Internet via a phone line, a modem, and an Internet service provider (ISP), or you can link to the Internet through a local area network (LAN), such as a company's network.

important

The exercises throughout this book assume you are connected to the Internet through either a LAN or a dial-up connection. For more information about establishing a dial-up connection, see Appendix A, "Installation and Setup Procedures."

Start Internet Explorer

In this exercise, you start Internet Explorer so you can begin exploring the Web.

Desktop Shortcut

● Click the Internet Explorer icon on your desktop.

The Internet Explorer window opens and displays your Internet home page.

If necessary, click the Maximize button to maximize the Internet Explorer window.

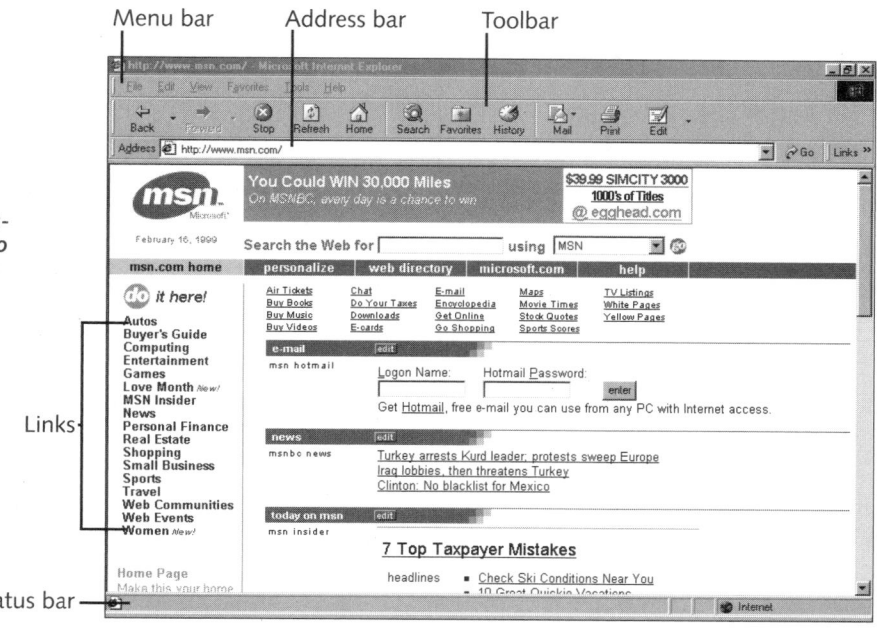

One of the Internet's greatest assets is that it can provide continuously updated content. Therefore, you might notice that the content on the page displayed on your screen is different from the content shown in the illustration.

Browsing a Web Site

After you connect to the Internet and open Internet Explorer, you're ready to start browsing for information. You can access Web pages in two ways: you can type an address in the Address bar, or you can click *hyperlinks* (also called *links*) to move from one Web page to another. Hyperlinks are Web page elements that connect Internet documents. They can appear as text (usually displayed in a different color and underlined) or graphical elements such as buttons. Click a hyperlink to a Web page, and almost instantly, you're there.

Both techniques—typing an address and clicking hyperlinks—use a *Uniform Resource Locator* (URL), or an Internet address. URLs are used to access a particular Internet document. When you enter an address in the Address bar, you manually enter the document's URL. When you click a hyperlink, the browser automatically places the URL in the Address bar and displays the document.

A URL identifies where a document is stored on the Internet. URLs are like street addresses. Just as a street address consists of several parts—number, street, city, state, and postal code—each URL consists of the parts of an Internet address—protocol, domain name, directory path, and filename.

The table below breaks down the following Lakewood Mountains Resort address: *http://mspress.microsoft.com/mspress/products/1349/recreation.htm.*

Example	Component	Definition
http://	Protocol	Indicates that your browser should transfer the document using the Hypertext Transfer Protocol (HTTP). (A *protocol* is a set of rules that one computer uses to "talk" to another computer.) Web documents always use the HTTP protocol.
mspress. microsoft.com	Domain name	Identifies the address of the computer (or *server*) where the document is stored. These are often divided into three parts: *mspress* (indicates that the document is on the Microsoft Press Web); *microsoft* (the name of the computer where the Web is stored, sometimes called the *second-level domain name*); and *com* (a two-letter or three-letter extension that identifies the Web page type, also called the *top-level domain*).

Example	Component	Definition
mspress/ products/1349	Folder path	Identifies where the document is stored. URLs can reference folders within folders, which is just like your desktop's file and folder organization.
recreation.htm	Filename	Names the specific Web page to be displayed in your browser. If no filename is specified in the URL, the browser displays the Web site's index.htm or default.htm Web page. These pages are generally the main or starting pages (usually called the *home* pages).

Top-Level Domain Names

Many types of organizations maintain Web sites. To make Web addresses easier to understand, they contain an identifier (or top-level Web domain) that classifies the type of organization the name represents. Following are the seven most common top-level domain extensions.

Extension	Organization
.com	Commercial organization within the United States
.edu	Educational institution
.gov	Agency or branch of the government
.int	International organization
.mil	U.S. military site
.net	Networking service (such as an ISP)
.org	Other organizations

In addition to these top-level domain names, a Web address can also supply a country code. For example, .jp is the code for a Japanese Web site and .il is the code for an Israeli Web site. You can view a list of these codes at *www.ics.uci.edu/pub/websoft/wwwstat/country-codes.txt*.

Common Internet Protocols

Occasionally, you'll need to retrieve an Internet file that isn't a Web page and doesn't use the Web's HTTP protocol. The following list provides some of the Internet's more common protocols and their descriptions.

Protocol	Definition
file://	Indicates a path to a file stored on your local hard disk drive or on your network. In Internet Explorer, instead of entering this protocol, you can simply enter your drive letter, such as C:\.
ftp://	Specifies the File Transfer Protocol. This protocol is used to send and retrieve entire documents without displaying the document in your browser. For example, you can use the FTP protocol to send a Microsoft Word document from your computer to another computer connected to the Internet. Then the recipient can open the document in Word.
gopher://	Distributes documents using a menu-based system. Gopher originated at the University of Minnesota (yes, it's named after their mascot), and it has been largely superseded by Web search engines.
http://	Specifies the Hypertext Transfer Protocol. This protocol is used to access Web pages on the Internet and other networks.
https://	Specifies the Hypertext Transfer Protocol, Secure. This is used to access Web pages on the Internet and other networks, using a more secure transmission procedure than the HTTP protocol.
telnet://	Enables you to log on to and work on a remote system just as if the programs and files stored on the remote computer were available on your own computer.
wais://	Stands for the Wide Area Information Server protocol. WAIS is a distributed information retrieval system similar to gopher and the Web.

Internet Explorer offers many helpful features that come into play when you enter a URL in the Address bar. For example, when you access a Web page, you don't need to type in the protocol. Furthermore, you can frequently guess a company's Web page address by inserting the company's name as the second-level domain name. For example, you can retrieve the home page of the Sears Web site by typing *www.sears.com* in the Address bar and pressing Enter. The http:// portion of the Sears URL is automatically inserted by Internet Explorer.

When you enter a URL in the Address bar or click a hyperlink, you spark a series of events. First you tell Internet Explorer which document you want to view. Then Internet Explorer contacts the computer storing the document. After the computer is located, Internet Explorer *downloads* the document to your computer. In other words, Internet Explorer copies and transfers the Web page data from the computer storing the Web page to your computer. Internet Explorer then interprets the data and displays the Web page on your screen.

Back

Forward

After you display a few Web pages, you can quickly navigate among the pages you have visited during the current session. To revisit a previously displayed Web page, you click the Back button on Internet Explorer's toolbar. Likewise, if you've used the Back button at least once, you can use the Forward button to return to a site you visited before going back.

Other times while you are accessing Web pages, you might change your mind about downloading a Web page. Maybe you mistyped the URL in the Address bar, or possibly you elected to open a particular site, only to find that you could rewrite the Constitution during the time it takes to download the graphics. Regardless of the reason, you might need to stop a page from downloading. You can stop a page from downloading by clicking the Stop button on the toolbar.

Stop

Another Web page display technique that you can use on occasion is called *refreshing* a page. Refreshing a page means that you instruct Internet Explorer to re-download the currently displayed page. You might want to do this for a number of reasons: to view updated sports scores, watch breaking news stories evolve, or reload a page you stopped. When you refresh a page, you ensure that you have the most up-to-date version of the Web page. To refresh a Web page, you simply click the Refresh button on the toolbar.

Refresh

In addition to refreshing the current page and moving among visited pages, you can return to your home page at any point during your browsing session.

Home

By default, clicking the Home button displays the MSN home page, or a home page provided by your computer manufacturer or your Internet service provider. The term *home page* can be confusing because it refers to the Internet home page that is always displayed when you start Internet Explorer, but it also refers to the main starting page at a particular Web site.

The final basic Web surfing skill that you need to learn involves finding specific text on a Web page. You can find text on a Web page just as you find text in a document. The Internet Explorer Edit menu contains a Find command that enables you to search the currently displayed Web page for a particular word or group of words.

You are just starting to represent Lakewood Mountains Resort for your public relations firm. You'll be flying out to visit the resort next week, but for now, your first order of business is to visit the resort's Web site.

Use the Address bar to access an Internet document

In this exercise, you use Internet Explorer's Address bar to display the Lakewood Mountains Resort main page.

❶   If necessary, start Internet Explorer, and click in the Address bar (the box next to the word *Address*).

   The currently displayed URL is selected. (If the URL is not selected, double-click it.)

❷   Type **mspress.microsoft.com/mspress/products/1349/default.htm** and then press Enter.

   The Lakewood Mountains Resort main page appears.

tip

If you type (in the Address bar) a URL that you've previously entered, Internet Explorer displays a list of addresses that are similar to the one you are entering. If you see the correct address in the list, simply click it. If Internet Explorer does not display the address you want, continue to enter the correct URL, and then press Enter to retrieve the Web page.

The Nature of Frames

Some Web pages are divided into *frames*. Frames enable Web page designers to show more than one Web document in your browser window at a time. Frames are commonly used to show a menu in one frame and the results of clicking menu items in another frame. The Lakewood Mountains Resort main page gives you the option to view the frames version or the no frames version of the Lakewood Mountains Resort home page. Web pages that do not have frames are created as a courtesy to those who use older browsers that cannot support frames.

Click hyperlinks to access Internet documents

In this exercise, you access a Web page by clicking hyperlinks on the Lakewood Mountains Resort home page.

1   On the Lakewood Mountains Resort main page, click the No Frames button.

The no frames version of the Lakewood Mountains Resort home page appears with a menu of different hyperlinks.

2   Type **mspress.microsoft.com/mspress/products/1349/default.htm** in the Address bar, press Enter, and then click the Use Frames button.

The frames version of the Lakewood Mountains Resort home page appears with a menu of different hyperlinks.

3   Click the Recreational Facilities hyperlink in the left frame.

Internet Explorer downloads the Recreation page. When the Web page is completely downloaded, the status bar displays the word *Done*.

You can tell when your mouse pointer is pointing to a hyperlink, because the pointer changes to a pointing hand.

tip

There might be times when you want to click a hyperlink, but you aren't finished with the currently displayed page. In those instances, you can open the document referenced by the hyperlink in a separate window. That way, you can have two Internet Explorer windows open—one displaying the original document and another displaying the document associated with the hyperlink. To view a linked document in a separate browser window, press the Shift key while you click a hyperlink.

Use the Back and Forward buttons

In this exercise, you use the Back and Forward buttons to redisplay Web pages you've visited during the current session.

If this URL aready appears in the Address bar, click at the end of the URL, and press Enter.

❶ Type **mspress.microsoft.com/mspress/products/1349/default1.htm** in the Address bar, and press Enter.

The Lakewood Mountains Resort home page appears.

❷ Click the Location hyperlink.

The Location page appears. Notice that the Back button is now displayed as an available option.

Back

❸ On the toolbar, click the Back button.

The Lakewood Mountains Resort home page appears. Notice that the Forward button is now displayed as an available option.

tip
You can click the drop-down arrows on the Back and Forward buttons to choose sites that you've already visited within a session.

Forward

❹ On the toolbar, click the Forward button.

The Location page appears.

Stop a page from downloading

You can stop a page from downloading if it is taking too long or if you decide you don't want to view the page. In this exercise, you stop loading a Web page.

Stop

● In the left frame, click the On The Town hyperlink, and then click the Stop button before the new Web page appears completely.

The new Web page stops downloading. Notice the empty placeholders where graphics should appear. (If your Internet access is 128 Kbps or faster, you might not see placeholder text.)

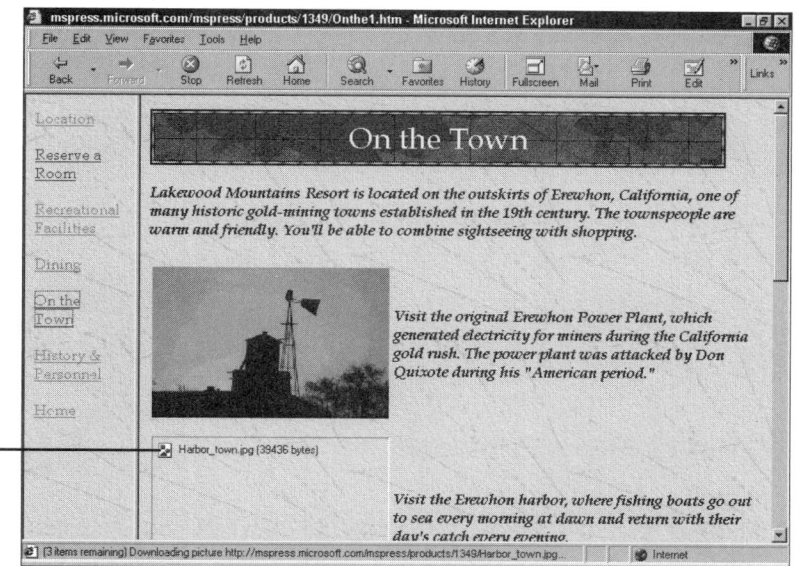

You can also press the Esc key to stop a page from downloading.

Empty place-holder

Refresh a Web page

In this exercise, you refresh a partially downloaded page.

Refresh

● On the toolbar, click the Refresh button.

Internet Explorer reloads the Web page you stopped loading. Notice that the page no longer displays empty placeholders.

tip

Sometimes you will be unable to access a Web page because the computer storing the Web site is too busy. You can click the Refresh button to take a second try at accessing the popular page.

Return to your home page

In this exercise, you return to your Internet home page by clicking the Home button.

Home

● On the toolbar, click the Home button.

Your Internet home page appears in your browser window.

Find text on a Web page

In this exercise, you find text on a Web page.

You can go to previously viewed Web pages by clicking the drop-down arrow to the right of the Address bar and then clicking the desired URL.

1 In the Address bar, type **mspress.microsoft.com/mspress/products/1349/default1.htm** and press Enter.

The Lakewood Mountains Resort home page appears.

2 Click the On The Town hyperlink in the left frame.

3 Click in the right frame.

4 On the Edit menu, click Find (On This Page).

The Find dialog box appears.

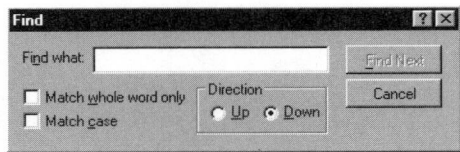

5 Type **Erewhon** in the Find What text box.

You might need to drag the Find dialog box to the left to see the highlighted word.

6 Click Find Next.

Internet Explorer highlights the first instance of the specified text.

7 Click Find Next again.

Internet Explorer highlights the next instance of the specified text.

8 Click Cancel to close the Find dialog box.

Creating a Desktop Shortcut to a Web Page

For a demonstration of how to create a desktop shortcut to a Web page, in the Multimedia folder on the Microsoft Internet Explorer 5 Step by Step CD-ROM, double-click the Shortcut icon.

As you probably know from working with Windows, desktop shortcuts let you open files and applications quickly. You can create shortcuts on your desktop that store Internet documents' URLs, which point to Internet pages. These shortcuts will allow you to go directly to a Web page without opening Internet Explorer and typing an address. Internet desktop shortcuts can be clicked, cut, copied, and pasted in the same manner as other shortcuts created in Windows.

As you continue to work on the Lakewood Mountains Resort project, you find that you frequently access the resort's Web page. You learn that you can create a desktop shortcut to a Web page, so you decide to create and use a desktop shortcut for the Lakewood Mountains Resort home page.

Create and use a desktop shortcut

In this exercise, you create a desktop shortcut for the Lakewood Mountains Resort home page. In addition, you use the desktop shortcut and delete it.

1 If necessary, start Internet Explorer.

2 In the Address bar, type **mspress.microsoft.com/mspress/products/1349/ default1.htm** and press Enter.

The Lakewood Mountains Resort home page appears.

3 On the File menu, point to Send, and then click Shortcut To Desktop.

A shortcut linking to the Lakewood Mountains Resort home page is created on your desktop.

Close

4 Click the Close button at the top-right corner of the Internet Explorer window, and minimize any open windows to display your desktop.

5 On your desktop, click the Lakewood Home Page shortcut. (The icon is labeled Default1.htm.)

Desktop Shortcut

Internet Explorer opens and the Lakewood Mountains Resort home page is displayed.

6 In the Internet Explorer window, click the Minimize button so that you can view your desktop.

Minimize

7 Right-click the Lakewood Home Page desktop shortcut.

A shortcut menu appears.

8 On the shortcut menu, click Delete.

A message box asks if you want to send the shortcut to the Recycle Bin.

9 Click Yes.

The shortcut is removed from your desktop.

10 Redisplay the Internet Explorer window.

Printing Web Page Information

Internet Explorer lets you print Web pages in a variety of ways. You can print entire Web pages, selected items, or frames. You can also print linked documents along with the currently displayed page, or you can print a table of links.

When you print an entire Web page, you can display the File menu and then click Print to display the Print dialog box (as shown in the following illustration). Or you can click the Print button on the toolbar.

Print

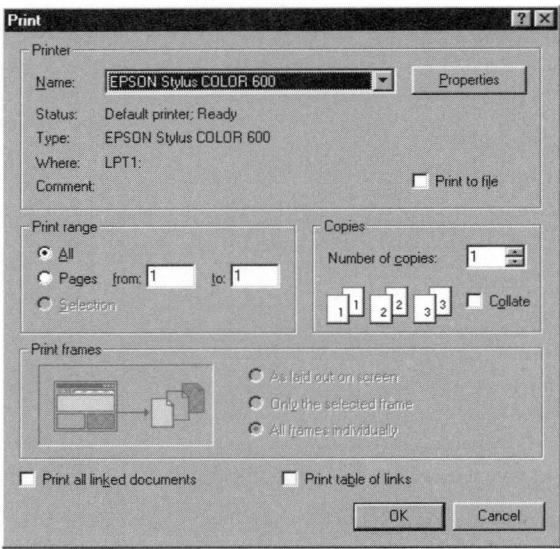

tip

When you print to a black and white printer, you might want to change your hyperlink colors to black before printing. Other colors might not appear when you print, leaving large blank areas in your printed document. Lesson 3, "Customizing Your Work Space," explains how to customize hyperlink colors in the "One Step Further: Specifying How Links Appear" section.

By default, Internet Explorer does not print Web page *backgrounds*. A Web page background is the color, texture, or picture that appears behind the text and graphics on a Web page. For example, the Lakewood Mountains Resort home page has a tan, adobe-textured type of background. Printing Web page backgrounds can waste your time and the printer's ink, as well as produce hard-to-read results. If you want to print a background, you must display the Tools menu, click Internet Options, click the Advanced tab, click the Print Background Colors And Images check box, and then click OK.

important

Your computer must be connected to a printer to complete the exercises in this section. In addition, you should verify that your printer is turned on.

Depending on your screen size, window size, and display settings, you might have to click the double-arrow symbol along the right edge of the toolbar to display the Print button. After you click the double-arrow symbol, Internet Explorer automatically creates a drop-down list (as shown below) if all the toolbar buttons cannot be displayed within the window's size constraints.

If the page you want to print doesn't contain frames, you can display the page and click the Print button to print the Web page.

tip

Be careful when using the Print button with framed pages. The Print button prints frames based on the previous setting stored in the Print dialog box. To be safe, on the File menu, click Print to display the Print dialog box when printing a framed page. That way, you can specify how you want the frames to be printed. If you want the framed page to be printed as it appears in your window, click the As Laid Out On Screen option.

Another Internet Explorer print option involves links. Internet Explorer gives you the option of printing not just the currently displayed page, but every other page to which it displays a link. This sounds like a handy option, but you should use it with caution. Depending on the number of links on a page, you might end up printing more linked pages than you want. In addition, Web pages are not bound by traditional paper sizes. If you print a single Web page, as many as 20 hard-copy pages could be printed. Instead of printing a Web page and its linked documents, you should consider printing a table of the documents linked to the current page.

You would like to make a hard copy of the Lakewood Mountains Resort Web site for the art department to review in this afternoon's meeting. You decide to print a copy of the Web site.

Beware of Copyrights

Copyright protection on the Internet is a sticky issue. To be safe, assume that all material contained in an Internet document is copyrighted. That means that you can print material for your own private use, but you can't reuse or redistribute the material without permission. If you want to reuse material, such as a photograph from the Lakewood Mountains Resort Web page, obtain permission from the Web site's "Webmaster" or the contact person listed on the page.

Occasionally, you'll run across a site that offers free use of graphics or other material. For example, there are a number of sites that provide icons, background patterns, and custom bullets for use without permission. In those instances, feel free to copy and use the resources you find.

Print a Web page

In this exercise, you print the Lakewood Mountains Resort home page.

1 If necessary, start Internet Explorer.

2 In the Address bar, type **mspress.microsoft.com/mspress/products/1349/default1.htm** and press Enter.

The Lakewood Mountains Resort home page appears.

3 On the File menu, click Print.

The Print dialog box appears.

4 In the Print Frames area, click the As Laid Out On Screen option, and then click the OK button.

The Lakewood Mountains Resort home page is printed.

Print selected items

In this exercise, you print only the address of the Lakewood Mountains Resort.

1 Select the resort's address (which appears below the picture of the resort).

2 On the File menu, click Print.

The Print dialog box appears.

3 In the Print Range area, click the Selection option.

❹ Click OK.

The selected text is printed.

❺ Click anywhere on the Web page to deselect the text.

Print each frame on a separate page

In this exercise, you print each frame of the Lakewood Mountains Resort home page on a separate page.

❶ On the File menu, click Print.

The Print dialog box appears.

❷ In the Print Frames area, click the All Frames Individually option, and then click OK.

Each frame is printed on a separate page.

Print a single frame

In this exercise, you print the main frame of the Lakewood Mountains Resort home page.

❶ Click the right frame of the Lakewood Mountains Resort home page. (This frame contains a picture of the resort as well as address and phone information.)

Internet Explorer internally marks this as the current frame.

❷ On the File menu, click Print.

The Print dialog box appears.

❸ In the Print Frames area, click the Only The Selected Frame option (if necessary).

tip
When you select the Only The Selected Frame option in the Print dialog box, the Print Frames illustration will not indicate which frame is the selected frame.

❹ Click OK.

The selected (right) frame is printed.

Print linked documents

In this exercise, you print the Lakewood Mountains Resort home page and all linked documents.

important

Printing linked documents can result in dozens or even hundreds of printed pages. In one instance, printing an Internet home page along with all its linked documents resulted in sending over 60 separate documents to the printer.

1 Click in the left frame, but not on a hyperlink.

Internet Explorer internally marks this as the current frame.

2 On the File menu, click Print.

The Print dialog box appears.

3 If necessary, click the Only The Selected Frame option.

4 Click the Print All Linked Documents check box.

This indicates that you want to print all linked documents as they appear in your browser. Any framed pages will be printed with all frames on one page.

5 Click OK.

The current frame and all linked pages are printed. Each linked document is treated as a separate printing process. In other words, if four Web pages are linked to the currently displayed page, your printer will process five consecutive documents (of varying page counts, because Web pages do not have to conform to standard printed page sizes).

Print a table of links

In this exercise, you print a table of links for the Lakewood Mountains Resort Web site.

1 Click in the left frame.

Internet Explorer internally marks this as the current frame.

2 On the File menu, click Print.

The Print dialog box appears.

3 Click the Only The Selected Frame option if necessary, and click the Print Table Of Links option.

4 Click OK.

The current frame is printed, followed by a two-column table. The left column presents each link's name and the corresponding right column shows each link's complete URL.

One Step Further Saving Web Pages

You do not need to be connected to the Internet to view saved Web pages.

A Web page contains *Hypertext Markup Language* (HTML) formatting tags, graphics, and multimedia files. HTML formatting tags are used to format text, manipulate graphics, add background colors, and customize Web pages. Because a single Web page can consist of a number of *embedded files* (each graphic on a Web page is a separate file linked to the Web page's text document), you can choose to save a Web page in four ways:

- Save a complete Web page. (This saves the HTML file and all additional files, such as images, embedded in the Web page.)
- Save an archive of a Web page. (This saves the entire Web page as a single, uneditable file.)
- Save only the HTML document. (This saves the HTML formatting tags, but does not save embedded files.)
- Save only the text appearing on the Web page.

When you save a complete Web page, Internet Explorer automatically creates a folder with the same name as the saved file. This folder is also placed in the same location as the saved file. When you open the Web page, Internet Explorer opens, and all elements appear in the Web page, just as if you were viewing the page online.

When you save a Web page as an archive file, you save the entire Web page without creating a separate folder to contain the Web page's embedded elements. You can open the archive file to view the entire Web page on your hard disk drive, but you cannot change the Web page in any way, nor can you access separate components of the saved Web page such as graphics files. Be aware that while an archive file is a single file, it takes up more space on your computer than a Web page saved as a complete Web page.

When you save an HTML file, you leave out the graphics and other embedded elements. You can read formatted text, but you won't be able to view graphics because they're not saved on your hard disk drive.

Finally, when you save a Web page as a text file, you are saving only the text appearing on the page without any HTML tags. The saved text will not include any formatting, graphics, or other page elements.

You decide that you want to save the no-frames version of the Lakewood Mountains Resort home page to your computer. You aren't sure how you want to save the Web page, so you try all four options. Then you view each option to see which version serves your needs best.

important

If you are saving a Web page with frames, you must save the document as a complete Web page. The other save options do not work with framed Web pages.

Save a complete Web page

In this exercise, you save the Lakewood Mountains Resort home page as a complete Web page.

1. If necessary, start Internet Explorer.
2. Type **mspress.microsoft.com/mspress/products/1349/default2.htm** in the Address bar, and press Enter.

   The no-frames version of the Lakewood Mountains Resort home page is displayed.
3. On the File menu, click Save As.

   The Save Web Page dialog box appears.
4. If necessary, click the Save In drop-down arrow, and click Desktop.
5. In the File Name text box, select the current filename, and type **Complete Web Page**.

   The document you are saving will be named Complete Web Page.
6. If necessary, click the Save As Type drop-down arrow, click Web Page, Complete (*.htm,*.html), and then click Save.

   A progress bar shows the progress of the operation as the page's elements are saved. The document and its folder are saved to your desktop.

Save an archived version of a Web page

In this exercise, you save the Lakewood Mountains Resort home page as an archive file.

1. On the File menu, click Save As.

   The Save Web Page dialog box appears.
2. If necessary, click the Save In drop-down arrow, and click Desktop.

③ In the File Name text box, type **Archived Web Page**.

④ Click the Save As Type drop-down arrow, click Web Archive For Email (*.mht), and click Save.

A progress bar shows the progress of the operation as the page's elements are saved. The document is saved to your desktop as an archive file.

Save only a Web page's HTML file

In this exercise, you save the Lakewood Mountains Resort home page as an HTML file.

① On the File menu, click Save As.

The Save Web Page dialog box appears.

② If necessary, click the Save In drop-down arrow, and click Desktop.

③ In the File Name text box, type **HTML Only**.

④ Click the Save As Type drop-down arrow, click Web Page, HTML Only (*.htm,*.html), and then click Save.

A progress bar shows the progress of the operation as the page's elements are saved. The document is saved on your desktop as an HTML file.

Save a Web page as a text file

In this exercise, you save the Lakewood Mountains Resort home page as a text file.

① On the File menu, click Save As.

The Save Web Page dialog box appears.

② If necessary, click the Save In drop-down arrow, and click Desktop.

③ In the File Name text box, type **Text File**.

④ Click the Save As Type drop-down arrow, click Text File (*.txt), and then click Save.

A progress bar shows the progress of the operation as the page's elements are saved. The document is saved as a text file, without HTML formatting.

Close

⑤ Click the Close button at the top-right corner of the Internet Explorer window, and minimize any open windows to display your desktop.

View saved Web pages

In this exercise, you view saved Web pages.

> # important
>
> The steps in this exercise assume that you are using the Web pages that you saved in the previous sections. If you didn't save these files, you can still open identical pages from the Lesson 1 folder in the Internet Explorer 5 SBS Practice folder on your hard disk drive.

1 If necessary, display your desktop.

2 Click the Complete Web Page icon on your desktop.

A complete copy of the saved Web page appears in Internet Explorer with all graphics and other components embedded in the Web page. The local address is displayed in the Address bar.

You can click hyperlinks on Web pages saved as complete or archived to access the linked Web pages on the Internet.

3 Close the Internet Explorer window.

4 Click the Complete Web Page Files icon on your desktop.

The folder's contents are displayed.

5 Click the Main Building file.

The picture of the Lakewood Mountains Resort appears in Internet Explorer.

6 Close the Internet Explorer window and the Complete Web Page_Files window.

7 Click the Archived Web Page icon on your desktop.

A complete copy of the Web page opens in Internet Explorer.

8 Close the Internet Explorer window.

9 Click the HTML Only icon on your desktop.

A modified version of the saved Web page appears in Internet Explorer. The graphics are not displayed, because they are not saved within the file.

10 Close the Internet Explorer window.

11 Click the Text File icon on your desktop.

A text file is displayed without any formatting. The text file appears in Notepad or another text editor instead of appearing in the Internet Explorer window.

12 Click the Close button at the top-right corner of the text editor.

Close

Finish the lesson

● Drag the icons for any Web page files on your desktop to the Recycle Bin. The saved Web page files are deleted.

Lesson 1 Quick Reference

To	Do this	Button
Start Internet Explorer	Click the Internet Explorer icon on your desktop.	
Browse to another Web page	Type a Web address in the Address text box and press Enter, or click a hyperlink on the currently displayed Web page.	
Redisplay Web pages viewed during the current session	Click the Back (or the Forward) button.	
Stop downloading a page	Click the Stop button.	
Redownload the current Web page	Click the Refresh button.	
Display your Internet home page	Click the Home button.	
Find text in the current Web page	Click Find (On This Page) on the Edit menu. Type the text you want to search for, and click the Find Next button to find each instance of the search term.	
Create a desktop shortcut	On the File menu, point to Send, and then click Shortcut To Desktop.	
Print a Web page	Click the Print button, or click Print on the File menu, select the desired options in the Print dialog box, and click OK.	
Print selected items	On a Web page, select an item such as a word. Click Print on the File menu. Click the Selection option in the Print dialog box, and click OK.	

Lesson 1 Quick Reference

To	Do this
Print frames on separate pages	Display a Web page that has frames. Click Print on the File menu. Click the All Frames Individually option in the Print dialog box, and then click OK.
Print a single frame	Display a Web page that has frames. Click a frame. Click Print on the File menu. Click the Only The Selected Frame option in the Print dialog box, and click OK.
Print linked documents	Click Print on the File menu. Click either the Only The Selected Frame or All Frames Individually option in the Print Frames section. Click the Print All Linked Documents check box in the Print dialog box, and click OK.
Print a table of links	Click Print on the File menu. Click either the Only The Selected Frame or All Frames Individually option in the Print Frames section. Click the Print Table Of Links option in the Print dialog box, and then click OK.
Save a Web page	Click Save As on the File menu. Use the Save Web Page dialog box to specify how and where you want to save the Web page content, and click Save.

LESSON

2

Finding and Managing Information

ESTIMATED TIME
30 min.

Managing Information

In this lesson you will learn how to:

✔ *Search for information on the Web.*

✔ *Create a Favorites list.*

✔ *Use Favorites.*

✔ *Manage your Favorites folder.*

✔ *Use and modify your History folder.*

Imagine that you're the account executive for Impact Public Relations' most prestigious client—Lakewood Mountains Resort. The resort's off-season is looming, so you're researching the feasibility of offering package deals to attract business groups and vacationers. You turn to the Internet to research current travel trends, prices, and schedules. Microsoft Internet Explorer 5 offers a number of tools that can help you find and store links to Internet information. As you find sites that interest you, you can create a site list for future reference.

In this lesson, you will learn how to use Internet Explorer to search for information on the World Wide Web. Then you will learn how to create, use, and manage a list of your favorite Internet sites. You'll also see how Internet Explorer keeps tabs on your Internet travels. Finally, you'll learn how you can use and manage Internet Explorer's history feature.

Searching for Information on the Web

The Internet contains so many documents that you'll frequently need help finding specific information. Internet Explorer makes finding Web information easy. You can search for information on the Web by using Internet Explorer's Address bar or by clicking the Search button on the toolbar, which opens the Search Assistant, as shown in the following illustration.

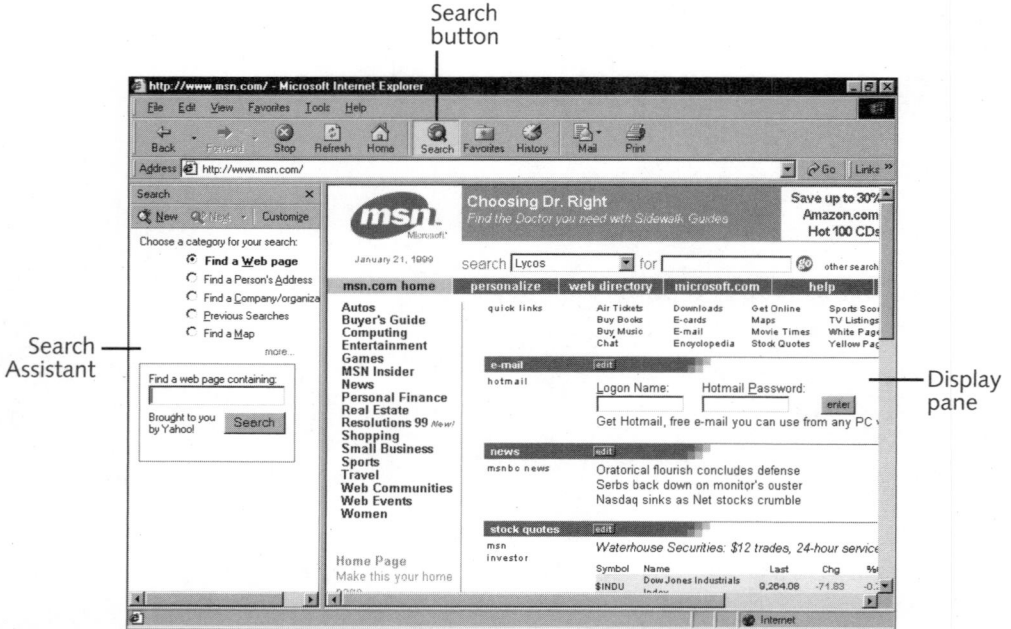

For a demonstration of how to search using the Search Assistant, in the Multimedia folder on the Microsoft Internet Explorer 5 Step by Step CD-ROM, double-click the Search icon.

The Search Assistant is a tool that helps you find information on the Internet. It gives you the choice to search for a subject word, or search for a subject word within a category. Searching by category helps to narrow down what you want to look for. After you type in a subject word and click the Search button, the Search Assistant will display a list of links to Web pages that contain information about your subject word. Just click the link to view the information.

The Search Assistant also gives you the option to choose a *search engine*. A search engine is a Web tool designed to look for Internet information based on subject words (also called *keywords*) or to browse for topics organized by subject groups. You can view other available search engines by clicking the drop-down arrow to the right of the Next button in the Search Assistant.

After you select a search engine, you can type in a keyword or click subject groupings to narrow your search. The more criteria you add to your search, the more likely you are to find the type of information you're seeking.

> ## tip
> When using a search engine, you can search for multiple terms by including a plus sign between words in the search text box. For example, you can enter *mountain+resort* in the search text box to find Web sites about mountains and resorts. Also, if you want to search for a phrase, you can surround the phrase with quotation marks. For example, you can enter *"bed and breakfast"* to find Web sites about bed and breakfast services. Most search engines include a page dedicated to Internet searching tips and techniques.

You can also search for Web sites using the Address bar. Internet Explorer provides one main Address bar search feature—*Autosearch*. Autosearch enables you to search for Web pages by word or phrase. In the Address bar, type *go*, *find*, or *?* followed by a space and a word or phrase, and then press Enter. The Autosearch Web page will appear with a list of hyperlinks to Web sites. Each Web site will have a short description listed below it. For example, you could type *go fish* to search for information related to fish. The Autosearch Web page will list hyperlinks related to fish. After you read the descriptions of the Web sites, simply click a hyperlink that interests you. The Web site you choose will appear in Internet Explorer.

You will use the Autosearch feature as you gather information for your client, Lakewood Mountains Resort.

Display the Search Assistant

In this exercise, you display and resize the Search Assistant in Internet Explorer.

Search

1 Start Internet Explorer.

2 On the toolbar, click the Search button.

The Search Assistant is displayed.

3 Click the Search button again.

The Search Assistant closes.

4 Click the Search button, and position your mouse pointer along the right edge of the Search Assistant.

The mouse pointer turns into a horizontal double arrow.

5 Drag the right edge of the Search Assistant to the right.

The Search Assistant appears wider, as shown in the illustration.

The AutoComplete dialog box might appear, asking if you want it to list suggestions of your previous search words as you type search words in the Search Assistant. Click Yes.

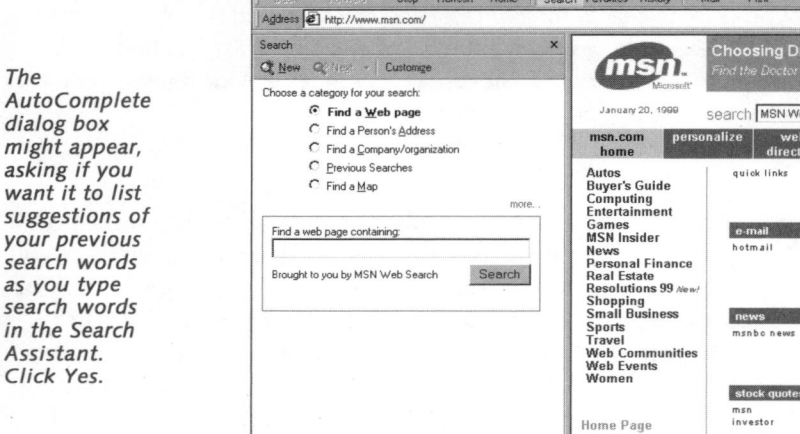

6 Drag the right edge of the Search Assistant to the left until it is close to its original size.

The Search Assistant becomes thinner.

7 Click the Close button at the top-right corner of the Search Assistant.

The Search Assistant closes.

Close

Search for a Web site

In this exercise, you use the Search Assistant to do a quick search for the word *airlines*.

1 On the toolbar, click the Search button.

The Search Assistant is displayed.

2 Type **airlines** in the Find A Web Page Containing text box.

This indicates that you want to search for Web sites containing the word *airlines*.

You can also start a search by pressing Enter after typing in a word.

❸ Click the Search button.

The search is performed. Links to categories and Web pages containing information matching your search criterion appear in the Search Assistant.

❹ Click a link in the Search Assistant.

A Web page matching your search criterion is displayed in Internet Explorer's display pane.

Your screen will differ from this one if you clicked a different hyperlink.

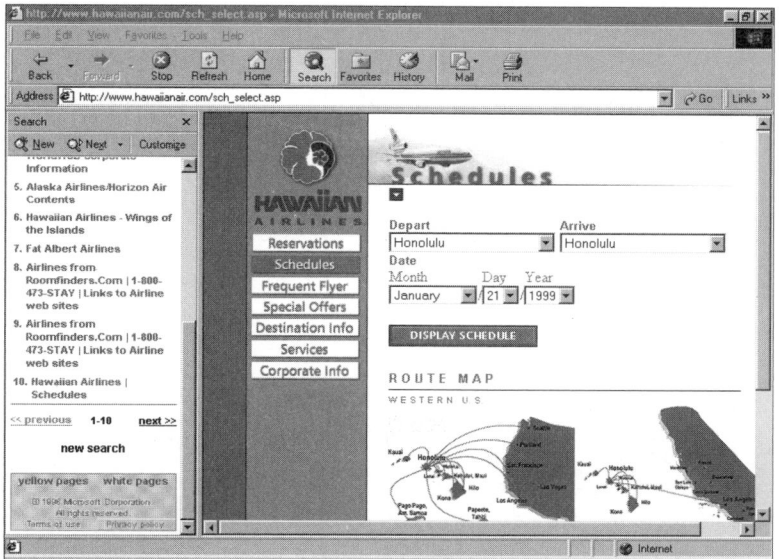

❺ In the Search Assistant, click the New button.

The Search Assistant is now ready for a new search.

❻ On the toolbar, click the Search button.

The Search Assistant closes.

Selecting Your Own Search Engine

There are several search engines (such as Yahoo, HotBot, and AltaVista) that you can use to find documents on the Internet. You might find over time that you prefer one search engine in particular. Internet Explorer lets you choose which search engine you want to use.

Select a search engine

In this exercise, you conduct a search on restaurants, and then you select a different search engine to conduct a new search on restaurants.

Search

1 On the toolbar, click the Search button.

The Search Assistant is displayed.

2 Type **restaurants** in the Find A Web Page Containing text box, and click Search.

A list of links related to the word *restaurants* appears.

If you click only the Next button and not the drop-down arrow, the next search engine in the list will conduct a search on restaurants.

3 In the Search Assistant, click the drop-down arrow to the right of the Next Button.

A list of search engines appears.

4 Click Yahoo!

Yahoo! displays a new list of links related to restaurants.

5 Click the New button.

A new search can now be conducted.

tip

You can change the order and content of your search engine list by clicking the Customize button in the Search Assistant. The Customize Search Settings window will appear, and you will see a list of search engines in the Find A Web Page section. Click a search engine in the list box, and then use the up or down arrow buttons to move the search engine to a different location in the list. You can change the content of the search engine list by deselecting or selecting the check boxes to the left of the search engines. When you are finished making changes, click OK.

Choose a category to narrow your search

In this exercise, you select different categories in the Search Assistant to narrow your search.

1 Click the Find A Business option.

A search for Web pages related to companies and organizations will be conducted.

You can select another search engine to conduct the same search by clicking the Next button in the Search Assistant.

❷ Type **Microsoft** in the Business text box, type **Redmond** in the City text box, type **WA** in the State/Province text box, and click the Search button.

A list of links related to Microsoft appears in the Search Assistant.

❸ Scroll down the list, and click one of the Microsoft Corporation links.

The InfoSpace Web page appears, displaying information about Microsoft.

❹ In the Search Assistant, click the New Button, and click the word *More*.

The list of categories becomes larger.

❺ Click the Find In Encyclopedia option.

The search will be conducted by Encarta.

❻ Type **elephants** in the Find Encyclopedia Articles On text box, and click Search.

Encarta conducts a search on elephants and lists the results.

❼ Click the Elephant link.

The Encarta Web page appears, displaying facts about elephants.

❽ On the toolbar, click the Search button.

The Search Assistant closes.

Search

Use Autosearch

In this exercise, you use Autosearch to find Web pages containing the word *boeing*.

❶ Click in the Address bar.

Internet Explorer selects the current text.

❷ Type **go boeing**, and then press Enter.

The Autosearch Web page appears with a list of hyperlinks related to the word *boeing*.

❸ Click any hyperlink on the Autosearch page to display a Web site related to the word *boeing*.

Internet Explorer displays the Web site of the hyperlink you clicked.

Creating a Favorites List

Imagine you've been working extensively with your Lakewood Mountains Resort client. You've been visiting the resort's Web site three or four times a day. You're tired of repeatedly typing the Web page address in the Address bar, so you would prefer to create a quicker way to access the page. You learn that you can add an entry to your Internet Explorer Favorites list that will enable you to access the Lakewood Mountains Resort Web page with a single click.

A *Favorites list* is a menu you create that contains a collection of shortcuts to Web pages. Your Favorites list contains at least five folders (you might have additional Favorite folders if you created them in previous versions of Internet Explorer or Windows): Channels (this folder contains *channels* or Web sites designed to deliver customized information to your computer based on an updated schedule), Imported Bookmarks (this folder contains bookmarks you might have created in other browsers before you installed Internet Explorer 5), Links, Media, and Software Updates.

Your Favorites list can store links to any Web page you choose. The simplest way to add a link is to display the Web page in your browser and then add the page to your Favorites list.

In addition to placing Web page links in your Favorites list, you can add links to local resources (such as your hard disk drive or files and folders that you access frequently). Adding a local resource to your Favorites list allows you to quickly display the resource by clicking its Favorites link. To view your Favorites list's contents, click the Favorites button on the toolbar. The Favorites bar is displayed in the left pane of the Internet Explorer window.

Add the current Web page to your Favorites list

In this exercise, you add the Lakewood Mountains Resort home page to your Favorites list.

1   Click in the Address bar, type **mspress.microsoft.com/mspress/product/ 1349/default1.htm** and press Enter.

       The Lakewood Mountains Resort home page is displayed.

Favorites

New!

2   On the toolbar, click the Favorites button.

       The Favorites bar is displayed.

3   On the Favorites bar, click the Add button.

       The Add Favorite dialog box appears as shown in the following illustration.

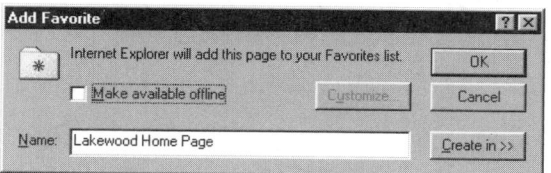

2

Managing Information

tip

You can also use the menu bar to add Favorites to your Favorites list. Display a Web page. On the Favorites menu, click Add To Favorites, and click OK.

4   In the Add Favorite dialog box, click OK.

The Favorites list now includes a link to the Lakewood Home Page as shown in the illustration.

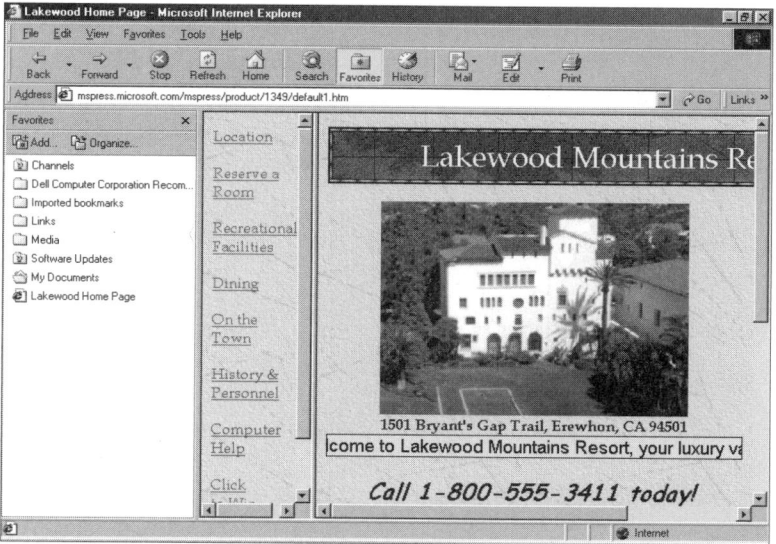

Favorites

5   On the toolbar, click the Favorites button.

The Favorites bar closes.

Add your desktop to your Favorites list

In this exercise, you add your desktop to your Favorites list.

❶ Click in the Address bar, type **desktop**, and press Enter.

The contents of your desktop appear.

❷ On the Favorites menu, click Add To Favorites.

The Add Favorite dialog box is displayed.

❸ In the Add Favorite dialog box, click OK.

Your desktop is added to your Favorites list.

❹ Click the Back button to return to the previously displayed Web page.

❺ On the toolbar, click the Favorites button.

The Favorites bar is displayed. Notice that the Favorites list now includes a link to your desktop.

Back

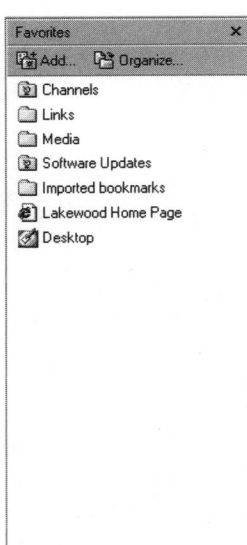

❻ On the toolbar, click the Favorites button.

The Favorites bar closes.

Favorites

Using Favorites

Creating Favorites means that you can visit Web sites without having to remember the address of a Web page or type a path in the Address bar. Instead, you can display the Favorites bar, find the link that you created, and click it to display the page. You can also access the Favorites list from the menu bar. You can even access the Favorites list without having Internet Explorer open. To do so, click the Start button, point to Favorites, and click a Favorites link.

When you click a Favorites link using the Start menu, Internet Explorer opens and displays the selected Web page.

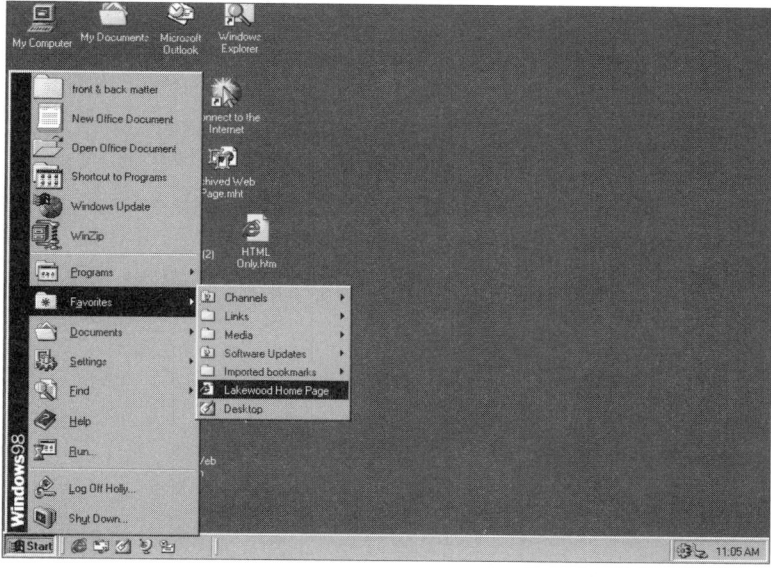

Use the Favorites bar

In this exercise, you add the Expedia Travel site to your Favorites list and then access the site using the Favorites bar.

1 Click in the Address bar, type **expedia.com**, and press Enter.

The Expedia Travel site is displayed.

Favorites

2 On the toolbar, click the Favorites button.

The Favorites bar is displayed.

3 On the Favorites bar, click the Add button, and click OK when the Add Favorite dialog box appears.

The Expedia Travel site appears as a link in your Favorites list.

Home

4 On the toolbar, click the Home button.

Your home page is displayed.

⑤ On the Favorites bar, click the Expedia link.

The Expedia Travel site is redisplayed.

⑥ On the toolbar, click the Favorites button.

The Favorites bar closes.

Use the Favorites menu

In this exercise, you use the Favorites menu to open a Web page.

① On the Favorites menu, click a Favorites link.

The Web site is downloaded and appears in Internet Explorer.

② On the toolbar, click the Back button.

Access Favorites from the Windows taskbar

In this exercise, you use the Windows Start menu to open a Favorites link.

① On the Windows taskbar, click the Start button, and point to Favorites.

The content of your Favorites list is displayed.

② On the Favorites menu, click a link.

The Web site associated with the Favorites link downloads and is displayed in Internet Explorer.

③ On the toolbar, click the Back button.

Managing Your Favorites List

You've decided that you want to create a folder to store links to Web pages associated with your project. Storing these links in a separate folder will help you find the Web pages quickly and organize links that have a similar topic or purpose. After you create the new folder, you decide to move existing Favorites into the folder. In addition, you want to add a new link directly into the folder.

While moving your Favorites, you notice a site with a long name and find that you can rename the Favorite with minimal effort. Finally, as you organize your Favorites, you realize that you no longer need some of the links, so you delete the links to minimize clutter. To accomplish these tasks, you use Internet Explorer's Organize Favorites dialog box.

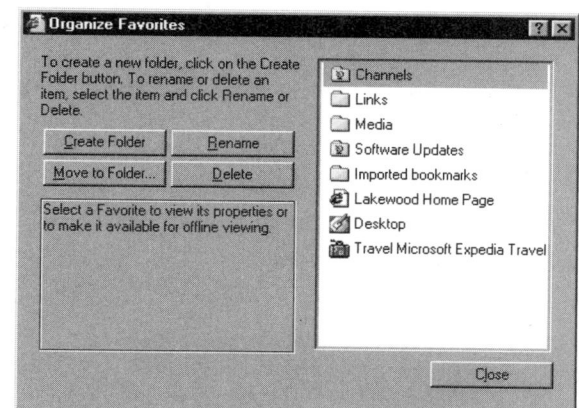

New!

Create a folder within your Favorites list

In this exercise, you create a folder to store Favorites links for your Lakewood Mountains Resort project.

1 On the toolbar, click the Favorites button.

The Favorites bar is displayed.

2 On the Favorites bar, click the Organize button.

The Organize Favorites dialog box is displayed.

3 Click the Create Folder button.

A folder named *New Folder* is added to the bottom of the list.

4 Type **Lakewood Mountains Resort**, and press Enter.

The new folder is renamed Lakewood Mountains Resort.

5 Click the Close button.

The Organize Favorites dialog box closes.

6 On the toolbar, click the Favorites button.

The Favorites bar closes.

Move an existing Favorites link into a folder

In this exercise, you move the Lakewood Home Page Favorites link to the Lakewood Mountains Resort folder.

This exercise assumes that you have created a Favorites link to the Lakewood Mountains Resort home page. If you have not, follow the steps in the exercise "Add the Current Web Page to Your Favorites List" earlier in this lesson.

1 On the toolbar, click the Favorites button.

The Favorites bar is displayed.

2 On the Favorites bar, click the Organize button.

The Organize Favorites dialog box is displayed.

3 In the Organize Favorites dialog box, click the Lakewood Home Page link.

The Lakewood Home Page link is selected.

4 Click the Move To Folder button.

The Browse For Folder dialog box is displayed.

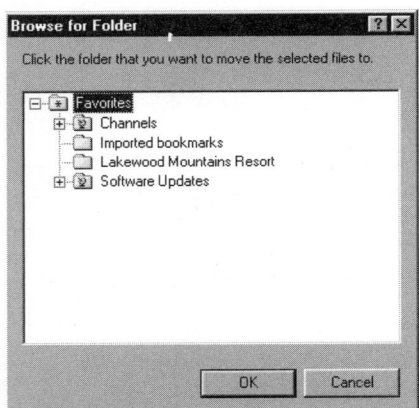

5 In the Browse For Folder dialog box, click the Lakewood Mountains Resort folder, and then click OK.

The Lakewood Home Page link is now stored in the Lakewood Mountains Resort folder. Notice the Lakewood Home Page link no longer appears in the top level of the Organize Favorites dialog box.

6 In the Organize Favorites dialog box, click the Close button.

The Organize Favorites dialog box closes.

7 On the Favorites bar, click the Lakewood Mountains Resort folder.

The Lakewood Home Page Favorites link appears below the Lakewood Mountains Resort folder.

8 Click the Lakewood Mountains Resort folder again.

The folder closes.

9 On the toolbar, click the Favorites button.

The Favorites bar closes.

Place a new Favorites link into a folder

In this exercise, you use the Add Favorite dialog box to place the Avis home page into the Lakewood Mountains Resort folder.

1 Click in the Address bar, type **www.avis.com**, and then press Enter.

The Avis home page is displayed.

2 On the toolbar, click the Favorites button.

The Favorites bar is displayed.

3 On the Favorites bar, click the Add button.

The Add Favorite dialog box is displayed.

4 If necessary, click the Create In button to expand the Add Favorite dialog box.

5 In the Create In area, click the Lakewood Mountains Resort folder, and then click OK.

The Avis home page link is stored in the Lakewood Mountains Resort folder.

6 If necessary, on the Favorites bar, click the Lakewood Mountains Resort folder.

The Avis home page link is displayed below the Lakewood Mountains Resort folder, as shown in the following illustration.

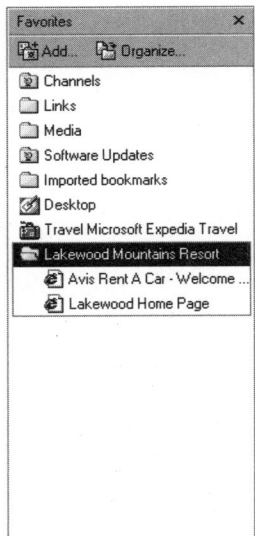

7 On the toolbar, click the Favorites button.

The Favorites bar closes.

Rename a Favorites link

In this exercise, you create a Favorites link to the Visa International home page, and then you rename the link.

1 Click in the Address bar, type **www.visa.com**, and then press Enter.

The Visa International home page is displayed.

2 On the toolbar, click the Favorites button.

The Favorites bar is displayed.

3 On the Favorites bar, click the Add button, and then click OK.

A Favorites link entitled Visa International appears on the Favorites bar.

4 On the Favorites bar, click the Organize button.

You can also right-click a link in the Favorites list and click Rename to rename a Favorites link.

5 In the Organize Favorites dialog box, click the Visa International link, click the Rename button, type **Visa**, press Enter, and then click the Close button.

The Visa International link is renamed *Visa*.

6 On the toolbar, click the Favorites button.

The Favorites bar closes.

tip

You can save time by naming your Favorites links as you create them. When the Add Favorite dialog box is displayed, select the current text in the Name text box, type a new name for the Favorites link, and click OK.

Deleting Favorites

The Internet constantly changes, which means that your Favorites links sometimes become outdated. In addition, your needs change over time. You should sort through your Favorites links occasionally to delete outdated and unwanted Favorites links. Otherwise, your Favorites folder could grow unwieldy.

Delete Favorites

In this exercise, you delete the Visa Favorites link.

You can also right-click a link or a folder in the Favorites list and click Delete to delete a Favorites link.

1 On the toolbar, click the Favorites button.

2 On the Favorites bar, click the Organize button.

3 In the Organize Favorites dialog box, click the Visa link.

4 Click the Delete button, and then click Yes to confirm the deletion.

The Visa Favorites link is deleted from your Favorites list.

5 Click the Close button.

The Organize Favorites dialog box closes.

6 On the toolbar, click the Favorites button.

The Favorites bar closes.

Using the History Folder

You just finished surfing the Internet for six hours, looking for information for your Lakewood Mountains Resort project. You realize too late that you forgot to add some helpful sites to your Favorites list. You groan as you wonder how you'll be able to retrace your steps. Fortunately, your partner walks by and notices your dismay. As you explain that you'll never "re-find" some sites, your partner stops you in mid-sentence to ask if you've checked the History folder.

Internet Explorer automatically records a history of each Internet browsing session. This record is in your History folder, which contains links to each site you visit on the Internet. Your History folder also stores other facts, such as the day you visited each Web page.

To view the contents of your History folder, simply click the History button on the toolbar. The History bar appears along the left side of the Internet Explorer window and has a search feature that allows you to type in a search word to locate a site that you visited.

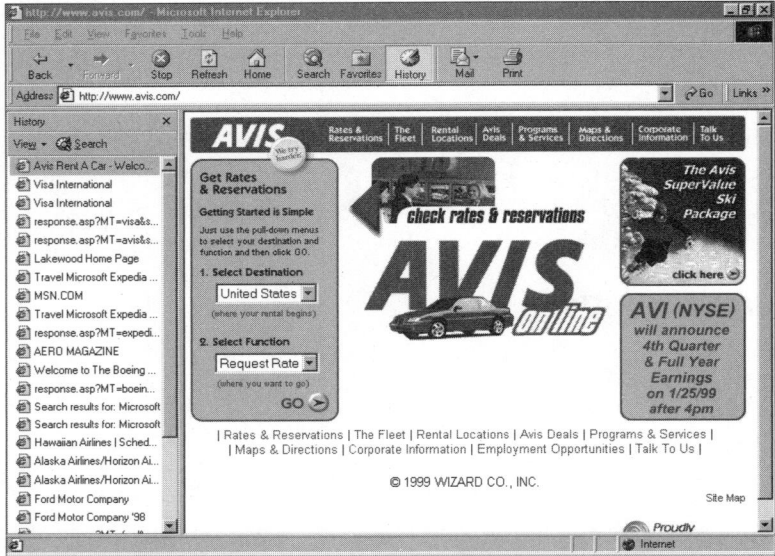

You can specify how long Internet Explorer saves items in your History folder. By default, the History folder stores links to all sites visited within the last 20 days. After an item has been stored for 20 days, it is deleted. For more control, you can manually delete links stored in the History folder. Microsoft refers to deleting all links in your History folder as *clearing* your history.

View your history

This exercise assumes that you have visited the Lakewood Mountains Resort Web site today.

You can view a history of your Internet explorations with a click of a button. In this exercise, you view the contents of your History folder.

❶ On the toolbar, click the History button.

The History bar appears.

❷ On the History bar, click the Search button.

The Search For text box appears.

❸ In the Search For text box, type **lakewood**, and click Search Now.

A list of Web sites that contain the word *lakewood* appears.

4 Click the View button.

   A drop-down list appears.

5 Click the By Date option.

*Click a folder
to open a list
of links, and
then click a
link to view a
Web page you
recently
visited.*

   A list of folders of Web sites that you visited today appears.

6 On the toolbar, click the History button.

   The History bar closes.

Configure your history settings

You can change the length of time that Internet Explorer stores your history information. In this exercise, you configure your History folder's settings.

1 On the Tools menu, click Internet Options.

   The Internet Options dialog box is displayed, as shown in the illustration.

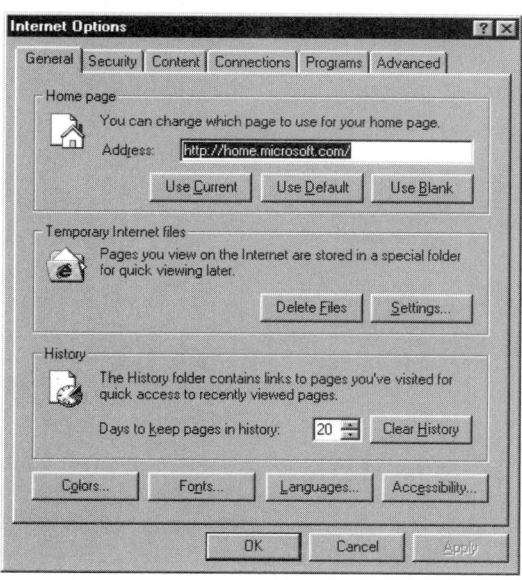

2 On the General tab in the History section, double-click the number in the Days To Keep Pages In History text box.

   The number in the text box is selected.

3 Type **30**.

   The setting changes to 30 days.

4 In the text box, delete 30, type **20**, and click OK.

   The setting returns to 20 days, and the Internet Options dialog box closes.

Clear your History folder

You can manually empty or "clear" your History folder. In this exercise, you clear all of the contents of your History folder.

1 On the Tools menu, click Internet Options.

The Internet Options dialog box is displayed.

2 On the General tab in the History section, click the Clear History button.

A message box appears, asking if you want to delete all items in your History folder.

3 Click OK.

The contents of your History folder are deleted.

4 Click OK.

The Internet Options dialog box closes.

5 On the toolbar, click the History button.

The History bar no longer displays a list of links.

6 Click the History button again.

The History bar closes.

One Step Further | Managing Your Temporary Internet Files

To help speed up your Internet browsing experience, Internet Explorer saves a "local" copy of every file you view to your hard disk drive. When you return to a Web site, Internet Explorer first checks to see if a local copy of the Internet site is on your computer. If it is, Internet Explorer displays the local files. You can display local files much more quickly than files from the Internet because retrieving a file from your hard disk drive is much quicker than retrieving it through your Internet connection. This process of saving and displaying local files is called *caching*. Internet Explorer places cached files in the Temporary Internet Files folder. You need to be aware of this, because the Temporary Internet Files folder can store a sizeable amount of information—and take up a sizeable amount of disk space.

Internet Explorer lets you configure your Temporary Internet Files settings. You can set how often Internet Explorer checks the Internet for new versions of Web pages stored in your Temporary Internet Files folder.

You can also dictate the amount of disk space to use for storing cached files. Increasing the size available for your Temporary Internet Files folder can increase how fast previously viewed Web pages are displayed, but large files decrease the amount of space available for other files on your computer.

Updating Stored Web Pages

You can choose from among four Internet Explorer options to check for new content on Web pages stored in your Temporary Internet Files folder.

Select this option	For this result
Every Visit To The Page	Internet Explorer checks for new content on a Web page each time you visit the page.
Every Time You Start Internet Explorer	Internet Explorer checks for new content only on pages you have viewed recently. It does not check for new content each time you view a Web page during the current session.
Automatically	Internet Explorer checks for new content only on pages you have viewed recently. Over time, if Internet Explorer determines that the Web site's files are changing infrequently, it will check for new content less often.
Never	Internet Explorer never checks for updates to stored Web pages. You must click the Refresh button on the toolbar to update a stored Web page.

Configure your temporary Internet files settings

In this exercise, you select how often you want Internet Explorer to check for newer versions of stored files, and you change the amount of disk space allotted for storing your temporary Internet files.

1   On the Tools menu, click Internet Options.

The Internet Options dialog box is displayed.

2   In the Temporary Internet Files section, click Settings.

The Settings dialog box appears, as shown in the following illustration.

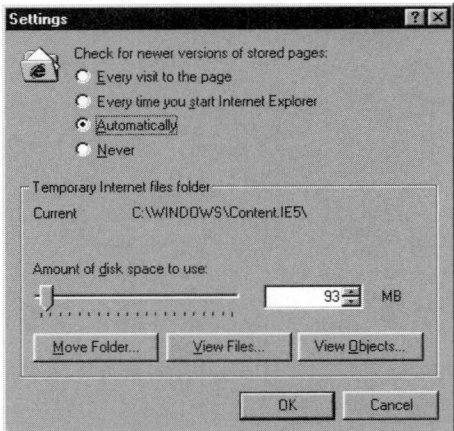

❸ Select how often you want Internet Explorer to check for newer versions of stored files. You can retain the Automatically default setting or select one of the other three options.

❹ Drag the slider (beneath the words *On the Amount Of Disk Space To Use*) to the left or right.

The allocation size for the disk cache changes for the Temporary Internet Files folder.

❺ Click OK to close the Settings dialog box, and click OK to close the Internet Options dialog box.

Delete temporary Internet files

As your Temporary Internet Files folder fills up, you might want to delete some of the saved Web page files. In this exercise, you delete temporary Internet files.

After you delete your temporary Internet files, Internet Explorer will download new files for each Web page you visit.

❶ On the Tools menu, click Internet Options.

The Internet Options dialog box is displayed.

❷ On the General tab in the Temporary Internet Files section, click Delete Files, and then click OK in the Delete Files dialog box.

The files stored in your Temporary Internet Files folder are deleted.

❸ Click OK.

The Internet Options dialog box closes.

Finish the lesson

❶ If necessary, display your Favorites bar, and delete any links or folders created in this lesson.

❷ Quit Internet Explorer.

Lesson 2 Quick Reference

To	Do this	Button
Display the Search Assistant	Click the Search button on the toolbar.	
Search for a Web site	Display the Search Assistant, enter a search word in the text box, and click the Search button.	
Select a search engine	Display the Search Assistant, type a search word in the text box, click the Search button, click the drop-down arrow to the right of the Next button and select a search engine.	
Choose a category to narrow down searches	Display the Search Assistant, and click a category.	
Use Autosearch	In the Address bar, type **go**, **find**, or **?**, press the Spacebar, type a word or phrase, and press Enter.	
Add the current Web page to your Favorites list	Display a Web page. Click the Favorites button on the toolbar. Click the Add button on the Favorites bar, and click OK.	
Add your desktop to your Favorites list	In the Address bar, type desktop, and press Enter. Click Add To Favorites on the Favorites menu, and click OK.	
Use the Favorites bar	Click the Favorites button on the toolbar, and then click a Favorites link on the Favorites bar.	
Use the Favorites menu	Click a Favorites link on the Favorites menu.	
Access Favorites from the Windows taskbar	On the Windows taskbar, click Start, point to Favorites, and then click a Favorites link.	
Create a folder within your Favorites list	Display the Favorites bar, click Organize, click the Create Folder button, type a name for the new folder, press Enter, and click the Close button.	

Lesson 2 Quick Reference

To	Do this	Button
Move an existing Favorites link into a folder	Display the Favorites bar, click Organize, select the item to be moved, click the Move To Folder button, select the folder to store the selected item, click OK, and click the Close button.	
Place a new Favorites link into a folder	Display a Web page. Display the Favorites bar, click Add, click the Create In button (if necessary), click the folder to store the new Favorites link, and click OK.	
Rename a Favorites link	Display the Favorites bar, click Organize, click the link to be renamed, click the Rename button, type a new name for the Favorites link, press Enter, and click the Close button.	
Delete Favorites	Display the Favorites bar, click Organize, select a Favorites link to delete, click the Delete button, click Yes, and click the Close button.	
View your Web usage history	Click the History button on the toolbar.	
Configure your history settings	Click Internet Options on the Tools menu, make desired changes in the History section, and click OK.	
Clear your History folder	Click Internet Options on the Tools menu, click Clear History, click OK, and click OK to close the Internet Options dialog box.	
Configure your Temporary Internet Files settings	Click Internet Options on the Tools menu, click Settings, make desired changes, click OK in the Settings dialog box, and click OK to close the Internet Options dialog box.	
Delete temporary Internet files	Click Internet Options on the Tools menu, click Delete Files, click OK in the Delete Files dialog box, and then click OK to close the Internet Options dialog box.	

LESSON

3

Customizing Your Work Space

ESTIMATED TIME
30 min.

In this lesson you will learn how to:

- ✔ *Specify your home page.*
- ✔ *Use the status bar.*
- ✔ *Customize your view.*
- ✔ *Customize the toolbar.*
- ✔ *Work with the Links toolbar.*
- ✔ *Specify how links appear.*

As you work with Microsoft Internet Explorer at Impact Public Relations, you find that you want to customize the browser's interface to suit your working style. You learn from a colleague that Internet Explorer has a number of features that enable you to change the way your browser looks and responds. Your colleague explains that you can assign which page is displayed when you click the Home button; you can even customize the appearance of the browser's toolbars and buttons. You can also specify how links appear on Web pages.

After learning about these Internet Explorer features, you decide to spend the last hour of the day experimenting with Internet Explorer's options. Because so many of your clients at Impact Public Relations want to have a strong Web presence, you decide that learning to get the most out of Internet Explorer will have a very positive impact on your relationships with your clients.

In this lesson, you will learn how to specify your own home page, hide and display the status bar, customize your view and toolbars, work with the Links toolbar, and specify how links should appear as you surf the Web.

Specifying Your Home Page

You can make the Home button point to any Internet document or any other file or folder on your hard disk.

You can click the Home button to return to your Internet home page—the page initially displayed each time you start Internet Explorer. But Internet Explorer also enables you to change your home page. By changing your home page, you can make the Home button display your company's Web site, a Web page you visit frequently, a file or folder stored on your computer, or even a blank page. To specify a different home page, click Internet Options on the Tools menu.

Notice that the Home Page section on the General tab contains an Address text box. You can type the address for your desired home page there. A good way to determine what your home page should be is to determine what you typically do first when you visit the Internet. For instance, some people check their local weather, some check sports scores, and others check their stock portfolio.

Specify a home page

In this exercise, you temporarily change your home page to the Lakewood Mountains Resort home page. Then you change your home page to the default setting.

1 Start Internet Explorer.

2 On the Tools menu, click Internet Options.

The Internet Options dialog box is displayed.

The Use Current button enables you to change your home page to the Web site that is currently displayed in Internet Explorer.

3 On the General tab in the Home Page area, type **mspress.microsoft.com/ mspress/products/1349/default1.htm** in the address text box, and click OK.

The Lakewood Mountains Resort is now your home page.

4 On the toolbar, click the Home button.

The Lakewood Mountains Resort home page is displayed.

5 On the Tools menu, click Internet Options.

The Internet Options dialog box is displayed.

6 On the General tab in the Home Page area, click the Use Default button.

The default home page address appears in the Address text box.

7 Click OK.

The Internet Options dialog box closes.

You can click the Use Blank button to assign a blank page to the Home button.

8 Click the Home button.

The default home page is displayed.

Using the Status Bar

The status bar appears along the bottom of the Internet Explorer window and provides tidbits of information as you browse the Web.

Link and download   Progress bar   Security zone
information

For the most part, the status bar displays hyperlink information. When you move your mouse pointer over a link, the link's address appears in the left portion of the status bar. When you click a link, the middle portion of the status bar reports on Internet Explorer's progress as it locates the linked Web page. Then, as the linked site opens on your computer, the status bar displays the download progress. (Notice the illustration indicates that there are five items remaining to be downloaded.) A progress bar is also displayed in the middle of the status bar while a page is downloaded. On the far right portion of the status bar, you can see the security zone setting for the current page. You can read more about security zones in Lesson 4, in the section "Customizing Internet Explorer's Security Settings." While the status bar can be a helpful tool, there might be times when you would rather have a larger viewing area than have constant feedback about your browser's activity. If you want, you can hide or display the status bar by clicking Status Bar on the View menu.

You're preparing for tomorrow's meeting with the CEO of Lakewood Mountains Resort. You want to use the Lakewood Mountains Resort home page as a basis for discussion. You decide that you want to hide the status bar to make the site look extra "clean."

Hide or display the status bar

In this exercise, you hide and display the status bar while viewing the Lakewood Mountains Resort home page.

1 Display the Lakewood Mountains Resort home page (*mspress.microsoft.com/mspress/products/1349/default1.htm*).

A check mark to the left of the Status Bar option on the View menu means that the status bar is currently displayed.

2 On the View menu, click Status Bar.

Internet Explorer no longer displays the status bar along the bottom edge of the browser window.

3 On the View menu, click Status Bar again.

The status bar is redisplayed in the browser window.

Customizing Your View

Internet Explorer provides options that enable you to change how a Web page is displayed. For example, you can change a Web page's text size and color, and you can specify a Web page's background color. Another view option enables you to maximize your browser's viewing area by displaying Web pages in Full Screen view. All the view options are easily accessible in Internet Explorer, and they can help you display Web sites to your best advantage.

Like people, no two Web pages are exactly alike. Some Web pages sport microscopic print while others blast your eyes with enormous text. You adjust text size by pointing to the Text Size command on the View menu. You can display Web page text as Largest, Larger, Medium, Smaller, or Smallest. You'll probably want to make this adjustment on a site-by-site basis, unless you have a general visual preference for larger or smaller type.

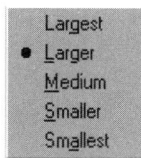

The following illustration shows the Lakewood Mountains Resort Web site's menu with the Smallest, Medium, and Largest text settings applied.

In addition to changing the text size on Web pages, you can specify the text and background colors used by Web pages. By default, Internet Explorer uses the colors specified by the Web page designer. However, occasionally, you'll come across a Web site that has content you want to view, but also has garish background color that makes it difficult to ready anything.

To change Web page color settings, you click Internet Options on the Tools menu and then click the Colors button.

The Colors dialog box assists you in assigning colors to Web page text and backgrounds. Notice the Use Windows Colors option is selected by default.

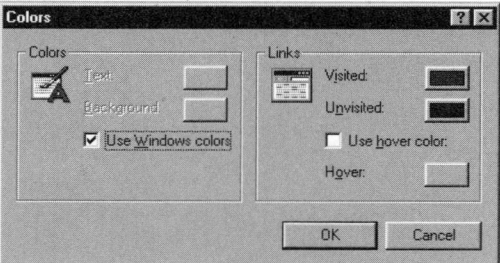

When the Use Windows Colors option is selected, Internet Explorer displays Web pages with the colors and text that the Web designer selected. The first step to changing text and background colors is clearing the Use Windows Colors check box. The Text color and Background color buttons then become activated. To select a color, you click either the Text color button or the Background color button, and select a color from the palette.

important

To make Internet Explorer use your colors in place of the Web page designer's colors, you need to adjust your Accessibility settings. To do so, click Internet Options on the Tools menu, and click the Accessibility button on the General tab in the Internet Options dialog box. In the Accessibility dialog box, click the Ignore Colors Specified On Web Pages check box, and then click OK.

Finally, along with changing your text and color scheme settings, you can choose to display Web pages in Full Screen view. When you choose Full Screen view, Internet Explorer displays the maximum amount of viewing area and a scaled-down toolbar, while it hides the menu bar, Address bar, and status bar.

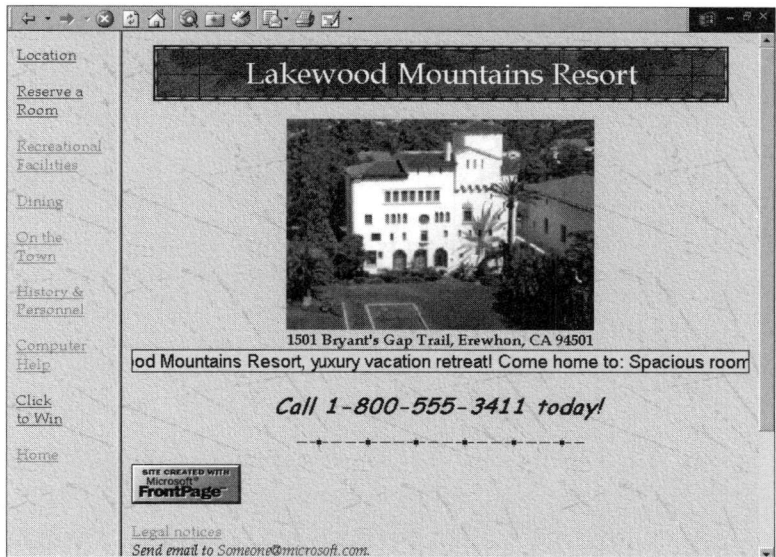

To shift to Full Screen view, you click Full Screen on the View menu. Then, when you want to return to the standard view, press F11.

Suppose that you are still in your office researching Internet Explorer's features. Most of your public relations campaigns use Web pages, so you want to be comfortable with Internet Explorer's view options. Furthermore, you often use clients' Web sites during marketing meetings and presentations. You foresee that it will be helpful to be able to customize views to suit particular situations.

Change the text size

In this exercise, you change the text size on the Lakewood Mountains Resort home page.

1 Display the Lakewood Mountains Resort home page (*mspress.microsoft.com/mspress/products/1349/default1.htm*).

2 On the View menu, point to Text Size, and click Smallest.

The Lakewood Mountains Resort home page is displayed with the smallest available text size.

❸ On the View menu, point to Text Size, and then click Largest.

The page is displayed with the largest available text size.

Medium-sized text is the default size in Internet Explorer.

❹ On the View menu, point to Text Size, and then click Medium.

The Lakewood Mountains Resort is displayed with medium-sized text.

Assign text and background colors

In this exercise, you change the text color to blue and the background color to white on the Lakewood Mountains Resort Recreation page.

❶ On the Lakewood Mountains Resort home page, click the Recreational Facilities link.

The Recreation Web page is displayed.

❷ On the Tools menu, click Internet Options.

The Internet Options dialog box is displayed.

❸ On the General tab, click the Colors button.

The Colors dialog box is displayed.

❹ In the Colors dialog box, clear the Use Windows Colors check box.

This activates the Text and Background color buttons.

❺ Click the Text color button, click a blue square on the color palette, and then click OK.

The text color is set to blue.

❻ Click the Background color button, click the white square on the color palette, and click OK.

The background color is set to white.

❼ Click OK to close the Colors dialog box.

❽ On the General tab, click the Accessibility button.

The Accessibility dialog box is displayed.

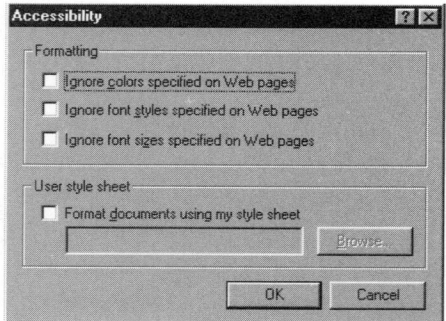

9 Click the Ignore Colors Specified On Web Pages check box, and click OK.

Web page color schemes will now be ignored and your color settings will be displayed.

10 Click OK to close the Internet Options dialog box.

The Recreation page is displayed with blue text on a white background.

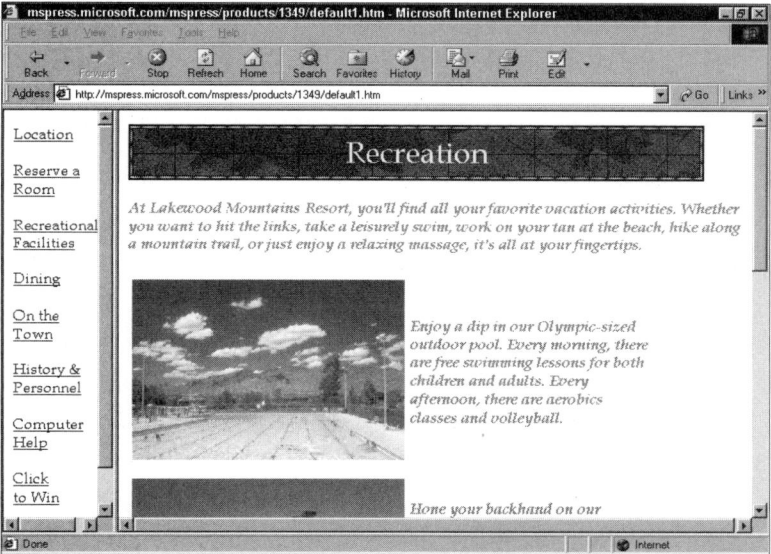

11 On the Tools menu, click Internet Options.

The Internet Options dialog box is displayed.

12 On the General tab, click Accessibility.

The Accessibility dialog box is displayed.

13 Clear the Ignore Colors Specified On Web Pages check box, and click OK.

The instruction to replace Web page settings with your color specifications is removed.

14 On the General tab, click the Colors button.

The Colors dialog box is displayed.

15 Click the Use Windows Colors option, click OK, and then click OK again to close the Internet Options dialog box.

The custom color settings are removed, and the default settings are restored. The Recreation page is displayed with the Web designer's selected colors.

> **tip**
> Keep in mind that when you assign default colors to Web pages, you might run into situations where you cannot see a Web page's links or graphic elements due to color issues. For example, a black or darkly colored background can make it difficult or impossible to see text and dark buttons. Generally, it is best to view Web sites using the Web designer's settings or change colors only when the Web designer's selections were poorly selected.

Alternate between standard view and Full Screen view

In this exercise, you display the Lakewood Mountains Resort Recreation page in Full Screen view, and then you revert to Internet Explorer's standard view.

1 On the View menu, click Full Screen.

Internet Explorer changes to Full Screen view. Notice the smaller toolbar and the lack of an Address bar, menu bar, and status bar.

2 Press F11.

Internet Explorer redisplays the Web page in the standard view.

Customizing the Toolbar

You can customize the Internet Explorer toolbar in a variety of ways:

- Add and remove toolbar buttons.
- Display the toolbar icons as small icons.
- Hide and display the toolbar's text labels.
- Change the position of buttons on the toolbar.

For a demonstration of how to add a button to the toolbar, in the Multimedia folder on the Microsoft Internet Explorer 5 Step by Step CD-ROM, double-click the Add Button icon.

You can add buttons to your toolbar so that you don't have to use the menu bar and you don't have to memorize shortcut keys. For example, if you add the Size button to the toolbar, you can quickly access the Text Size menu. Just click the Size button to view the Text Size menu options (Largest, Larger, Medium, Smaller, and Smallest). If you add the Full Screen button to the toolbar, you won't have to switch to Full Screen view via the View menu, and you won't have to memorize that you must press F11 to change back to standard view. Just click the Full Screen button to switch between views. To add buttons to your toolbar, you display the View menu, point to Toolbars, and click Customize. In the Available Toolbar Buttons list, select a button and click the Add button.

To save space on your toolbar, you can make the buttons smaller and hide the buttons' labels. Below the Available Toolbar Buttons list in the Customize Toolbar dialog box are text and icon options. If you click the drop-down arrow to the right of the Icon Options box and select Small Icons, Internet Explorer will display the toolbar with small icons.

If you click the drop-down arrow to the right of the Text Options box and select No Text Labels, Internet Explorer will display the toolbar without text labels, whether small or large icons are displayed.

New!

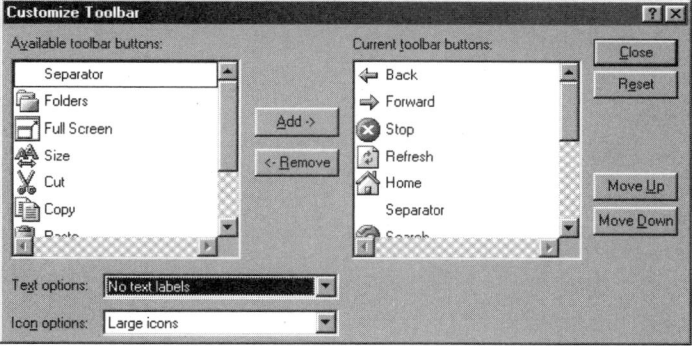

You can also use the Customize Toolbar dialog box change the position of buttons on the toolbar by using the Move Up and Move Down buttons.

Add and remove buttons

In this exercise, you display the Size button and the Full Screen button on the toolbar and then you hide the Size button.

You can quickly display the Customize Toolbar dialog box by right-clicking an empty area of the toolbar and clicking Customize.

1 On the View menu, point to Toolbars, and click Customize.

The Customize Toolbar dialog box is displayed.

2 In the Available Toolbar Buttons list, click the Size button.

The Size button is selected.

3 Click Add.

The Size button is now listed in the Current Toolbar Buttons list.

4 In the Available Toolbar Buttons list, click the Full Screen button.

The Full Screen button is selected.

5 Click Add.

The Full Screen button is now listed in the Current Toolbar Buttons list.

6 Click the Close button.

The Customize Toolbar dialog box closes, and the Size and Full Screen buttons are displayed on the toolbar.

Size

7 Click the Size button. (You might have to click the double-arrow to the right of the toolbar to display this button.)

Internet Explorer displays the Text Size menu.

Full Screen

8 Click the Full Screen button. (You might have to click the double-arrow to the right of the toolbar to display this button.)

Internet Explorer is displayed in Full Screen view.

9 Click the Full Screen button again.

Internet Explorer is displayed in standard view.

10 On the View menu, point to Toolbars, and click Customize.

The Customize Toolbar dialog box is displayed.

11 In the Current Toolbar Buttons List, click the Size button.

12 Click Remove.

The Size button is moved back to the Available Toolbar Buttons list.

13 Click the Close button.

The Size button is removed from the toolbar.

Display small icons

In this exercise, you display small icons on the toolbar buttons and then you revert to the toolbar's large icon view.

1 On the View menu, point to Toolbars, and click Customize.

The Customize Toolbar dialog box is displayed.

2 Click the drop-down arrow to the right of the Icon Options box, select Small Icons, and click the Close button.

The Customize Toolbar dialog box closes, and the toolbar now displays small icons.

3 On the View menu, point to Toolbars, and then click Customize.

The Customize Toolbar dialog box is displayed.

4 Click the drop-down arrow to the right of the Icon Options box, click Large Icons, and click the Close button.

The toolbar buttons revert to the large icon size.

Hide and display text labels

In this exercise, you hide and display text labels on the toolbar buttons.

1 On the View menu, point to Toolbars, and then click Customize.

The Customize Toolbar dialog box is displayed.

2 Click the drop-down arrow to the right of the Text Options box, click No Text Labels, and click the Close button.

The text labels are removed from the toolbar buttons.

3 On the View menu, point to Toolbars, and then click Customize.

The Customize Toolbar dialog box is displayed.

4 Click the drop-down arrow to the right of the Text Options box, click Show Text Labels, and click the Close button.

The text labels are displayed on the toolbar buttons.

Change the position of buttons on the toolbar

In this exercise, you use the Customize Toolbar dialog box to change the position of buttons on the toolbar.

1 On the View menu, point to Toolbars, and then click Customize.

The Customize Toolbar dialog box is displayed.

2 If necessary, click at the top of the Customize Toolbar dialog box and drag it down so you can see your toolbar.

3 In the Current Toolbar Buttons list, click the Refresh button, and then click the Move Up button until the Refresh button is at the top of the list.

The Refresh button moves to the beginning of the Current Toolbar Buttons list and is displayed on the far-left end of the toolbar.

Your toolbar is updated as you make changes in the Customize Toolbar dialog box, so you can view your settings without closing the dialog box.

4 Click the Move Down button once.

The Refresh button moves down one space in the Current Toolbar Buttons list and is positioned between the Back and Forward buttons on the toolbar.

5 In the Customize Toolbar dialog box, click the Reset button.

The toolbar is reset to its default settings.

6 Click the Close button.

The Customize Toolbar dialog box closes.

Working with the Links Toolbar

The Links toolbar is a highly customizable toolbar that you can use to store and access links to frequently visited Web pages. Unlike your Favorites list, there's room for only a few buttons on the Links toolbar, so you should add buttons for only your top four or five Web sites. The links toolbar makes it easy for you to access your favorite Web sites because after a Web site is added, you need only to click the link to revisit it. To show the Links toolbar, drag the word *Links* (located to the right of the Address bar) below the Address bar.

| Links | Best of the Web | Channel Guide | Customize Links | Free HotMail | Internet Start | Microsoft | Windows Update | » |

To display the Web page associated with a Links item, click the link on the Links toolbar. You can add items to the Links toolbar in a number of ways; however, dragging a link to the Links toolbar is the easiest approach. You can drag Web page addresses from the Address bar onto the Links toolbar, or you can drag links from Web pages onto the Links toolbar. To remove a link, right-click the link you want to remove, and then click Delete on the shortcut menu. Add a link to the Links toolbar if you visit a site frequently. Remove a link if your visitations to the site begin to drop off so that you can create room for adding a more frequently used link.

You decide that you want to add the Lakewood Mountains Resort home page to your Links toolbar. Then you add the Location page to your Links toolbar.

Add and remove links

In this exercise, you add the Lakewood Mountains Resort home page and the Location page to your Links toolbar, and then you remove them from the Links toolbar.

❶   If necessary, display the Lakewood Mountains Resort home page (*mspress.microsoft.com/mspress/products/1349/default1.htm*).

❷   Drag the word *Links* located to the right of the Address bar downward.

The Links toolbar is displayed below the Address bar.

important

To place a link on the Links toolbar, position the pointer between two existing links before releasing the mouse button. If you try to place a link on top of an existing link, Internet Explorer will not add it to the Links toolbar.

Click the double-arrow character at the end of the Links toolbar to see more Links.

❸ In the Address bar, drag the icon appearing to the left of the Lakewood Mountains Resort URL to the Links toolbar, and when the pointer changes to an insertion mark, release the mouse button.

The Lakewood Home Page link is displayed on the Links toolbar.

❹ In the left frame of the Lakewood Mountains Resort home page, drag the Location link to the Links toolbar.

A link to the Location page appears on the Links toolbar.

❺ On the Links toolbar, right-click the Lakewood Home Page link.

A shortcut menu is displayed.

❻ Click Delete on the shortcut menu, and click Yes to confirm the deletion.

The Lakewood Home Page link is removed from the Links toolbar.

❼ On the Links toolbar, right-click the Location link.

A shortcut menu is displayed.

❽ Click Delete on the shortcut menu, and click Yes to confirm the deletion.

The Location link is removed from the Links toolbar.

❾ Click the word *Links* and drag it up to the Address bar and over to the far-right corner of the Address bar.

The Links bar is restored to its default setting.

tip

Click Customize Links on the Links toolbar to display a Web page that tells you more about working with the Links toolbar.

One Step Further

Specifying How Links Appear

You can customize link colors just as you can customize text and background colors for Web pages. You can also specify a color for links you've already clicked, which helps you to keep track of what Web pages you recently visited. Furthermore, you can add a *hover* color to links. To *hover* means to place your mouse pointer over a link without clicking the link.

When you add a hover color to links, Internet Explorer changes the color of links when you point to them with the mouse pointer. When you move the mouse pointer away from the link, the link reverts to its specified link color. Some Web designers automatically build the hover color feature into their Web page designs. (Many Microsoft sites take advantage of this feature.) Finally, you can customize when (and if) links should appear underlined. Links that become underlined after your mouse pointer passes over them are easier to see.

tip

If you are printing a Web page on a black and white printer, consider temporarily changing the default link colors to black. That way, the links will be printed clearly. Some link colors are printed faintly on a black and white printer or not at all.

Change link colors

In this exercise, you change link colors and view the color changes on the Lakewood Mountains Resort home page.

1. If necessary, display the Lakewood Mountains Resort home page (*mspress.microsoft.com/mspress/products/1349/default1.htm*).
2. On the Tools menu, click Internet Options.
    The Internet Options dialog box is displayed.
3. On the General tab, click the Colors button.
    The Colors dialog box is displayed.
4. In the Links area, click the Visited color button
    The Color dialog box is displayed.
5. Click a gray square on the Color palette, and click OK.
    Links that you have clicked will appear gray.
6. In the Links area, click the Unvisited color button, click a purple square on the Color palette, and click OK.
    Links that you have not clicked will appear purple.
7. Click OK.
    The Colors dialog box closes.
8. Click the Accessibility button.
    The Accessibility dialog box is displayed.

9   Click the Ignore Colors Specified On Web Pages check box, and click OK.

The link colors you selected will override any settings created by Web page designers.

10   Click OK.

The Internet Options dialog box closes. Notice that the links on the Lakewood Mountains Resort menu are displayed in purple and gray text and the background color changed to white.

11   On the Tools menu, click Internet Options.

The Internet Options dialog box is displayed.

12   Click the Accessibility button, clear the Ignore Colors Specified On Web Pages check box, and click OK.

The option to override Web page designers' color settings is turned off and the Accessibility dialog box closes.

13   Click OK again.

The Internet Options dialog box closes. The Lakewood Mountains Resort home page is displayed with its default settings.

Use the hover color feature

In this exercise, you turn on the hover color feature and display links in green whenever the mouse pointer moves over a link.

1   On the Tools menu, click Internet Options.

The Internet Options dialog box is displayed.

2   On the General tab, click the Colors button.

The Colors dialog box is displayed.

3   Click the Use Hover Color check box.

The hover feature is turned on.

4   Click the Hover color button, click a green square in the Color palette, and click OK.

Links will be displayed in green text when the mouse pointer moves over a link.

5   Click OK.

The Colors dialog box closes.

6   Click OK again.

The Internet Options dialog box closes.

7 Move the mouse pointer (without clicking) over the links in the Lakewood Mountains Resort left frame.

Each link in the Lakewood Mountains Resort left frame temporary is displayed in green text as the mouse pointer moves over the link.

8 On the Tools menu, click Internet Options.

The Internet Options dialog box is displayed.

9 On the General tab, click the Colors button.

The Colors dialog box is displayed.

10 Clear the Use Hover Color check box.

The hover feature is turned off.

11 Click OK.

The Colors dialog box closes.

12 Click OK again.

The Internet Options dialog box closes. The links in the Lakewood Mountains Resort left frame are returned to their default settings.

Customize link underlines

In this exercise, you display links with underlines only when you hover over the link.

1 On the Tools menu, click Internet Options.

The Internet Options dialog box is displayed.

2 Click the Advanced tab.

3 Scroll down to Underline Links under the Browsing heading.

4 Click the Hover option, and then click OK.

Links will now be displayed with an underline only when you move the mouse pointer over the link.

5 Move the mouse pointer slowly over the left frame's links.

Each link is displayed with an underline as you move the mouse pointer over the link. The underline disappears when the mouse pointer is no longer over the link.

6 On the Tools menu, click Internet Options.

The Internet Options dialog box is displayed.

7 Click the Advanced tab in the Internet Options dialog box.

8 Scroll down to the Underline Links option listed under the Browsing heading, click the Always option, and then click OK.

The link underline feature is returned to the default setting.

Finish the lesson

● Quit Internet Explorer.

Lesson 3 Quick Reference

To	Do this	Button
Specify a home page	Click Internet Options on the Tools menu, enter an address in the Address text box, and click OK.	
Hide or display the status bar	Click Status Bar on the View menu.	
Change text size	On the View menu, point to Text Size, and click a size setting, *or* click the Size button on the toolbar, and choose a size setting.	
Assign text or background colors	Click Internet Options on the Tools menu, click the Colors button on the General tab, clear the Use Windows Colors check box, click the Text or Background color button, select a color on the color palette, click OK, and click OK to close the Colors dialog box. Click the Accessibility button on the General tab, click the Ignore Colors Specified On Web Pages check box, and click OK. Click OK to close the Internet Options dialog box.	
Alternate between standard and Full Screen view	Click Full Screen on the View menu, and Press F11, *or* click the Full Screen button on the toolbar.	
Add or remove toolbar buttons	On the View menu, point to Toolbars, and click Customize. In the Available Toolbar Buttons list, click a button, click Add, or in the Current Toolbar Buttons list, click a button, click Remove, and then click the Close button.	

Lesson 3 Quick Reference

To	Do this
Display small icons	On the View menu, point to Toolbars, and click Customize. Click the drop-down arrow to the right of the Icon Options box, select Small Icons, and click the Close button.
Hide or display text labels	On the View menu, point to Toolbars, and then click Customize. Click the drop-down arrow to the right of the Text Options box, click No Text Labels, or click Show Text Labels, and click the Close button.
Change the position of toolbar buttons	On the View menu, point to Toolbars, and then click Customize. Click a button in the Current Toolbar Buttons list, and click the Move Up or Move Down button, and click the Close button.
Display the Links toolbar	Click the word *Links* to the right of the Address bar, and then drag it under the Address bar.
Add links to the Links toolbar	Drag the icon to the left of a URL in the Address bar onto the Links toolbar, *or* drag a link on a Web page onto the Links toolbar.
Remove links from the Links toolbar	Right-click a link on the Links toolbar, click Delete on the shortcut menu, and then click Yes.
Change link colors	Click Internet Options on the Tools menu, and click the Colors button on the General tab. Click the Visited color button or the Unvisited color button, select a color, and click OK. Click OK to close the Colors dialog box. Click the Accessibility button on the General tab, click the Ignore Colors Specified On Web Pages check box, and click OK. Click OK to close the Internet Options dialog box.
Use the hover color feature	Click Internet Options on the Tools menu, and click the Colors button on the General tab. Click the Use Hover Color check box, click the Hover color button, select a color, and click OK. Click OK to close the Colors dialog box, and click OK to close the Internet Options dialog box.
Customize link underlines	Click Internet Options on the Tools menu, and click the Advanced tab. Scroll down to the Underline Links option listed under the Browsing heading, click the Always, Hover, or Never option, and then click OK.

Review & Practice

ESTIMATED TIME
20 min.

You will review and practice how to:

✔ *Browse Web sites.*

✔ *Create and delete shortcuts to Web sites.*

✔ *Search for information.*

✔ *Customize Internet Explorer's view.*

✔ *Manage Web information on your hard disk drive.*

Before you move on to Part 2, you can practice the skills you learned in Part 1 by working through this Review & Practice. In this section, you will browse Web sites and create and delete shortcuts to Web pages. You will search for information and customize your browser's view. Finally, you will manage your hard disk drive by clearing your History and Temporary Internet Files folders.

Scenario

Business is booming at Impact Public Relations. The Lakewood Mountains Resort account is flourishing so much that you've recently hired an assistant. The assistant's sole responsibility will be to handle the day-to-day affairs for the Lakewood Mountains Resort account. You've taken it upon yourself to train the assistant. Today's agenda includes showing the assistant how to use Internet Explorer's basic features. You will show the assistant how to browse Web sites, manage shortcuts to Web pages, search for information, customize the browser's view, and manage the History and Temporary Internet Files folders on the computer's hard disk drive.

Step 1:   Open Internet Explorer and View Web pages

The first step in using Internet Explorer is to open the browser and display Web pages. Therefore, you show the assistant how to open Internet Explorer and access the Lakewood Mountains Resort home page. Then you show her how to click hyperlinks to open related Web pages, and use the Back and Forward buttons to navigate among the pages you've visited during the current session. Finally, you print the Lakewood Mountains Resort reservation form.

❶   Click the Internet Explorer desktop icon to open Internet Explorer.

❷   Use the Address bar to access the Lakewood Mountains Resort home page (*mspress.microsoft.com/mspress/products/1349/default1.htm*).

❸   Navigate among various Lakewood Mountains Resort Web site pages by clicking hyperlinks.

❹   Use the Back and Forward buttons on the toolbar to view pages you visited recently during this session.

❺   Open the Lakewood Mountains Resort Reserve A Room Web page, and then print it.

For more information about	See
Opening Internet Explorer	Lesson 1
Using the Address bar	Lesson 1
Clicking hyperlinks	Lesson 1
Moving forward and backward	Lesson 1
Printing Web pages	Lesson 1

Step 2:   Create and Remove Shortcuts to Web Sites

Now that your assistant feels comfortable viewing Web pages, you show her how to streamline Web surfing by using shortcuts to Web sites. You demonstrate how to create Favorites folders and links, add links to the Links toolbar, create desktop shortcuts, and change the home page.

❶   Create a Favorites folder named Lakewood, and add a Favorites link within the folder to the Lakewood Mountains Resort Web site (*mspress.microsoft. com/mspress/products/1349/default1.htm*).

❷   Drag the Reserve A Room Web page link from the Lakewood Mountains Resort menu to your Links toolbar.

❸   Use the File menu's Send command to create a desktop shortcut for the Lakewood Mountains Resort Web site.

❹ Display the General tab in the Internet Options dialog box, and change the home page address setting to the Lakewood Mountains Resort home page (*mspress.microsoft.com/mspress/products/1349/default1.htm*).

For more information about	See
Managing Favorites	Lesson 2
Customizing the Links toolbar	Lesson 3
Creating desktop shortcuts	Lesson 1
Changing the home page	Lesson 3

Step 3:   Find Information

You discover that your assistant has some great marketing ideas that involve researching information on the Web. You demonstrate how to search for information on the Internet as well as how to find information on a page when it's displayed in the browser.

❶ Open the Search Assistant.

❷ Search for Web sites related to the term *resorts* by using a search engine in the Search Assistant.

❸ Open a site that matches your search criterion.

❹ Use the Find (On This Page) command on the Edit menu to find the word *restaurant* on the page.

❺ Close the Search Assistant.

❻ Use the Address bar to find Web sites about restaurants.

For more information about	See
Opening and closing the Search Assistant	Lesson 2
Searching for Web sites using search engines	Lesson 2
Scanning for specific text on a Web page	Lesson 1
Finding Web pages using the Address bar	Lesson 2

Step 4:   Customize Internet Explorer's View

Your assistant has become familiar with basic browsing and searching activities, so you show her how to customize the browser's view. You demonstrate how to hide and display the status bar, add and remove toolbar buttons, toggle between Full Screen and standard view, configure how hyperlinks appear, and change text and background colors.

❶ Hide and redisplay the status bar using the View menu.

❷ Add the Copy button to the toolbar, and display toolbar buttons without text labels.

❸ Revert the toolbar to its default settings.

❹ Change Internet Explorer's view to Full Screen view, and then return to standard view.

❺ Add a red hover color to hyperlinks.

❻ Change the default Web page colors to black for the background, white for the text, yellow for unvisited hyperlinks, and bright green for visited links.

❼ Configure your browser to ignore colors specified on Web pages.

For more information about	See
Toggling the status bar on and off	Lesson 3
Customizing the toolbar	Lesson 3
Changing to Full Screen view	Lesson 3
Applying a hover color to hyperlinks	Lesson 3
Assigning Web page colors	Lesson 3

Step 5:   Manage Web Information on Your Hard Disk

Your assistant is ready to get to work, but first you explain how to manage Internet information that automatically accumulates on the computer. You describe how the History folder and the Temporary Internet Files folder store information about sites that are visited on the Internet. Then you show how to view the default settings for emptying the folders, and you demonstrate how to empty the folders manually.

❶ Use the Internet Options dialog box to view the History folder and Temporary Internet Files folder settings.

❷ Use the Internet Options dialog box to clear the contents of the History folder.

❸ Delete temporary Internet files by using the Internet Options dialog box.

For more information about	See
Viewing History and Temporary Internet Files folder settings	Lesson 2
Clearing the History folder contents	Lesson 2
Deleting temporary Internet files	Lesson 2

Finish the Review & Practice

1   Delete the Lakewood folder and its contents.

2   Remove the Reserve A Room link from the Links toolbar.

3   Drag the Lakewood Mountains Resort desktop shortcut to the Recycle Bin.

4   Remove the option to ignore Web page colors.

5   Revert to the default Windows colors setting, and clear the Use Hover Color option.

6   Reset the home page to the default setting by clicking the Use Default button on the General tab in the Internet Options dialog box.

7   Quit Internet Explorer.

PART 2

Optimizing Internet Explorer 5 Features

4

Activating Security and Personal Information Settings

ESTIMATED TIME
40 min.

In this lesson you will learn how to:

✔ *Customize Internet Explorer's security settings.*

✔ *Set Content Rating preferences.*

✔ *Add personal information to Microsoft Wallet.*

✔ *Add a component to Internet Explorer.*

As you and your partners at Impact Public Relations have worked with clients on their Web-based marketing, they've asked often about security. In particular, your clients are concerned about downloading content from the Internet that might damage data on their computers. Other security-related issues voiced by clients have involved controlling access to Web sites based on content and how to transfer private information (such as credit card information) securely and easily across the Internet. These topics are important for Impact Public Relations employees as well as for your clients. Microsoft Internet Explorer addresses these issues by providing security zones, control over sensitive Web content (Content Advisor), and secure Web purchasing (Microsoft Wallet).

In this lesson, you will explore Internet Explorer's security zones to see how they help you monitor Web sites. You will also walk through the steps of activating Internet Explorer's Content Advisor tool and configure Internet Explorer's Microsoft Wallet feature. Finally, you will learn how to download and install Internet Explorer components that can expand your browser's capabilities.

Customizing Internet Explorer's Security Settings

Internet security is a hot topic—and for good reason. Both Internet content providers and Web page visitors need to be aware of security issues to help protect data. As an Internet user, you want to avoid downloading content that can damage the data you have stored on your computer. To help you control what types of content you download from the Internet, Internet Explorer provides *security zones*. Security zones help you to accept, monitor, and reject certain types of content stored on Web pages.

Using security zones is a two-tier process. First, you classify Web pages into zones; second, you apply a security level to each zone.

You can classify a page as belonging to the Local Intranet zone, Trusted Sites zone, Restricted Sites zone, or Internet zone. Then you can assign a security level to each zone—High, Medium, Low, or Custom.

Default Security Zones

Zone	Description	Security
Local Intranet	Typically contains resources that are part of your company's internal network (or *intranet*).	Medium
Trusted Sites	Contains sites from which you believe you can download content without concern, such as an official Microsoft download site.	Low
Restricted Sites	Includes Web sites that you do not trust. You assign sites to this zone if you're not sure that you can download and run files from the site without damaging your computer or data.	High
Internet	Applies to any files that are not on your computer, your intranet, or assigned to another zone. Most Web pages on the Internet fall into the Internet zone category.	Medium

When you assign a security level, you are concerned about the type of content that is allowed to be downloaded from Web pages. Basically, the security levels determine what action Internet Explorer takes when it encounters a Web page with a *component* or extra feature that could damage data on your computer. Keep in mind that to say that Web page content is "potentially damaging" does not mean that it is somehow nefarious or criminal. It means only that certain types of Web page content, such as *ActiveX controls* (small components, embedded in Web pages, that run on your computer), have the ability to cause harm if their author designed them to do so or designed them poorly. Using security zones to prevent "potentially damaging" content from downloading to your computer is just a matter of playing it safe—not a matter of paranoia.

Here's how each level reacts to a potentially damaging Web page component:

■ High security: Internet Explorer blocks any potentially dangerous content or processes from downloading onto your computer. You will receive a message box stating that the content may not be displayed correctly due to the High security setting.

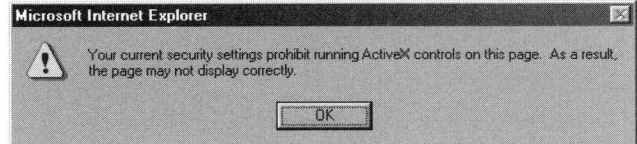

■ Medium security: Internet Explorer provides a Security Warning dialog box when you visit a site that attempts to download content to your hard disk drive, as shown below. You use this dialog box to continue to download the content.

You can choose to always accept content from a trusted source by clicking the Always Trust Content From (name of source) check box.

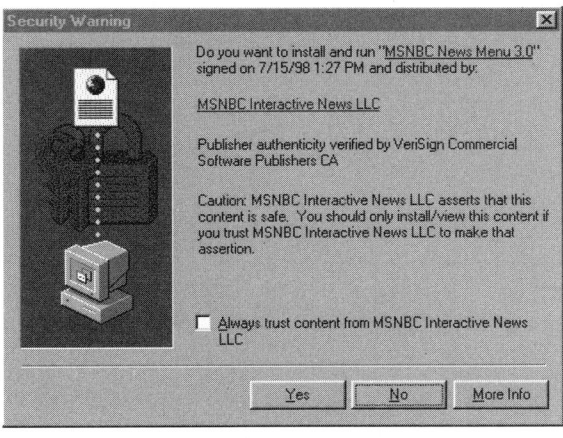

■ Low security: Internet Explorer ignores any potentially dangerous content and displays the content without presenting any dialog boxes stating that potentially damaging data exists on the Web page.

■ Custom security: Internet Explorer enables you to define what types of information can be downloaded. (Microsoft recommends this option for expert users only.)

Security Zones vs. Security Level

A *security zone* is the group to which a Web page belongs: Local Intranet, Trusted Sites, Restricted Sites, or Internet. A *security level* describes how to treat Web pages belonging to a security zone—with High, Medium, Low, or Custom precautions.

To manage your security zones and security levels, you use the Security tab in the Internet Options dialog box, as shown in the illustration.

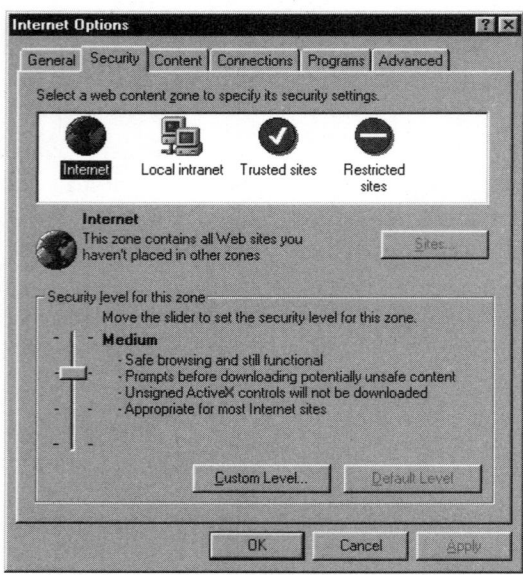

View security zones

In this exercise, you review the security zones available in Internet Explorer.

1 Start Internet Explorer.

2 On the Tools menu, click Internet Options.

The Internet Options dialog box appears.

3 On the Internet Options dialog box, click the Security tab.

The Internet zone is selected by default, and the Medium security level is displayed in the lower portion of the dialog box.

4 Click Trusted Sites.

The Security tab shows information about the Trusted Sites zone, and the Low security level is displayed in the lower portion of the dialog box by default.

5 Click Restricted Sites.

The Security tab shows information about the Restricted Sites zone, and the High security level is displayed in the lower portion of the dialog box by default.

6 Click Local Intranet.

The Security tab shows information about the Local Intranet zone, and the Medium security level is selected in the lower portion of the dialog box by default.

7 Click OK.

The Internet Options dialog box closes.

Change a zone's security level

In this exercise, you reconfigure the Internet zone to have a High security level and then you restore the Internet zone's default Medium security level.

tip

You can create custom security settings by clicking the Custom Level button on the Security tab. If you are not well-versed in topics such as ActiveX controls, Java applets, scripting, and other Internet processes, you should use only the High, Medium, and Low security levels in Internet Explorer.

Activating Security 4

❶ On the Tools menu, click Internet Options.

The Internet Options dialog box appears.

❷ Click the Security tab.

❸ Move the slider up one level and click Apply.

The security level for the Internet zone is reassigned from a Medium security level to a High security level.

❹ Click OK.

All Web pages falling into the Internet zone classification will be treated with High security level precautions.

❺ In the Address bar, type **msnbc.microsoft.com**, and press Enter.

The MSNBC page attempts to open on your computer, but you receive a message that your current security settings prohibit running ActiveX controls so the page may not be displayed correctly.

❻ Click OK.

Internet Explorer downloads the MSNBC page without downloading the unsafe content.

❼ On the Tools menu, click Internet Options.

The Internet Options dialog box appears.

❽ Click the Security tab.

❾ Click the Default Level button, click Apply, and then click OK.

The Internet zone security level is reassigned to Medium.

❿ On the toolbar, click the Refresh button.

Internet Explorer displays a Security Warning dialog box, notifying you that the site will attempt to download content to your hard disk drive.

Refresh

⓫ Click Yes to indicate that you trust this site.

Internet Explorer downloads the MSNBC content to your hard disk drive.

Assigning Web Pages to Security Zones

In addition to controlling the security level for each security zone, you can assign pages to the Trusted Sites and Restricted Sites zones. Your administrator should handle assigning Web pages and resources to the Local Intranet zone. All other Web pages fall into the Internet zone, which means that Web pages on the Internet are met with Medium security settings by default. If you want to assign Web pages to the Trusted Sites zone or the Restricted Sites zone, you need to add the pages manually to the appropriate zone.

tip

You cannot add Web sites to the Internet zone, because it includes all documents (aside from the documents on your computer) that do not belong to any other zone. You should assign a Web page to the Trusted Sites zone when you want to use powerful applications on the Web site without being interrupted by the Security Warning dialog box.

You can manage your Trusted Sites zone and Restricted Sites zone by adding and removing sites from each zone's Web page list.

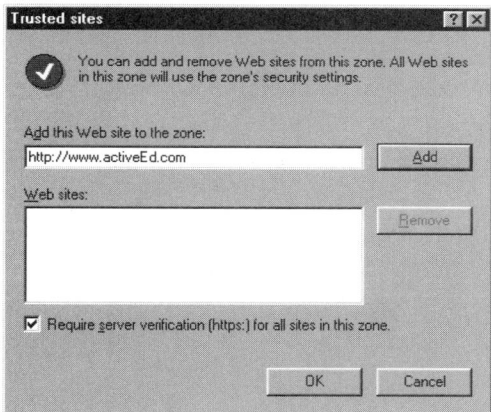

tip

The Trusted Sites dialog box includes an option to require that trusted sites use the HTTPS protocol. (HTTPS is a more secure version of the HTTP protocol.) If you want to include Web pages that do not use the HTTPS protocol in your Trusted Sites zone, you should clear the Require Server Verification (HTTPS:) For All Sites In This Zone check box.

Add and remove Web pages from security zones

In this exercise, you add the Lakewood Mountains Resort home page to your Trusted Sites zone. Then, before closing the Trusted Sites dialog box, you remove the site from your Trusted Sites zone.

❶ On the Tools menu, click Internet Options

The Internet Options dialog box appears.

❷ Click the Security tab.

❸ Click Trusted Sites.

The Security tab shows the Trusted Site zone's security level in the lower portion of the dialog box.

❹ Click the Sites button.

The Trusted Sites dialog box is displayed.

❺ Clear the Require Server Verification (HTTPS:) For All Sites In This Zone check box.

The option is turned off.

❻ In the Add This Web Site To The Zone text box, type **mspress.microsoft.com/mspress/products/1349/default1.htm,** and click the Add button.

The Web Sites text box shows the Lakewood Mountains Resort home page listed as a trusted site.

❼ In the Web Sites text box, select the Lakewood Mountains Resort entry, and then click the Remove button.

The Lakewood Mountains Resort home page entry is deleted, and the site is no longer considered a trusted site.

❽ Click OK

The Trusted Sites dialog box closes.

❾ Click OK.

The Internet Options dialog box closes.

Setting Content Rating Preferences

Rumor has it that some employees at Impact Public Relations have been surfing the Web for entertainment instead of using the Internet to complete their work tasks. Internet Explorer's Content Advisor feature can help you control what types of sites users can visit on the Internet.

In conjunction with the Recreational Software Advisory Council on the Internet (RSACi), Microsoft provides a method to limit the types of sites users can view. Basically, you can define an allowable level of sex, nudity, violence, and language that can appear on a Web page. To use Internet Explorer's Content Advisor, you access the Content Advisor section in the Internet Options dialog box.

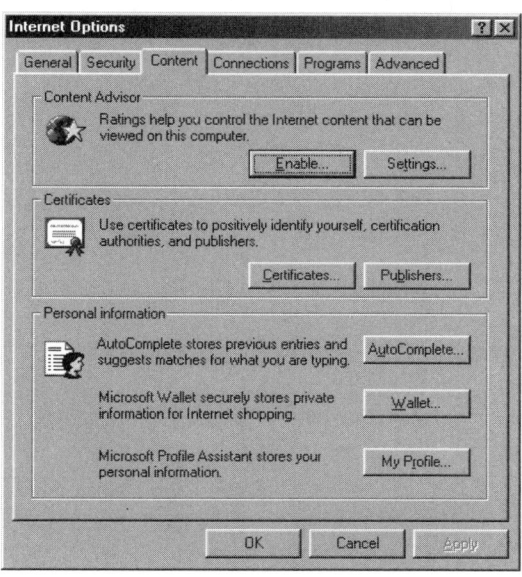

For a demonstration of how to set a content rating level, in the Multimedia folder on the Microsoft Internet Explorer 5 Step by Step CD-ROM, double-click the Content Rating icon.

To turn on the Content Advisor, you click the Enable button on the Content tab. Then you configure what level of language, nudity, sex, and violence is acceptable on Web pages. If a rated Web page exceeds the acceptable level defined by your Content Advisor, the page will not be shown. By default, the Content Advisor is set to the most conservative (least likely to offend) settings when you first enable it. Therefore, you should manually configure your settings to suit your needs after you turn on the Content Advisor.

When you configure the Content Advisor settings, you rate the level of acceptable content for language, nudity, sex, and violence. The rating levels range from Level 0, which allows only the least offensive content, through Level 4, which is the most liberal setting.

For more information about Web page ratings, you can visit the RSACi Web page (*www.rsac.org/ratingsv01.html*), shown in the following illustration.

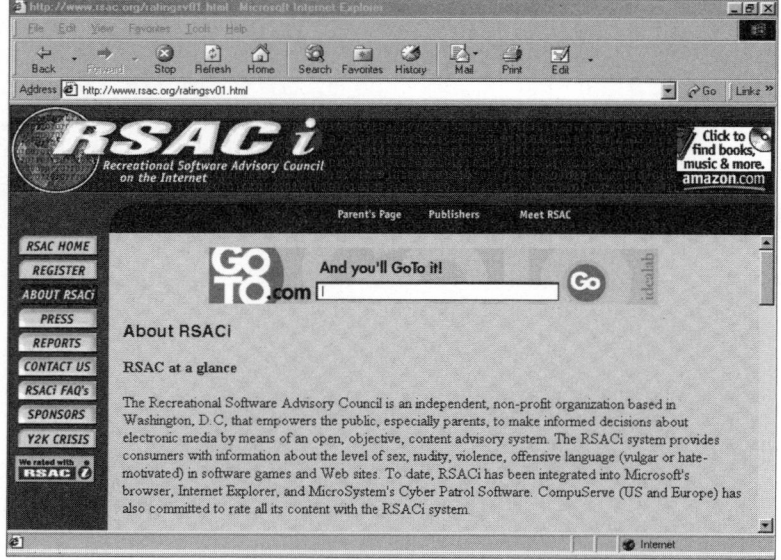

You can also access the RSACi Web page by clicking the More Info button on the Ratings tab in the Content Advisor dialog box.

To configure your rating level, you use the Ratings tab in the Content Advisor dialog box, as shown in the illustration.

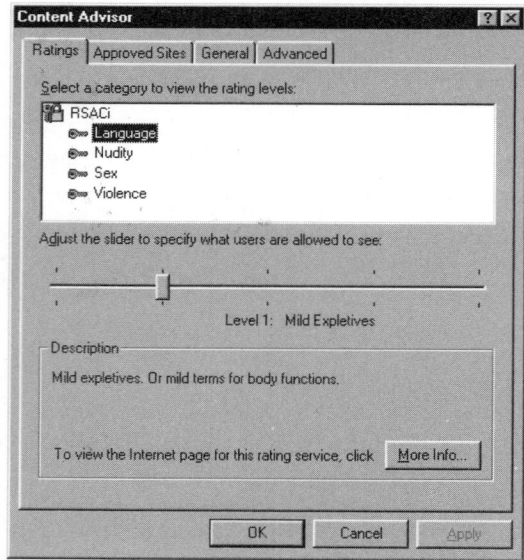

At present, Web page ratings are voluntary. In other words, Web sites register with RSACi to obtain a rating. Because not all sites are registered, you must choose whether you want viewers to be able to view nonrated sites.

For all Content Advisor actions—enabling, disabling, and configuring settings—you need to supply a password. Make sure you choose a password you can remember easily. If you forget your password, visit the Microsoft Product Support Services page (*www.microsoft.com/support*) and call the appropriate number for assistance.

Enable the Content Advisor

In this exercise, you create a supervisor password and you activate Internet Explorer's Content Advisor to limit the content that is automatically available to Web users.

1   On the Tools menu, click Internet Options.

The Internet Options dialog box is displayed.

2   Click the Content tab.

3   Click the Enable button.

The Create Supervisor Password dialog box appears.

Unless you want to change your password, you will have to create a supervisor password only once.

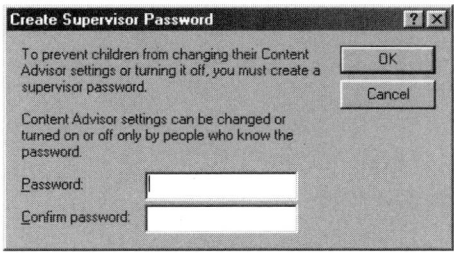

4   Enter a password in the Password text box, press Tab, retype your password in the Confirm Password text box, and then click OK.

The Create Supervisor Password dialog box closes, and the Content Advisor alert box appears, informing you that the Content Advisor has been turned on.

5   Click OK.

The Content Advisor alert box closes.

6   Click OK.

The Internet Options dialog box closes.

Configure the Content Advisor settings

In this exercise, you change the language rating level to Level 1: Mild Expletives in the Content Advisor dialog box.

❶   On the Tools menu, click Internet Options.

The Internet Options dialog box is displayed.

❷   Click the Content tab.

❸   Click the Settings button, type your password in the Supervisor Password Required dialog box, and click OK.

The Language category on the Ratings tab is selected by default.

❹   Drag the slider to the next hash mark.

The words *Level 1: Mild Expletives* appear beneath the slider, and explanatory text is displayed in the Description area.

❺   Click Apply, and then click OK.

A Level 1 rating setting is applied to the Language category, and the Content Advisor dialog box closes.

❻   Click OK.

The Internet Options dialog box closes.

Handle nonrated sites

In this exercise, you configure the Content Advisor so that users can view nonrated Web sites.

❶   On the Tools menu, click Internet Options.

The Internet Options dialog box is displayed.

❷   Click the Content tab.

The Content tab is displayed.

❸   Click the Settings button, type your password in the Supervisor Password Required dialog box, and click OK.

The Content Advisor dialog box appears.

❹   Click the General tab.

❺   In the User Options section, click the Users Can See Sites That Have No Rating check box, and click Apply.

Users will now be able to view nonrated sites.

❻   Clear the same check box, and click Apply.

The default settings are restored, and users are not allowed to view nonrated Web sites.

7 Click OK.

The Content Advisor dialog box closes.

8 Click OK.

The Internet Options dialog box closes.

Change the supervisor password

In this exercise, you replace your existing Content Advisor supervisor password with a new password.

1 On the Tools menu, click Internet Options.

The Internet Options dialog box is displayed.

2 Click the Content tab.

3 Click the Settings button, type your password in the Supervisor Password Required dialog box, and click OK.

The Content Advisor dialog box appears.

4 Click the General tab.

5 In the Supervisor Password section, click the Change Password button.

The Change Supervisor Password dialog box appears.

6 In the Old Password text box, type your current password, and press Tab.

7 In the New Password text box, type your new password, and press Tab.

8 In the Confirm New Password text box, retype your new password, and then click OK.

An alert box appears, stating that the password was successfully changed.

9 Click OK.

The new password is activated, and the old password can no longer be used to open the Content Advisor.

10 Click OK.

The Content Advisor dialog box closes.

11 Click OK.

The Internet Options dialog box closes.

Disable the Content Advisor

In this exercise, you disable the Content Advisor.

1 On the Tools menu, click Internet Options.

The Internet Options dialog box appears.

2 Click the Content tab.

3 In the Content Advisor section, click the Disable button.

The Supervisor Password Required dialog box prompts you to enter the password.

4 Type your password, and then click OK.

An alert box is displayed, stating that the Content Advisor is turned off.

5 Click OK.

The message box closes.

6 Click OK.

The Internet Options dialog box closes.

Adding Personal Information to Microsoft Wallet

Recently, many of your clients at Impact Public Relations have wanted to add credit card purchasing capabilities to their Web sites. Your clients want to know if Internet Explorer can help users supply credit card information securely and privately over the Internet. In response, you tell your clients that Internet Explorer users can use Microsoft Wallet to assist them in processing credit card transactions.

For additional information about Microsoft Wallet, visit the Microsoft Wallet site at www.micro-soft.com/wal-let.

Microsoft Wallet is Internet Explorer's key component for processing credit card and personal information transactions on the Internet. You can store credit card and personal information in Microsoft Wallet just as you store information in your regular wallet. Then, when you're ready to purchase items on the Web, you show your credit card credentials to the vendor and the transaction takes place. If the vendor supports Microsoft Wallet, you will not have to reenter your credit card and personal information.

When you configure Microsoft Wallet, you enter and store your private credit card information on your computer. Microsoft Wallet stores the information in *encrypted* (or encoded) form to ensure that no one with unauthorized access will be able to read the data. For added security, you assign a separate password for each credit card number.

Security while sending your information depends on the merchant's Web site configuration. You should ensure that you work with merchants who use the HTTPS protocol when you send order information, and choose to shop at sites that can produce valid *digital certificates*. Digital certificates are electronic certificates issued by certification organizations, such as VeriSign, Inc., that are sent with encrypted content to verify that the sender is the entity identified in the transmission.

Currently, many services and goods are available for online purchase. To get a taste of Internet fare, visit *www.microsoft.com/wallet/directory*. Every site listed in this directory supports Microsoft Wallet and conforms to Microsoft's security model.

tip

When you send information across the Internet, it can be routed through a number of host computers along its path. If your information stops at another computer, anyone can read it. Therefore, you should be careful when using a credit card on the Internet. Most vendors provide secure sites, which means that your information will be encrypted so that the data can be decoded only by the vendor. You can tell if a site is secure, because Internet Explorer shows a small padlock on the right side of the status bar when you are viewing the secure site.

Add your address information

In this exercise, you add address information that can be automatically accessed by Microsoft Wallet.

important

You must have Microsoft Wallet installed on your computer before you can complete the exercises in this section. Some Internet Explorer installations do not automatically install Microsoft Wallet. If you need help installing Microsoft Wallet on your computer, refer to the "One Step Further: Adding Components" section later in this lesson.

1 On the Tools menu, click Internet Options.

The Internet Options dialog box opens.

2 Click the Content tab.

See Lesson 7, "Managing Your Electronic Mail," for more information about the Personal Address book and online communication.

3 In the Personal Information section, click the My Profile button.

The Address Book - Choose Profile dialog box is displayed, which lists the addresses stored in your Personal Address book.

4 Verify that the Create A New Entry In The Address Book To Represent Your Profile option is selected, and click OK.

The Main Identity Properties dialog box is displayed.

5 On the Personal tab, enter information in the First, Last, and E-mail Addresses text boxes.

6 Click the Home tab.

You can press Tab to move smoothly from field to field as you enter data into the Properties dialog box.

7 Enter information in the Street Address, City, State/Province, Zip Code, and Country/Region text boxes.

8 Click OK.

The Properties dialog box closes.

9 On the Content tab, click the My Profile button.

Your personal Properties dialog box is displayed, containing the information you entered in the Properties dialog box.

10 Click OK.

The Properties dialog box closes.

11 Click OK again.

The Internet Options dialog box closes.

Add and delete your payment information

In this exercise, you add and delete information that you can use to make credit card purchases on the Internet.

If the Installing Payment Extensions dialog box appears, click the Install button if you would like to add the Discover card as an available payment method.

1 On the Tools menu, click Internet Options.

The Internet Options dialog box opens.

2 Click the Content tab.

3 In the Personal Information section, click the Wallet button.

The Payment Options dialog box appears.

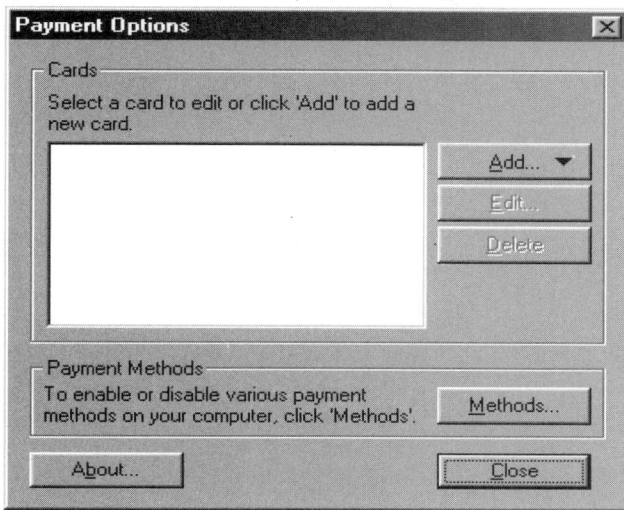

❹   Click the Add button.

A drop-down menu appears.

The license agreement will appear only once. The next time you add payment information, the license agreement will not appear.

❺   Click the type of credit card for which you want to create an entry in Microsoft Wallet.

A dialog box presents you with a license agreement for Microsoft Wallet.

❻   Click the I Agree button.

The Add A New Credit Card dialog box appears as shown on the following page.

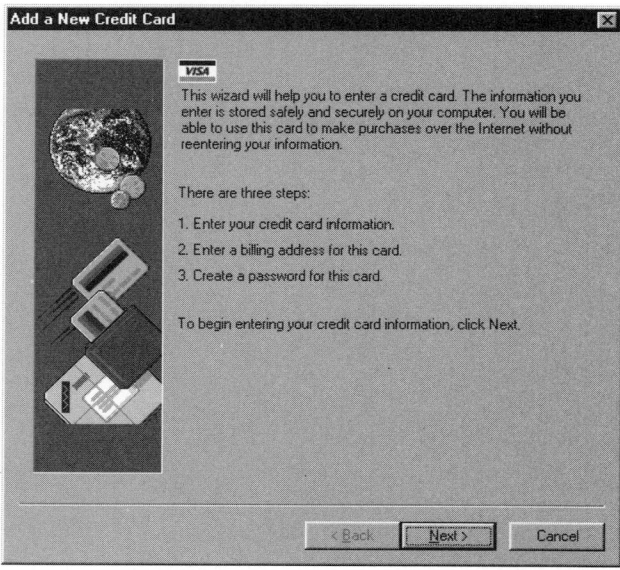

7 Click Next.

The Credit Card Information dialog box appears.

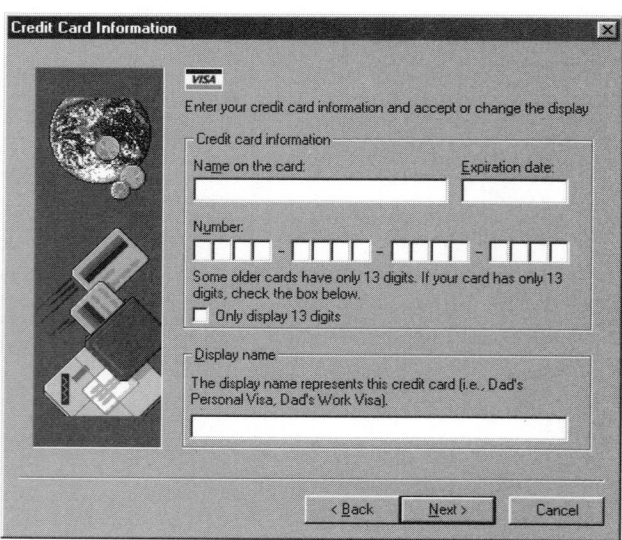

8 In the Credit Card information dialog box, enter the appropriate information in each text box, and then click Next.

The Credit Card Billing Address dialog box appears.

9   Click the New Address button.

The Add A New Address dialog box appears.

10   Click the Address Book button.

The Select From Windows Address Book dialog box appears.

tip

If you do not have an Address Book entry containing your personal information, you can enter your information in the New Address dialog box instead of clicking the Address Book button.

11   In the Type Name Or Select From List text box, start to type your name.

Your name and address appear in a box to the right of the Select From Windows Address Book dialog box.

12   Click your Address Book entry and press Enter.

The Credit Card Billing Address dialog box displays the billing address you selected.

13   Click Next.

The Credit Card Password dialog box is displayed.

14   In the Password text box, type a password, press Tab, retype your password in the Confirm Password text box, and click Finish.

The Credit Card Password dialog box closes, and the newly added credit card entry appears in the Payment Options dialog box.

15   In the Payment Options dialog box, ensure that the entry you just created is selected, click Delete, and click Yes.

The new credit card entry is deleted.

16   Click Close.

The Payment Options dialog box closes.

17   Click OK.

The Internet Options dialog box closes.

**One
Step
Further**

Adding Components

Adding and upgrading Internet Explorer components is similar to adding programs to your computer. The first step toward adding or upgrading a component is to display your Control Panel window.

To upgrade or install a component, click the check box to the left of the component name or names. You can install and upgrade as many components at one time as necessary. Keep in mind that the more components you select for installation, the longer the download time will be. Some of the available components include:

■ Microsoft NetMeeting: Enables you to use audio, video, and other communication tools for conducting online conferences.

■ Microsoft Outlook Express: Provides electronic messaging capabilities, such as sending and receiving e-mail messages.

■ Microsoft FrontPage Express: Enables you to edit and create Web pages.

■ Multilanguage Support: Enables you to view Web pages created and displayed using text characters other than your default language's text characters.

Add Internet Explorer Components

In this exercise, you use the Windows Update program to download one or more Internet Explorer components.

1 On the Windows taskbar, click the Start button, point to Settings, and click Control Panel.

2 Double-click the Add/Remove Programs icon.

The Add/Remove Programs Properties dialog box appears.

3 Scroll down if necessary, click Microsoft Internet Explorer 5 And Internet Tools, and click the Add/Remove button.

The Internet Explorer 5 And Internet Tools dialog box is displayed as shown on the following page.

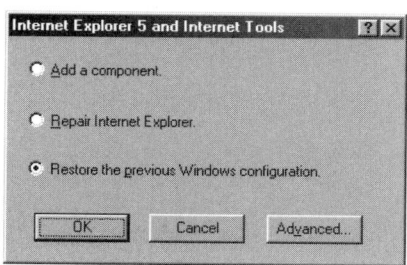

❹ Click the Add A Component Option, and click OK.

The Windows Update: Internet Explorer And Internet Tools dialog box is displayed.

❺ In the list of components, click the check boxes for the components you want to install, and then click the Next button.

An alert box might appear, indicating that files need to be downloaded from the Internet.

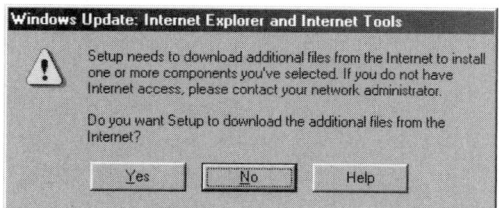

❻ If necessary, click Yes.

The Download Sites dialog box might appear.

❼ If necessary, click the Region drop-down arrow, and click your region, and in the Download Sites section, click the download site closest to you, and click the Next button.

The Windows Update program downloads the selected components to your hard disk drive.

❽ Click the Finish button.

Depending on which component(s) you choose to download, Windows might restart your computer.

Finish the lesson

● Quit Internet Explorer.

Lesson 4 Quick Reference

To	Do this
View a security zone	Click Internet Options on the Tools menu, and click the Security tab. Click a security zone.
Change a security zone's level	Click Internet Options on the Tools menu, click the Security tab, click the security zone that you want to configure, move the slider up or down, and then click OK.
Assign a Web page to a security zone	Click Internet Options on the Tools menu, and click the Security tab. Select the Trusted Sites zone or Restricted Sites zone. Click the Sites button, clear the Require Server Verification (HTTPS:) For All Sites In This Zone check box. Type a Web address in the Add This Web Site To The Zone text box, click Add, and click OK. Click OK to close the Internet Options dialog box.
Enable the Content Advisor	Click Internet Options on the Tools menu, click the Content tab, and click the Enable button. Type a supervisor password and click OK. Click OK in the Content Advisor alert box, and then click OK in the Internet Options dialog box.
Configure Content Advisor settings	Click Internet Options on the Tools menu, and click the Content tab. Click the Settings button, enter your password, and click OK. Click a category, drag the slider left or right, click Apply, and then click OK. Click OK to close the Internet Options dialog box.
Handle nonrated sites	Click Internet Options on the Tools menu, and click the Content tab. Click the Settings button, enter your password, and click OK. Click the General tab, click the Users Can See Sites That Have No Rating check box, click Apply, and click OK. Click OK to close the Internet Options dialog box.

Lesson 4 Quick Reference

To	Do this
Change the supervisor password	Click Internet Options on the Tools menu, and click the Content tab. Click the Settings button, type your password, and click OK. Click the General tab, and then click the Change Password button. Enter your existing password, press Tab, enter a new password, press Tab, reenter the new password, and click OK. Click OK to close the Content Advisor alert box, click OK to close the Content Advisor dialog box, and click OK to close the Internet Options dialog box.
Disable the Content Advisor	Click Internet Options on the Tools menu, click the Content tab, click the Disable button, enter a password, and click OK. Click OK to close the alert box, and click OK again to close the Internet Options dialog box.
Add your address information	Click Internet Options on the Tools menu, click the Content tab, and click the My Profile button. Verify that the Create A New Entry In The Address Book To Represent Your Profile option is selected, and click OK. Enter your information into the Properties dialog box, click OK, and click OK to close the Internet Options dialog box.
Add and delete your payment information	Click Internet Options on the Tools menu, and click the Content tab. Click the Wallet button, click the Add button, click the type of credit card for which you want to create an entry, click the I Agree button if the license agreement is displayed, and click Next. Enter your credit card information, click Next, enter a billing address, and click Next. Enter and confirm a password, and click Finish. In the Payment Options dialog box, select an entry, click Delete, and click Yes. Click Close, and then click OK.

4

Activating Security

Lesson 4 Quick Reference

To	Do this
Add Internet Explorer components	On the Windows taskbar, click the Start button, point to Settings, and click Control Panel. Double-click the Add/Remove Programs icon. Scroll down if necessary, click Microsoft Internet Explorer 5 And Internet Tools, and click the Add/Remove button. Click the Add A Component option, and click OK. Click the check boxes for the components you want to install, and click the Next button. If necessary, click Yes. If necessary, click the Regions drop-down arrow and click your region, and in the Download Site section, click the download site closest to you, and then click the Next button. Click the Finish button.

5

Working Offline

Working Offline

In this lesson you will learn how to:

✔ *Mark Web sites for offline viewing.*

✔ *Synchronize offline Web pages.*

✔ *Automate offline Web page synchronization.*

✔ *Work offline.*

✔ *Manage offline Web pages.*

**ESTIMATED TIME
20 min.**

Imagine that the president of Impact Public Relations has asked you to present this year's marketing campaign to the management staff at Lakewood Mountains Resort. Your flight leaves tomorrow morning, and it's a three-hour trip. You don't want the three hours to go to waste, so you decide to review the Lakewood Mountains Resort Web site on your laptop computer. "If only the plane had an Internet connection...."

Fortunately, when you use Microsoft Internet Explorer, you can view Web pages without being connected to the Internet. Internet Explorer enables you to download Web pages while you are connected to the Internet and store them on your computer's hard disk drive. After the pages are stored on your hard disk drive, you can view the Web pages even without a "live" Internet connection. This is called *working offline*.

Working offline is especially helpful for users who have dial-up connections or use laptop computers. A person with a dial-up connection who pays for an Internet connection based on Internet usage (such as per hour or per minute) can see significant savings by working offline.

The user can download Web pages of interest while connected to the Internet, disconnect from the Internet, and then leisurely browse the Web pages offline, without having to worry about racking up a sizable bill. Similarly, laptop computer users can benefit from working offline, because often they might not have access to a phone line or other means of connecting to the Internet. A laptop user can download Web pages while connected to the Internet, and then later, when an Internet connection is unavailable, the user can view stored Web pages offline.

In this lesson, you'll learn how to mark Web sites for offline viewing. In addition, you'll learn some key offline management techniques, such as updating (or *synchronizing*) offline pages, working in offline mode, and deleting offline Web page data. Finally, you'll learn how to manage offline Web pages.

Marking Web Sites for Offline Viewing

While using Internet Explorer, you've noticed menu commands using the word *offline*. You've already decided that you would like to work with the Lakewood Mountains Resort Web page in offline mode as you travel. To prepare a site for offline viewing, you must mark it for offline availability in your Favorites list. You can do that either when you first add the Web site to your Favorites list or later on.

To mark a Web page for offline viewing when you create a Favorites list entry, you turn on the Make Available Offline option while the Add Favorite dialog box is open, as shown in the illustration. To open the Add Favorite dialog box, open the Favorites menu, and click Add To Favorites.

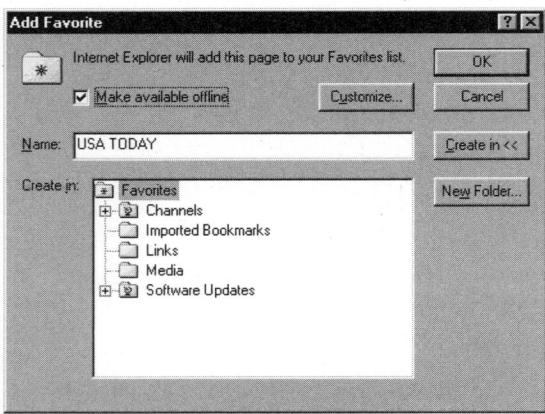

To mark an existing Favorite for offline viewing, you use the Organize Favorites dialog box. To open the Organize Favorites dialog box, click Organize Favorites on the Favorites menu. After you select a link, a Make Available Offline check box appears, as shown in the illustration.

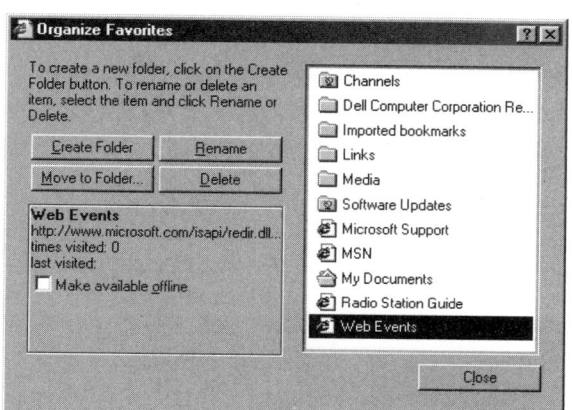

For a demonstration of how to make a Web site available for offline viewing, in the Multimedia folder on the Microsoft Internet Explorer 5 Step by Step CD-ROM, double-click the View Offline icon.

If you click the Make Available Offline check box, you can set download options for a selected Favorite. The main options specify when to download content, and whether to download linked pages. By default, only the page associated with the Favorite is downloaded (without linked pages), and you will have to manually update (or *synchronize*) your offline Web pages.

Configure a new Favorites link for offline viewing

In this exercise, you create a Favorites link to the Lakewood Mountains Resort home page, and you make the page available offline.

1 Start Internet Explorer.

2 Display the Lakewood Mountains Resort home page (*mspress.microsoft.com/mspress/products/1349/default1.htm*).

The Lakewood Mountains Resort home page appears.

3 On the Favorites menu, click Add To Favorites.

The Add Favorite dialog box opens.

4 Click the Make Available Offline check box, and click OK.

The Synchronizing message box appears, as shown in the illustration. The message box shows a progress bar as the Lakewood Mountains Resort home page content is downloaded to your computer.

Working Offline

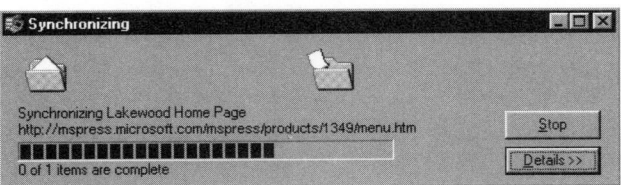

5 On the toolbar, click the Favorites button.

Favorites that are marked for offline availability are easy to spot because they appear in the Favorites bar with a shortcut icon.

The Lakewood Home page Favorites link appears on the Favorites bar with a shortcut icon, indicating that the Web site's content is now stored on your hard disk drive.

6 On the toolbar, click the Favorites button.

The Favorites bar closes.

Configure an existing Favorites link for offline viewing

In this exercise, you modify an existing Favorites link to be available for offline viewing.

1 On the Favorites menu, click Organize Favorites.

The Organize Favorites dialog box opens.

2 In the Organize Favorites dialog box, click the Links folder.

The content of the Links folder appears.

3 Click the Best Of The Web link.

Information about the link is displayed in the lower-left section of the Organize Favorites dialog box.

4 Click the Make Available Offline check box.

The Best Of The Web link is specified as a Favorites link that will be available for offline viewing.

5 Click Close.

The Synchronizing message box appears while the Best Of The Web content is downloaded to your hard disk drive.

Favorites

6 On the toolbar, click the Favorites button.

The Favorites bar opens.

7 On the Favorites bar, click the Links folder.

Shortcut

The links stored in the Links Favorites folder appear. Notice that the Best Of The Web link is accompanied by a shortcut icon.

Favorites

8 On the toolbar, click the Favorites button.

The Favorites bar closes.

tip

By default, offline Web page files are stored in a folder named Offline Web pages within your Windows folder. For example, if your Windows folder is stored on your computer's drive C, your offline pages will appear in C:\Windows\Offline Web Pages.

Synchronizing Offline Web Pages

Imagine it's 7:30 A.M. You're just about to leave your office for the airport to catch your flight to Lakewood Mountains Resort. Before you disconnect your laptop from the Internet, you want to download the latest information for the Web pages marked to be available for offline viewing. In other words, you want to make sure that the offline Web pages saved on your hard disk drive are in sync with the most up-to-date versions of the Web pages on the Internet.

tip

To *synchronize* means to download the latest information for a Web page stored on your computer. Synchronizing ensures that the copy of the Web page stored on your computer is in sync with the Web page stored on the Internet. Many Web pages are updated frequently, on a daily, hourly, or even minute-by-minute basis. Therefore, synchronizing offline Web pages is often necessary to ensure that you are viewing up-to-date information when working offline.

When you store pages offline, it's very likely that some of the pages will become outdated. Many Web pages are notorious for changing content regularly. Sports, news, and stock exchange Web pages can change rapidly. You can keep your offline copies of Web pages up-to-date by using Internet Explorer's Synchronize feature.

The Process of Synchronization

Synchronizing your offline files is like updating your wardrobe. When you update your style, you don't start by throwing out all of your clothes; you purchase items that reflect the newest trends and integrate them into your collection. Similarly, when you synchronize your offline Web pages, Internet Explorer doesn't start by deleting all your old files; Internet Explorer scans the Internet Web pages for new content and then downloads only the Web page files that contain new content.

When you mark a Web page to be available for offline viewing, the Web page is configured for manual synchronization by default. Manually synchronizing your offline pages means that you must click an Internet Explorer command to update your pages. You can manually synchronize a single Web page, or you can manually synchronize all offline pages at once.

Manually synchronize a single offline Web page

This exercise assumes that you have configured the Lakewood Home Page Favorites link for offline viewing. If you have not, follow the steps in the exercise "Configure a New Favorites Link for Offline Viewing" earlier in this lesson.

In this exercise, you synchronize a single Web page.

① On the toolbar, click the Favorites button.

The Favorites bar appears.

② On the Favorites bar, right-click the Lakewood Home Page link.

A shortcut menu appears.

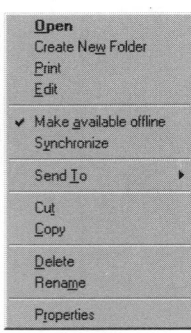

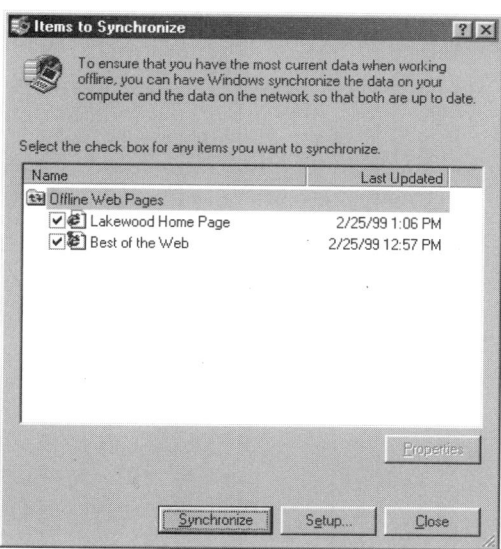

❸ Click Synchronize.

The Synchronizing message box appears as the Lakewood Home Page's content is downloaded to your computer.

❹ On the toolbar, click the Favorites button.

The Favorites bar closes.

Favorites

Manually synchronize all offline Web pages

In this exercise, you use the Items To Synchronize dialog box to manually synchronize all the files for Web pages that you have marked to be available offline.

❶ On the Tools menu, click Synchronize.

The Items To Synchronize dialog box appears.

You can deselect Favorites in the Items To Synchronize dialog box by clearing the check boxes.

❷ Ensure that each check box is selected.

❸ Click Synchronize.

The Synchronizing message box appears as the Favorites' content is downloaded to your computer.

Working Offline

Automating Offline Web Page Synchronization

As you synchronize the Lakewood Mountains Resort Web page, you realize that you can use the synchronization feature for more than viewing Web pages during flights. You can also use the synchronization feature to update specified Web sites on a regular basis. For example, you can set up Internet Explorer on your home computer to update selected news sites each morning. The sites can be synchronized automatically as you're getting dressed. Then when you are ready to check the daily news as you drink your coffee, you can quickly browse through the offline versions of the news sites. In this case, synchronizing is a time-saver, because you can view the offline pages without having to sit impatiently while graphics and other Web page elements are downloaded. Furthermore, you are saving on connection time, because you can disconnect from the Internet as soon as the content is downloaded to your computer.

When you configure Internet Explorer to synchronize offline pages automatically, you set up a schedule indicating when the updates should take place. Therefore, you no longer have to remember to manually update your offline pages—they will be automatically updated periodically. To set up synchronization schedules, you use the Offline Favorite Wizard.

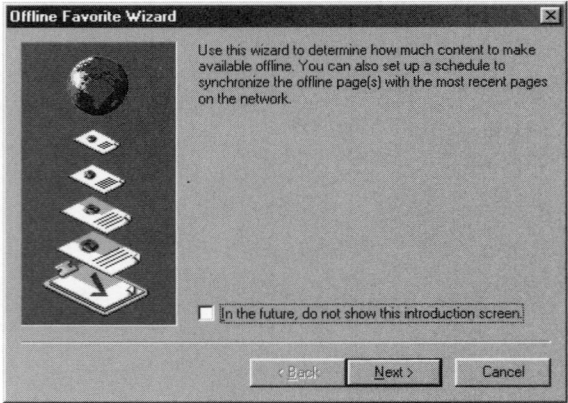

As you work your way through the wizard's dialog boxes, you can specify manual or automatic synchronization, choose to download pages linked to the Web page marked for offline viewing, and store any required passwords.

important

You should be cautious about downloading linked pages with the Offline Favorite Wizard. If a page contains several hyperlinks, you could end up downloading enormous amounts of information. On the other hand, if you don't choose to download linked pages, you won't be able to view any pages linked to the offline Web page without connecting to the Internet. You should carefully plan what you want to view offline, and delete outdated offline information often, as described in the "One Step Further: Managing Offline Web Pages" section later in this lesson.

You can apply a synchronization schedule to an existing Favorites link, or you can apply a schedule when you are creating a Favorites link. In either situation, the process of applying a synchronization schedule involves choosing the frequency and time of day at which updates occur.

You can also name a particular synchronization schedule and assign a number of Web pages to the named schedule. This enables multiple offline pages to be updated simultaneously. To continue the news site example, you could create a schedule and name it *News*. Then you could add the New York Times, Reuters, and MSNBC sites to the News synchronization group. When the News synchronization is activated, all three news sites will be updated simultaneously.

Customize a synchronization schedule

In this exercise, you create a synchronization schedule named News and you configure the schedule to be updated each day at 6:00 A.M.

1 Click in the Address bar, type **www.reuters.com**, and press Enter.

The Reuters home page appears.

2 On the Favorites menu, click Add To Favorites.

The Add Favorite dialog box appears.

3 Click the Make Available Offline check box.

The option to make the currently displayed page available for offline viewing is selected.

4 Click the Customize button.

The Offline Favorite Wizard dialog box appears.

Favorites

5 In the Offline Favorite Wizard dialog box, click Next.

The next Offline Favorite Wizard dialog box appears.

6 To indicate that you want to download pages that are linked to the Favorite, click the Yes option.

The Reuters home page and linked pages that are one link deep from the Reuters home page will be downloaded.

7 Click Next.

The next Offline Favorite Wizard dialog box appears.

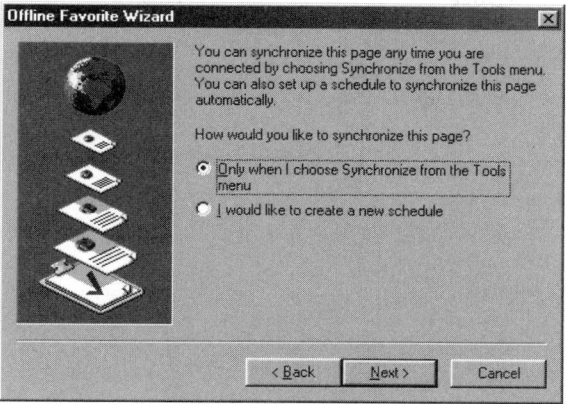

8 Click the I Would Like To Create A New Schedule option, and click Next.

The next Offline Favorite Wizard dialog box appears.

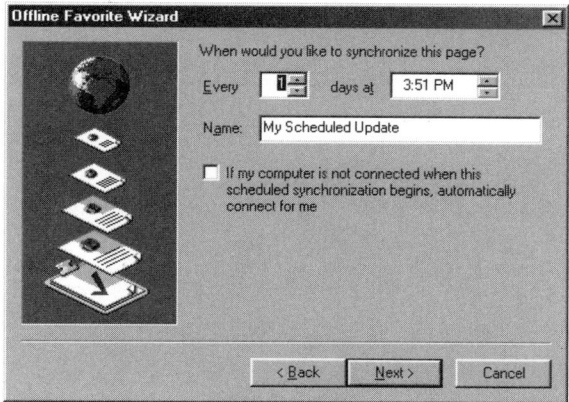

9 Press Tab. In the Days At text box type **6**, press the Right arrow key, type **00**, press the Right arrow key again, and type **A**.

The synchronization schedule is set to be updated every day at 6:00 A.M.

Notice that you have the option to have Internet Explorer automatically connect your computer to the Internet when the synchronization is scheduled to begin.

10 In the Name text box, select the default text, and then type **News**.

The synchronization schedule is named News.

11 Click Next.

The final Offline Favorite Wizard dialog box appears, enabling you to specify a password if the site requires one.

12 Click Finish.

The Offline Favorite Wizard closes, and the Add Favorite dialog box reappears.

13 Click OK.

The Add Favorite dialog box closes, and then the Synchronizing message box appears while the Reuters content is downloaded to your hard disk drive.

tip
Sometimes the initial download process for an offline Favorite takes a little while to complete. If you'd like, you can start the next exercise while the Reuters information is downloading. On the File menu, point to New, and then click Window. This will display a new window that you can use to start the next exercise.

Add a Favorites link to an existing synchronization schedule

In this exercise, you add the USA Today Web page to an existing synchronization schedule named News.

1 Click in the Address bar, type **www.usatoday.com**, and press Enter.

The USA Today home page appears.

2 On the Favorites menu, click Add To Favorites.

The Add Favorite dialog box appears.

3 Click the Make Available Offline check box.

The option to make the currently displayed page available for offline viewing is selected.

4 Click the Customize button.

The first Offline Favorite Wizard dialog box appears.

5 Click Next.

The next Offline Favorite Wizard dialog box appears.

6 Verify that the No option is selected.

Linked pages will not be downloaded along with the USA Today home page.

7 Click Next.

The next Offline Favorite Wizard dialog box appears.

8 Click the Using This Existing Schedule option, click the drop-down arrow, and then click News.

The USA Today synchronization schedule will be the same as the schedule for the other offline pages assigned to the News synchronization schedule.

❾ Click Next.

The final Offline Favorite Wizard dialog box appears, enabling you to specify a password if the site requires one.

❿ Click Finish.

The Offline Favorite Wizard closes, and the Add Favorite dialog box reappears.

⓫ Click OK.

The Add Favorite dialog box closes, and then the Synchronizing message box appears while the USA Today information is downloaded to your hard disk drive.

⓬ When the synchronization is complete, quit Internet Explorer.

Viewing Offline Web Pages

Your plane has just settled into its flight pattern and the passengers have been given permission to start electronic equipment. You open your laptop computer, ready to visit the Lakewood Mountains Resort Web page. After all your preparation to make Web pages available for offline viewing, you are rewarded with the ease of viewing the Web pages offline.

To view offline Web pages, you first need to disconnect from the Internet by using the Dial-Up Connections dialog box. After you've started Internet Explorer, you can verify whether you are connected to the Internet by clicking File on the menu bar. If Work Offline has a check mark next to it, you are working offline. You can switch back to online mode by clicking Work Online to clear the check mark.

important

There are several ways to connect to the Internet. For home users, the most common way is through a dial-up connection using a standard modem. However, it's becoming increasingly popular for home users and businesses to install faster, full-time connections such as a DSL (digital subscriber line) or a cable modem. These types of connections allow you to connect to the Internet 24 hours a day without incurring any extra charges or using your standard telephone line. If you are connected to the Internet through a dedicated, full-time-connetion, you will never need to work offline.

After you have determined that you are working offline, you can click a Favorites link that is available for offline viewing on the Favorites bar. You can tell which Web pages are available for offline viewing because they appear normally on the Favorites bar. Unavailable Favorites appear grayed out, as shown in the illustration.

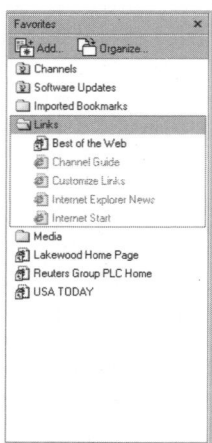

As you work offline, you might click a hyperlink that links to a Web page that is not stored on your computer. If you click a hyperlink pointing to a Web page that has not been downloaded to your computer, Internet Explorer displays a dialog box asking if you want to continue to work offline or if you'd like to connect to the Internet.

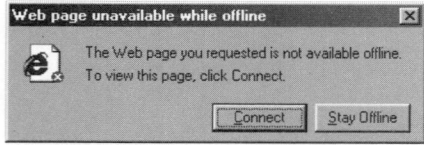

To continue to work offline, click the Stay Offline button. To connect to the Internet (if possible), click the Connect button.

Set Internet Explorer to work offline if your computer is configured to automatically connect to the Internet

In this exercise, you set Internet Explorer to work in offline mode.

➊   If necessary, quit Internet Explorer.

tip

For more information about setting up Internet Explorer and setting your dial-up connection, see Appendix A, "Installation and Setup Procedures."

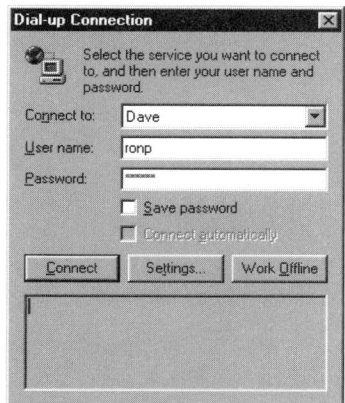

Close

❷ Start Internet Explorer, and click the Close button in the top-right corner of the Dial-Up Connection dialog box.

Internet Explorer opens without connecting to the Internet.

❸ Open the File menu and verify that the Work Offline option appears with a check mark.

View pages offline

This exercise assumes that you have con-figured the Lakewood Home Page Favorites link for offline viewing. If you have not, follow the steps in the exercise "Configure a New Favorites Link for Offline View-ing" earlier in this lesson.

In this exercise, you open a Favorites link that is available for offline viewing.

❶ Click the Favorites button on the toolbar.

The Favorites bar opens.

❷ Click the Lakewood Home Page Favorites link.

The Lakewood Home Page is displayed.

❸ On the toolbar, click the Favorites button.

The Favorites bar closes.

One Step Further   Managing Offline Web Pages

Your presentation was a resounding success. You are now relaxing on the flight home, and you decide to free some space on your laptop before you catch a quick nap. You can remove the offline Web page files stored on your computer. You can also change the status of Favorites links available for offline viewing.

Removing offline Web page content from your computer is similar to deleting cached files in your Temporary Internet Files folder, as discussed in the "One Step Further: Managing Your Temporary Internet Files" section in Lesson 2. You remove all Web page files associated with the offline Web page, but you do not remove the specification to make the Web page available for offline viewing. After you remove offline Web page content, you will not be able to view the Web page offline until you synchronize it. The next time you synchronize the offline Web page, the files will be downloaded to your computer.

Removing a Favorite specified as available for offline viewing is a little different from simply clearing the files from your offline folder. When you remove a Favorites link's offline availability, you remove the synchronization capabilities for the Favorites link. The Web pages will no longer be updated according to a synchronization schedule and the pages will not be updated when you manually synchronize all pages marked for offline availability.

Delete offline content

This exercise assumes that you have configured a link for offline viewing. If you have not, follow the steps in the exercise "Configure a New Favorites Link for Offline Viewing" earlier in this lesson.

In this exercise, you delete offline Web page content stored on your hard disk drive.

1 On the Tools menu, click Internet Options.

The Internet Options dialog box appears.

2 In the Temporary Internet Files section, click the Delete Files button.

The Delete Files dialog box appears.

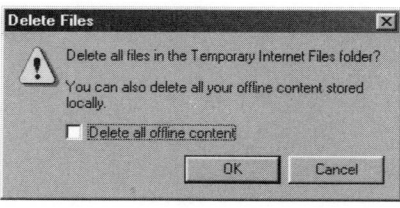

❸   In the Delete Files dialog box, click the Delete All Offline Content check box, and click OK.

The Web page files stored for offline pages are deleted, and the Delete Files dialog box closes.

❹   Click OK.

The Internet Options dialog box closes.

Remove offline availability status

In this exercise, you remove the offline availability status from the Lakewood Mountains Resort Favorites link.

❶   If necessary, connect to the Internet.

❷   On the Favorites menu, click Organize Favorites.

The Organize Favorites dialog box opens.

tip
You can also click the Organize button on the Favorites bar to open the Organize Favorites dialog box.

❸   Click the Lakewood Home Page Favorites link.

Information about the link is displayed in the lower-left section of the Organize Favorites dialog box.

❹   Clear the Make Available Offline check box.

The Lakewood Home Page Favorites link is no longer specified as available for offline viewing.

❺   Click Close.

The Organize Favorites dialog box closes.

Finish the lesson

❶   On the Favorites menu, click Organize Favorites. Use the Organize Favorites dialog box to delete the Lakewood Home Page, Reuters, and USA Today Favorites links by selecting a Favorites link, clicking the Delete button, and clicking Yes.

❷   In the Organize Favorites dialog box, click the Links folder icon, click the Best Of The Web Favorites link, clear the Make Available Offline check box, and click Close.

❸   Quit Internet Explorer.

Lesson 5 Quick Reference

To	Do this
Configure a new Favorites link for offline viewing	Display a Web site. Click Add To Favorites on the Favorites menu, click the Make Available Offline check box, and click OK.
Configure an existing Favorites link for offline viewing	Click Organize Favorites on the Favorites menu, click a Favorites link, click the Make Available Offline check box, and click Close.
Manually synchronize a single offline Web page	Click the Favorites button on the toolbar, right-click a Favorites link, and click Synchronize.
Manually synchronize all offline Web pages	Click Synchronize on the Tools menu, make sure all of the check boxes for the Favorites links that you want to synchronize are checked, and then click Synchronize.
Customize a synchronization schedule	Display a Web site. Click Add To Favorites on the Favorites menu, click the Make Available Offline check box, and click the Customize button. Click Next in the first Offline Favorite Wizard dialog box, make any desired selections, and click Next in the second wizard dialog box. Click the I Would Like To Create A New Schedule option, and click Next in the third wizard dialog box. Set a time in the Days At text box, type a new name in the Name text box, and click Next. Click Finish, and then click OK.
Add a Favorites link to an existing synchronization schedule	Display a Web site. Click Add To Favorites on the Favorites menu, click the Make Available Offline check box, and then click the Customize button. Click Next in the first Offline Favorite Wizard Synchronization dialog box, make any desired selections, and click Next in the second wizard dialog box. Click Using This Existing Schedule option, use the drop-down list to select a synchronization schedule name, and click Next. Click Finish, and click OK.
Set Internet Explorer to work offline	Start Internet Explorer. Click the Close button in the top-right corner of the Dial-up Connection dialog box if your computer automatically connects to the Internet.

Lesson 5 Quick Reference

To	Do this	Button
View pages offline	Set Internet Explorer to work off-line, click the Favorites button on the toolbar, and click the available Favorites link.	
Delete offline content	Click Internet Options on the Tools menu, click the Delete Files button, click the Delete All Offline Content check box, click OK, and then click OK again.	
Remove offline availability	Click Organize Favorites on the Favorites menu, click a Favorites link, clear the Make Available Offline check box, and click Close.	

Working Offline

6

Enjoying Multimedia on the Web

**ESTIMATED TIME
20 min.**

In this lesson you will learn how to:

✔ *Recognize graphics file formats.*
✔ *Use the Windows Media Player.*
✔ *Configure multimedia options.*
✔ *Use Shockwave.*

As you use Microsoft Internet Explorer, you notice that while there's a lot of text information on the Internet, there are also many different types of *multimedia*, which is any combination of text, video, audio, and animation. When the Internet first started, it was almost entirely text-based. Internet transmissions consisted of text, followed by text, and then more text. With the advent of the World Wide Web, the Internet became a medium for sending graphics along with text. Now, a few short years later, text and simple graphics compete with video, audio, animation, and other file formats for the most prominent positions within Web pages.

Fortunately, Internet Explorer has kept pace with multimedia technologies. It can run most multimedia files automatically, and you can control which multimedia files Internet Explorer opens for you. Because multimedia files can take a while to download and because they use computer resources (such as memory), you might choose to configure Internet Explorer to not show or run certain multimedia formats.

Turning off Internet Explorer multimedia options can help you speed up your Web surfing sessions and increase your productivity.

In this lesson, you will learn how to recognize graphics file formats and use Microsoft Windows Media Player to run audio and video files. You will also configure Internet Explorer's multimedia options so that you can control the use of multimedia on your computer. Finally, you will view a Macromedia Shockwave presentation that uses audio and video technologies.

important

The exercises in this lesson assume that you are using a multimedia computer that is capable of running audio and video file formats. Most computers sold today are multimedia systems.

Recognizing Graphics File Formats

As you cruise the Web, you run into all kinds of graphics. On Web pages, graphics take the form of illustrations, photographs, and animations. Because graphics continue to play a strong role in Web communication, you should become familiar with the types of graphics you'll find on the Web. Familiarizing yourself with graphics can help you make educated browsing decisions such as whether to allow graphics to download on Web pages.

Illustrations account for the majority of Web page graphics. They are usually page design elements (such as backgrounds and logos), content references (such as maps or drawings), page elements (such as bullets and divider lines, called *rule lines*), and interface elements (such as buttons and menu bars). Illustration files often have a .GIF or .PNG extension. GIFs and PNGs are usually small files that transfer quickly across the Internet. The illustration shows a GIF graphic from the Lakewood Mountains Resort Web page, which is used as a page design element.

Recreation

tip

An *extension* is the part of a filename that describes a file's type. For example, Welcome.doc is a Microsoft Word document while Welcome.gif is a GIF graphics file.

Photographs are high-color, detailed pictures on the Web. Usually, Web photographs have been scanned from hard-copy. (*Scanning* a photograph is similar to photocopying a photograph, except that scanning makes a copy of the image to a computer file instead of to a sheet of paper.) Photo files on the Web have a .JPEG or .JPG extension. JPEGs usually appear as pictures. Detailed, high-color artistry also uses the JPEG format. The illustration shows a photograph saved as a JPEG file.

Animations can be used to display short action sequences. GIF files are often used to create repeating movements on Web pages, such as bouncing balls, spinning globes, flashing lights, and other repetitive types of animation. Graphics created in this way are called *animated GIFs*. They are created using special programs that layer GIF files and then display them quickly, one after another, similar to old-fashioned flip-card animations. The illustration shows several frames of an animated GIF in which a bee flies to a sunflower.

Graphics File Formats

Web graphics files are most often in one of the following formats:

Format	Description
GIF	Stands for *Graphics Interchange Format.* These are small files that load fast and are limited to 256 colors. GIFs support *transparency,* which means that you can make one color in a graphic disappear. You can design icons and other elements that appear to be cut out to have the Web page's background show through. A GIF can also be *interlaced,* where the entire image is displayed at a blurred or jagged resolution and then gradually becomes clearer.
JPEG	Created by and is named after the *Joint Photographic Experts Group.* These files are usually photographs and can consist of millions of colors. JPEGs can be formatted to load *progressively.* When an image loads progressively, the viewer sees the top of the image first and then gradually sees lower portions until the entire graphic has been loaded.
PNG	Stands for *Portable Network Graphics.* Similar to GIFs, these are small files that load fast and are limited to 256 colors. PNG files transmit faster than GIFs, but they are supported by only newer browsers (including Internet Explorer 5). Therefore, they are not yet widely used on the Internet. Like GIFs, PNG files can also be displayed in interlaced format.

You can determine a graphic element's format by right-clicking the graphic and clicking Properties on the shortcut menu. Because Web pages are created from embedded elements, each component of the Web page is saved as a separate file. Similar to classic ransom note letters, each graphic is "cut out" and "pasted" onto a Web page. Each graphic's Properties dialog box indicates the filename and extension of the graphic.

View properties

In this exercise, you view the properties of a banner on the Lakewood Mountains Resort home page.

❶ Start Internet Explorer.

❷ In the Address bar, type **mspress.microsoft.com/mspress/products/1349/ default1.htm** and press Enter.

The Lakewood Mountains Resort home page appears.

❸ Right-click the Lakewood Mountains Resort banner, which appears along the top of the main window.

A shortcut menu appears.

❹ Click Properties.

The Properties dialog box appears and indicates in the filename that the element is a GIF file, as shown in the illustration.

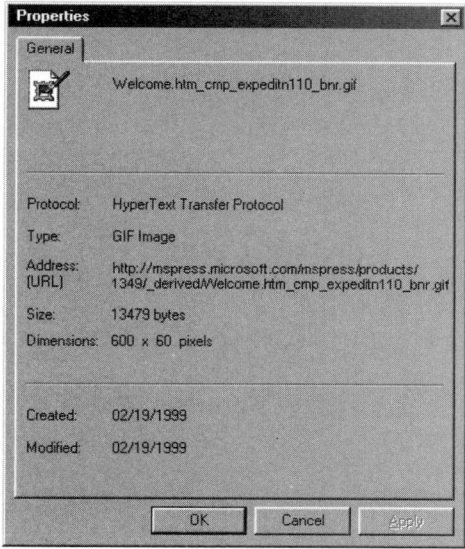

❺ Click the Cancel button.

The Properties dialog box closes.

View photographs

In this exercise, you view the hotel photograph on the Lakewood Mountains Resort home page.

❶ Right-click the picture of Lakewood Mountains Resort's hotel, and click Properties on the shortcut menu.

The Properties dialog box appears and indicates in the filename that the element is a JPEG file, as shown in the illustration on the following page.

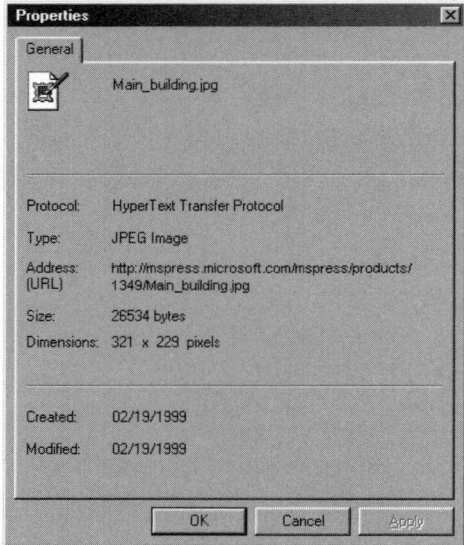

❷   Click the Cancel button.

The Properties dialog box closes.

View animated GIFs

In this exercise, you view an animated GIF on the Lakewood Mountains Resort Recreation page.

> ### tip
>
> Because animated GIFs are created from collections of GIF files, the Properties dialog box indicates only that the graphic is a GIF file. There is not a special file extension for animated GIFs.

❶   On the Lakewood Mountains Resort home page, click the Recreational Facilities hyperlink.

The Recreation page opens.

❷   Scroll down until you see the photograph (JPEG image) of the sail boats.

The boats image is shown accompanied by text and an animated GIF of swimming fish as shown on the following page.

Do you dream of sailing the ocean blue, or just of catching that once-in-a-lifetime marlin? Charter one of our power yachts for an afternoon at sea with a captain who knows where the fish are.

Using Windows Media Player

Windows Media Player is your Internet Explorer gateway to audio and video on the Internet. In the past, Internet surfers had to download and use a variety of multimedia applications to listen to sound files and view videos. Now Internet Explorer combines all the multimedia players into a single application called Windows Media Player.

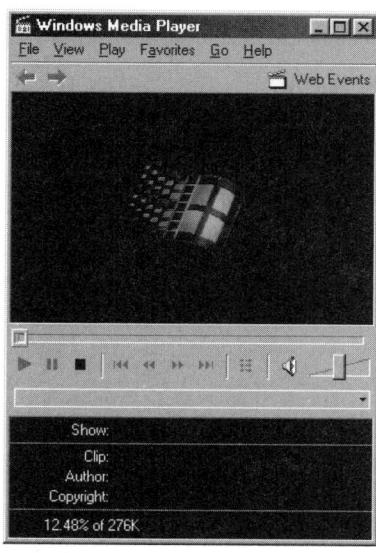

Windows Media Player can be opened directly from the Start menu. You can also open Media Player by clicking a sound or video file hyperlink on a Web page. Clicking a sound or video hyperlink opens Media Player automatically. After Media Player opens, the file downloads or *buffers* and then begins to play.

Enjoying Multimedia   6

Local vs. Streaming Multimedia

A multimedia file can be run locally or it can be *streamed*. When a file runs locally, the file plays after it is completely downloaded to your computer. When a file is streamed, your computer downloads signals and then begins to play the file while the download process continues. The slight delay at the beginning of the download creates a *buffer* (or a partially stored file) as the signals are sent across the Internet. Streaming enables you to listen to live and recorded radio, television, and other broadcasts aired on the Internet. Media Player recognizes most multimedia file formats. These formats are shown below.

A buffer stores the first part of the file before playing it and then stores the next part while the first part is playing. This lets the file play continuously.

File extension	Format	Multimedia type
ASF, ASX	Advanced Streaming Format	Synchronized streaming audio, video, animation, and text
AU, SND	Audio	Audio
AVI	Audio Video Interleave	Video
MID, RMI	Musical Instrument Digital Interface	Synthesized music
MOV	Moving JPEG	Video
MPEG (1, 2, and MP3)	Moving Pictures Expert Group	Combined audio and video
QT, AUF, AIFC, and AIFF	QuickTime	Streaming synchronized graphics, sound, video, and music
RA, RAM, RM, and RMM	Real Video/Real Audio	Streaming audio and video (usually live broadcasts)
WAV	Audio for Windows	Audio

Listen to sound files

In this exercise, you play an audio file by clicking a hyperlink on the Lakewood Mountains Resort Web page.

important

In order to listen to this sound file, your computer needs to be equipped with speakers and a sound card.

1 Start Internet Explorer.

2 Display the Lakewood Mountains Resort home page (*mspress.microsoft. com/mspress/products/1349/default1.htm*) and click the History & Personnel hyperlink.

The Lakewood Mountains Resort History And Personnel page opens.

3 Click the John Gardner hyperlink.

Media Player opens, and after the sound file is downloaded, the Welcome audio file plays.

You can click the Web Events button on Media Player to display the Web Events page. The Web Events page provides links to news, radio, audio, and video resources on the Web.

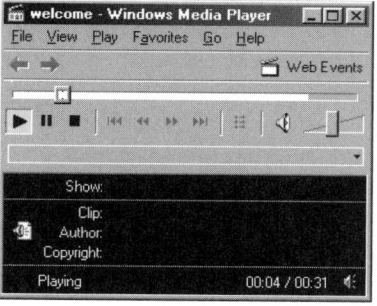

tip

When an audio file plays, Media Player's video pane automatically closes. You can adjust Media Player's window view manually by selecting Standard, Compact, or Minimal on Media Player's View menu.

Stop

4 While the sound file is playing, click the Stop button.

The audio file stops.

5 Click the Play button.

The audio file resumes.

Play

6 While the sound file is playing, move the volume slider to the right.

The volume increases.

Enjoying Multimedia 6

Volume

If the Sound control panel is already set for maximum volume, you might not be able to increase the volume with the volume slider.

7 While the sound file is playing, move the volume slider to the left.

The volume decreases.

8 Quit Media Player.

> ## tip
> Sound files on the Web take a number of forms. They can play as background music, sound-clip audio files displayed as links, broadcasts transmitted over the Internet, and video and animation accompaniment.

View video files

In this exercise, you visit Lakewood Mountains Resort's Computer Help Web page and view a video file.

1 Click the Computer Help hyperlink in the left frame of the Lakewood Mountains Resort home page.

The Lakewood Mountains Resort Computer Help Is Available page opens.

2 Click the Show Me How To Move An Application hyperlink.

Media Player opens. The video file is downloaded and then opens.

It might take a few minutes for the video file to download and play.

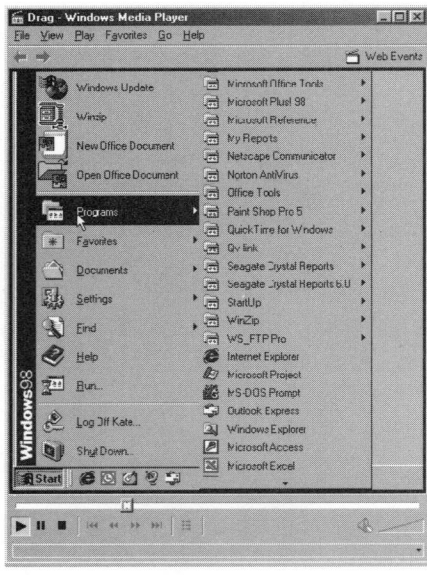

❸ Click the video picture.

   The video pauses.

❹ Click the video picture again.

   The video resumes.

❺ Quit Media Player.

Configuring Multimedia Options

You can specify whether you want multimedia elements to run automatically when you surf the Web. By default, Internet Explorer plays all multimedia elements, including pictures, animations, videos, and sounds. Internet Explorer's multimedia options include the following.

- Play animations: Enables animation files, such as animated GIFs, to appear and run on your computer.

- Play sounds: Enables audio files, such as MIDs, WAVs, and AUs, to play on your computer.

- Play videos: Enables movie files, such as AVIs, MOVs, and ASFs, to run on your computer.

- Smart Image Dithering: Enables Internet Explorer to smooth images' edges so that they appear less jagged when you view them.

- Show pictures: Enables graphics images, such as GIFs, JPEGs, and PNGs, to appear on your computer.

You can change Internet Explorer's default settings by turning off multimedia options. You might want to turn off multimedia elements to save time as well as space on your computer because all Web page files are stored in your Temporary Internet Files folder, which takes up hard disk space.

To change Internet Explorer's multimedia settings, you use the multimedia check boxes on the Advanced tab of the Internet Options dialog box as shown on the following page.

6

Enjoying Multimedia

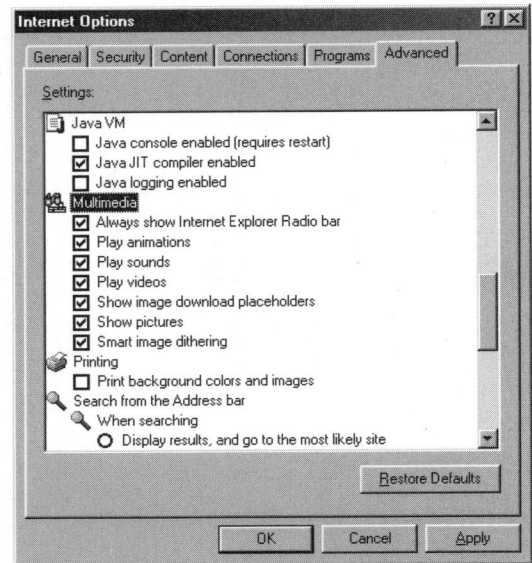

For a demonstration of how to turn off a multimedia setting, in the Multimedia folder on the Microsoft Internet Explorer 5 Step by Step CD-ROM, double-click the Multimedia Options icon.

After you turn off a multimedia element such as Show Pictures, placeholder icons appear on Web pages in place of multimedia items. You can right-click any placeholder icon and open the multimedia item by selecting it from the shortcut menu that appears.

Deactivate multimedia options

In this exercise, you turn off Internet Explorer's Show Pictures multimedia option.

important

This exercise assumes that you do not have the Lakewood Mountains Resort home page open.

1 On the Tools menu, click Internet Options.

The Internet Options dialog box appears.

When you turn off the Show Pictures option, graphics will not be downloaded to your computer when you visit Web pages.

2 Click the Advanced tab.

3 In the Settings list, scroll down until you see the Multimedia options.

4 Clear the check box next to the Show Pictures option.

5 Click OK.

The Internet Options dialog box closes.

6 Click the Address bar, type **mspress.microsoft.com/mspress/products/ 1349/onthe.htm** and press Enter.

The Lakewood Mountains Resort On The Town page appears with place-holders instead of graphics.

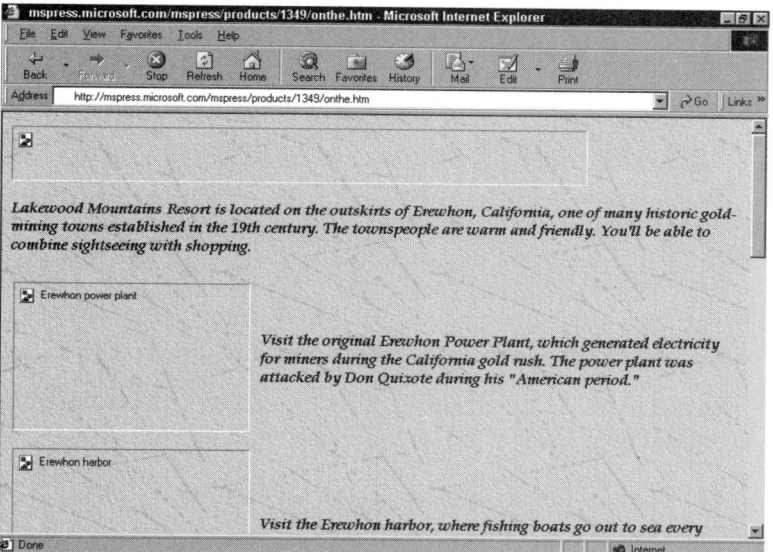

Activate selected multimedia elements

In this exercise, you view a single picture while Internet Explorer's Show Pictures option is turned off.

1 Right-click anywhere within the Erewhon Power Plant placeholder.

A shortcut menu appears.

2 On the shortcut menu, click Show Picture.

The Erewhon Power Plant graphic appears as shown on the following page.

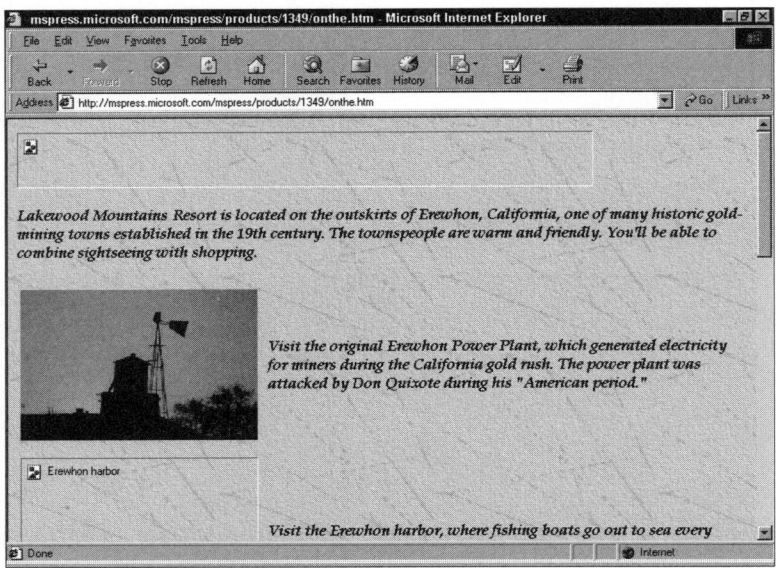

Reapply the default multimedia settings

In this exercise, you reset Internet Explorer's advanced multimedia settings to the default configuration.

1   On the Tools menu, click Internet Options.

The Internet Options dialog box opens.

2   Click the Advanced tab.

3   In the Multimedia section, click Show Pictures.

Internet Explorer's settings revert to the default configuration.

4   Click OK.

The Internet Options dialog box closes.

Refresh

5   On the toolbar, click the Refresh button.

All of the graphics on The On The Town page are downloaded.

One Step Further	# Using Shockwave

Macromedia Shockwave is a popular "cutting-edge" multimedia format. Using Shockwave with Internet Explorer, you can view high-quality streaming content within your browser. When you perform a Typical installation of Internet Explorer, Shockwave Director and Shockwave Flash components are installed automatically with Internet Explorer. If your installation of Internet Explorer does not include Shockwave, you can install Shockwave components. This process is described in Lesson 4, in the section "One Step Further: Adding Components."

With Shockwave, you can enjoy a variety of multimedia presentations on the Web, including games, animations, streaming CD-quality audio, interactive demonstrations, and video presentations. To find out more about Shockwave, visit Shockwave's home page at *www.macromedia.com/shockwave*. Click the Gallery hyperlink to access some examples of Shockwave's capabilities.

View a Shockwave application

Notice that Macromedia calls this the Shockrave site instead of the Shockwave site.

In this exercise, you visit Macromedia's Shockrave site and view an animation.

important

This exercise assumes that Shockwave components are installed on your computer. If they are not, follow the steps in the exercise "Add Internet Explorer Components" in Lesson 4.

● Click in the Address bar, type **www.shockrave.com/members/toons/ peanuts/piano/piano1.swf** and press Enter.

The Macromedia Shockrave page displays a Peanuts animation.

tip

If this address is no longer valid, or if you would like to view something other than the Peanuts "toon," type **www.shockrave.com**, click the Enter Shockrave Now hyperlink, click a category (such as Games, Toons, or Music) that interests you, and click the hyperlink of the item you want to view.

Finish the lesson

● Quit Internet Explorer.

Lesson 6 Quick Reference

To	Do this
View graphics information	Open a Web page, right-click a graphic, and click Properties.
View animated GIFs	Open a Web page that contains an embedded animated GIF.
Listen to sound files	Click a sound file hyperlink on a Web page.
View video files	Click a video file hyperlink on a Web page.
Change multimedia options	Click Internet Options on the Tools menu, click the Advanced tab, scroll down to the Multimedia section, check or clear check boxes next to multimedia options as desired, and click OK.
Activate a picture	Right-click a multimedia element's placeholder icon, and then click Show Picture.
View a Shockwave application	Ensure that the Shockwave components are installed on your computer. In the Address bar, type a URL that has a Shockwave application, and press Enter. *Or* type **www.shockrave.com** in the Address bar, click the Enter Shockrave Now hyperlink, click a category that interests you, and click the hyperlink of the item that you want to view.

Review & Practice

**ESTIMATED
TIME
20 min.**

You will review and practice how to:

✔ *Customize security settings.*
✔ *Apply content rating levels.*
✔ *Set up Microsoft Wallet.*
✔ *Add a component to Internet Explorer.*
✔ *Customize multimedia options.*
✔ *Work offline.*

Before you move on to Part 3, you can practice the skills you learned in Part 2 by working through this Review & Practice. In this section, you will customize Microsoft Internet Explorer by configuring your browser's security settings, content rating levels, Microsoft Wallet options, add-on components, and multimedia options. Then you will use Internet Explorer to make Web pages available for offline viewing.

Scenario

You've customized Internet Explorer's settings on your office computer, and now you want to configure Internet Explorer's settings on your home computer. You use your home computer for recreational Internet surfing and for after-hours work tasks, so many of the settings you implemented at the office will be useful at home. Further, because you will be doing some after-hours work on your home computer, you want to be able to view your clients' Web pages offline on your hard disk drive.

Step 1:   **Customize Your Personal Settings**

You are prepared to configure Internet Explorer's personal settings on your home computer. You want to configure your security, content, and Microsoft Wallet settings. The first task is to add the Lakewood Mountains Resort Web site (*mspress.microsoft.com/mspress/products/1349/default1.htm*) to your Trusted Sites zone. Next you want to turn on Internet Explorer's Content Advisor to limit the types of sites your kids can view on your home computer. And finally, you want to expedite online purchases by adding credit card information to Microsoft Wallet.

❶   Use the Security tab on the Internet Options dialog box to add the Lakewood Mountains Resort Web site to your Trusted Sites zone.

❷   Use the Content tab on the Internet Options dialog box to enable the Content Advisor, and configure the desired Content Advisor settings.

❸   Use the Microsoft Wallet dialog box to add a credit card entry.

For more information about	See
Viewing security zones	Lesson 4
Assigning Web pages to security zones	Lesson 4
Enabling the Content Advisor	Lesson 4
Configuring Content Advisor settings	Lesson 4
Adding credit card information to Microsoft Wallet	Lesson 4

Step 2:   **Select Multimedia Options**

As you use your home computer to surf the Internet, you find that background sounds sometimes slow down your sessions. In the past, you pressed the Esc key to turn off the music, but this has become a nuisance. You decide to turn off the Internet Explorer option that automatically plays sounds. Later, you go to a another Web site to view a Shockwave application.

❶   Use the Advanced tab on the Internet Options dialog box to turn off the Play Sounds option.

❷   If necessary, use the Windows Update: Internet Explorer And Internet Tools dialog box to install Internet Explorer's Shockwave add-on.

❸   View a Shockwave application.

For more information about	See
Turning off multimedia options	Lesson 6
Installing Internet Explorer add-on components	Lesson 4
Viewing a Shockwave application	Lesson 6

Step 3:   Work with Web Pages Offline

The last few evenings, you've been doing some quality work time on your home computer. However, you've found that you are frequently connecting to and disconnecting from your Internet service provider to view the Lakewood Mountains Resort Web site. Therefore, you decide to configure Internet Explorer so that you can work on the resort's Web site offline.

In addition to your work with the Lakewood Mountains Resort Web site, you often scan a few key news sites. For example, you visit the MSNBC Web site almost every day. Therefore, you decide to configure Internet Explorer to automatically download the MSNBC Web site pages once a day.

❶ Add the Lakewood Mountains Resort Web site to your Favorites list, and then use the Organize Favorites dialog box to make the Lakewood Mountains Resort Favorites link available for offline viewing.

❷ Configure the MSNBC Web site to be automatically synchronized for offline viewing once per day.

For more information about	See
Marking Web sites available for offline viewing	Lesson 5
Customizing a synchronization schedule	Lesson 5

Finish the Review & Practice

❶ Delete the Lakewood Mountains Resort Web site information from your Trusted Sites zone list.

❷ Disable the Content Advisor.

❸ Delete your credit card entry.

❹ Turn on the Play Sounds option on the Advanced tab in the Internet Options dialog box.

❺ Delete the offline viewing settings for the Lakewood Mountains Resort site and MSNBC site.

❻ Quit Internet Explorer.

PART 3

Communicating on the Internet

7

Managing Your Electronic Mail

In this lesson you will learn how to:

**ESTIMATED
TIME
40 min.**

- ✔ *Start Outlook Express.*
- ✔ *Create and send messages.*
- ✔ *Receive and respond to messages.*
- ✔ *Print messages.*
- ✔ *Manage your Address Book.*
- ✔ *Use electronic business cards.*
- ✔ *Find electronic mail addresses on the Internet.*
- ✔ *Use digital IDs.*

Impact Public Relations' employees have used electronic mail (e-mail) to communicate with each other for a couple of years. This has been a convenient tool for communicating within the office, but employees now find that they need to send e-mail messages around the world. Impact Public Relations' network administrator has suggested that employees use Microsoft Outlook Express, the Internet e-mail application that is integrated with Microsoft Internet Explorer.

In this lesson, you will start Outlook Express and create, send, receive, respond to, and print e-mail messages. You'll manage your Address Book and learn how to use electronic business cards, called *vCards*. Then you will learn how to find e-mail addresses that are cataloged in Internet directory services. Finally, you'll learn how to obtain and use digital IDs.

important

The exercises in this lesson assume that you have an e-mail account. (An e-mail account allows you to send and receive messages electronically across the Internet through the use of an Internet service provider's mail services.) Further, Outlook Express must be selected as your default e-mail service. To verify that Outlook Express is your default e-mail service, start Internet Explorer, click Internet Options on the Tools menu, and then click the Programs tab. Outlook Express should appear in the E-mail text box. If it does not, click the drop-down arrow, click Outlook Express, and click OK.

Starting Outlook Express

When you install Internet Explorer, Outlook Express is installed by default. Although Outlook Express comes with Internet Explorer, it is a separate program. Therefore, you can open and use Outlook Express independently of Internet Explorer. When you start Outlook Express, it opens in a new window separate from the Internet Explorer window.

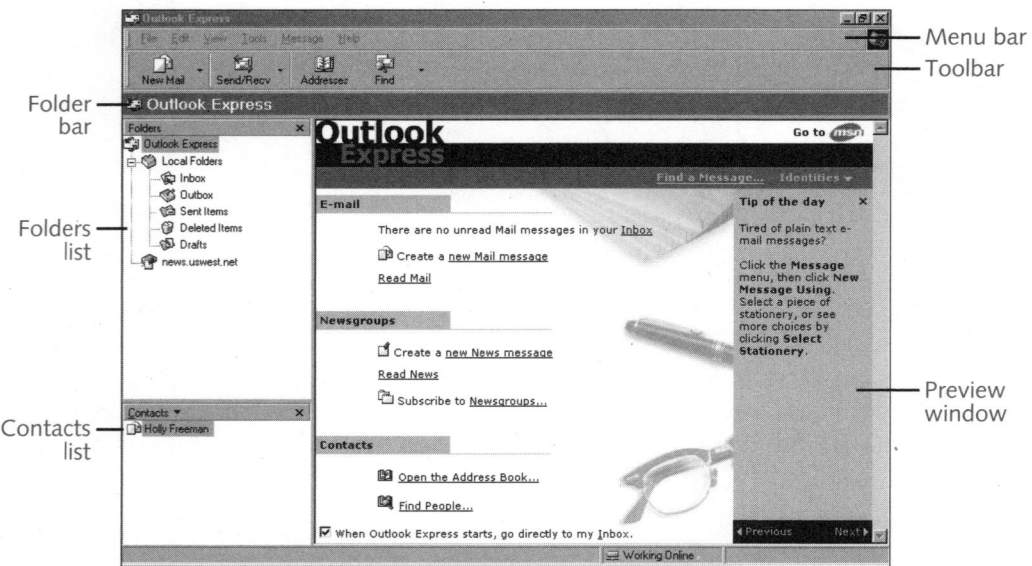

Starting Outlook Express

You can start Outlook Express in a variety of ways:

- Click the Mail button on the Internet Explorer toolbar, and then click Read Mail on the drop-down menu.

- Click the Launch Outlook Express icon on the Quick Launch toolbar. (This option is unavailable in Microsoft Windows NT.)

- On the Windows taskbar, click the Start button, point to Programs, and click Outlook Express.

After you start Outlook Express, you can customize its layout. You can change Outlook Express' message viewing area by hiding or displaying the Folders or Contacts lists.

Modify the layout of Outlook Express

In this exercise, you experiment with some of Outlook Express' layout options.

important

If you use a dial-up connection and are not connected to the Internet, the Dial-Up Connection dialog box appears. Click the Connect button if the Connect Automatically option isn't already selected.

If a message box appears, asking you if you want Outlook Express to be your default mail client, click Yes.

1 On the Windows taskbar, click Start, point to Programs, and click Outlook Express.

Outlook Express starts.

2 In the Folders list, click Inbox.

Your Inbox appears.

3 On the View menu, click Layout.

The Window Layout Properties dialog box opens.

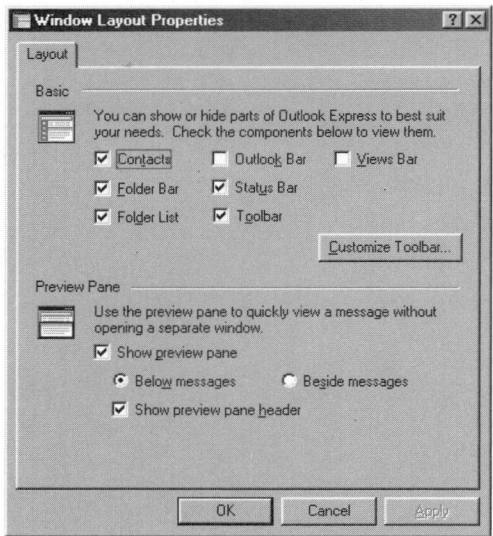

4   In the Window Layout Properties dialog box, clear the Folder List check box, and click the Apply button.

The Folders list closes in the Outlook Express window.

5   Drag the Windows Layout Properties dialog box to the right side of your screen.

Notice that the Folders list is no longer displayed.

6   In the Window Layout Properties dialog box, clear the Contacts check box, and click Apply.

The Contacts list closes in the Outlook Express window.

7   Click the Folder List and the Contacts check boxes, and then click Apply.

The Folders and Contacts lists appear in the Outlook Express window.

8   Click OK.

The Window Layout Properties dialog box closes.

Creating and Sending Messages

Creating and sending e-mail messages is similar to creating and sending traditional mail (which is now sometimes called *snail mail* because it's so slow compared to e-mail). E-mail is like snail mail only in that you must include an address on every message that you create and send. An e-mail address generally consists of a user name, an ampersand (@), and a domain name: for example, *someone@microsoft.com*.

On the other hand, e-mail is noticeably different than snail mail. When you use e-mail, you don't have to wait for a daily visit from your neighborhood mail carrier. Instead of getting messages once per day, you often receive e-mail messages throughout the day, every day, including holidays. This has proven to be an enormous time-saver for many people.

Before you can send e-mail, you must first learn how to create e-mail messages. To create an e-mail message, you open the New Message window in Outlook Express by clicking the New Mail button. You can create plain text messages, which consist of only text, or you can create HTML messages, which enable you to add graphics and other elements to your e-mail message.

Plain Text vs. HTML

When you create e-mail messages in plain text, you can include only unformatted text. The plain text format is the most commonly used e-mail format, because it keeps the e-mail file size small and is transmitted across the Internet quickly.

When you create e-mail messages in HTML, you can include pictures, *stationery* (e-mail messages that contain borders, backgrounds, font colors, font styles, and graphics—similar to commercial stationery used for snail mail), copies of Web pages, multimedia files, hyperlinks, and formatted text. HTML can communicate your ideas more graphically than plain text, but the messages are larger than plain text messages, which means that they take longer to be transmitted across the Internet. Generally, it is considered ill-mannered to send HTML messages that take more than 30 seconds to send. Moderately sized HTML messages are often welcome, as long as the recipient has an application that can display HTML messages. If you are unsure whether your recipient's e-mail program can read HTML messages, it is safer to send the message as plain text.

After you create e-mail messages, you are ready to send them. You can send messages instantly, by clicking the Send button, or you can store your messages in your Outbox and then send all your messages at once. When you store undelivered e-mail messages in your Outbox is especially useful when you want to create e-mail messages while you are not connected to the Internet. Then later, when you are connected to the Internet, you can send all the messages stored in your Outbox. By default, Outlook Express is configured to immediately send messages.

For a demonstration of how to add attachments, in the Multimedia folder on the Microsoft Internet Explorer 5 Step by Step CD-ROM, double-click the Attach File icon.

Another way that you can increase the usefulness of e-mail is to send *attachments*. Attachments are files sent along with an e-mail message. Attachments are instrumental when you want to send more than a simple message to a recipient. For example, you might want to send a spreadsheet showing next year's budget for a particular account. You could create an e-mail message explaining the spreadsheet and then attach the spreadsheet file to the e-mail message as a separate document. When you attach a file, a copy of the document is sent with the e-mail message. The file stored on your computer remains intact.

After you feel comfortable with creating and sending e-mail messages, you can customize your e-mail messages by creating a *signature*. A signature is text that is automatically added to the end of e-mail messages you create. When you create a signature, you specify the closing text that you want to appear at the end of every e-mail you send. E-mail users often configure signatures to provide their name, e-mail address, company name, and other pertinent data. Often people also include clever, witty, or inspirational sayings within their signature.

Before you start to create and send e-mail messages, you should view the Options dialog box. The Options dialog box displays message sending options such as how often to check for e-mail, or whether to create e-mail messages in plain text or HTML. Viewing the available options will give you an idea of which settings you want to configure.

MSN Hotmail

MSN Hotmail is a free Internet e-mail service. An MSN Hotmail e-mail account enables you to access messages from any computer on the Internet. To obtain an MSN Hotmail e-mail account, visit the MSN Hotmail home page at *www.hotmail.com*. Click the Sign Up Here button on the MSN Hotmail home page, and work through the sign-up pages.

View your send options

In this exercise, you open the Options dialog box and view the available message-sending options.

❶   If necessary, start Outlook Express.

❷   On the Tools menu, click Options.

The Options dialog box appears.

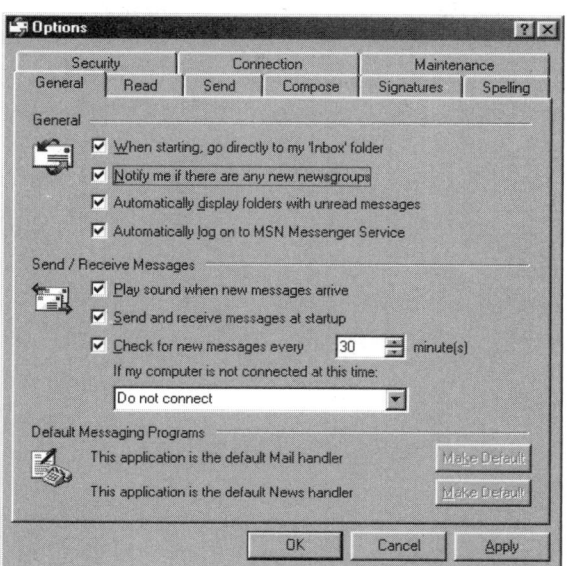

If necessary, click the Check For New Messages Every check box to activate the Minute(s) text box.

❸ Double-click the number in the Minute(s) text box, type **15**, and click Apply.

Outlook Express is configured to send messages stored in your Outbox every 15 minutes, and it will check for incoming mail every 15 minutes.

❹ In the Options dialog box, click the Send tab.

Managing Your E-mail   7

5 On the Send tab, clear the Send Messages Immediately check box.

When you create a message and then click the Send button, the message will be placed in your Outbox folder instead of being sent immediately to the message recipient.

If you plan to compose messages offline, you should leave the Send Messages Immediately check box cleared.

6 Click the Send Messages Immediately check box.

When you create a message and then click the Send button, the messages will be sent immediately to the message recipient.

7 In the Mail Sending Format section, click the Plain Text option.

When you create a new message, the message will be created and sent in plain text format.

You can click the HTML Settings and Plain Text Settings buttons on the Send tab to customize those settings.

8 Click the HTML option.

When you create a new message, the message will be created and sent in HTML format.

9 Click OK.

The Options dialog box closes.

Create and send a message

In this exercise, you create and send a test message to Microsoft.

1 On the toolbar, click the New Mail button.

The New Message window opens.

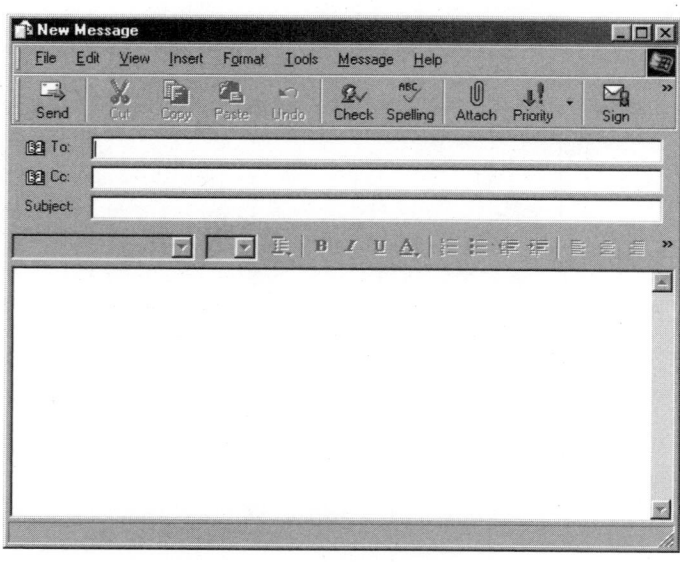

② Type **someone@microsoft.com** in the To text box.

③ Press Tab twice, and type **Test e-mail** in the Subject text box.

④ Press Tab, and type **Just testing my e-mail.** in the message box.

    The e-mail message is ready to be sent.

A reply from Microsoft will eventually appear in your message list.

⑤ Click the Send button on the toolbar.

    The message is sent to Microsoft.

Create a message using stationery

In this exercise, you use stationery to format a New Message window.

① On the toolbar, click the drop-down arrow on the New Mail button, and click Select Stationery.

    The Select Stationery dialog box appears.

② Click the Ivy selection.

    The Ivy stationery appears in the Preview box.

③ Click OK.

    A New Message window appears formatted with the Ivy stationery.

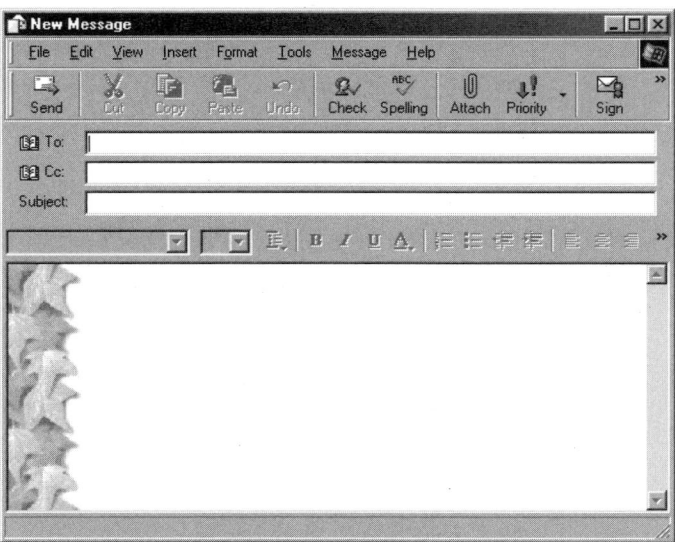

④ In the New Message window, click Close on the File menu.

    The New Message window closes.

Finding Additional Stationery

New!

You can download and create additional stationery packages:

❶ On the Tools menu, click Options.

❷ In the Options dialog box, click the Compose tab.

The Compose tab contains two buttons in the Stationery section—Create New and Download More. Clicking the Create New button starts the Stationery Setup Wizard. You can create and name custom stationery using this wizard. Clicking the Download More button opens the More Outlook Express Stationery Web page in Internet Explorer. To download a stationery pack, click the Get It Now! hyperlink below a stationery design description that interests you. The stationery is free for you to use.

Create a signature

In this exercise, you create a signature that you can attach to your e-mail messages.

❶ On the Tools menu, click Options.

The Options dialog box appears.

❷ Click the Signatures tab.

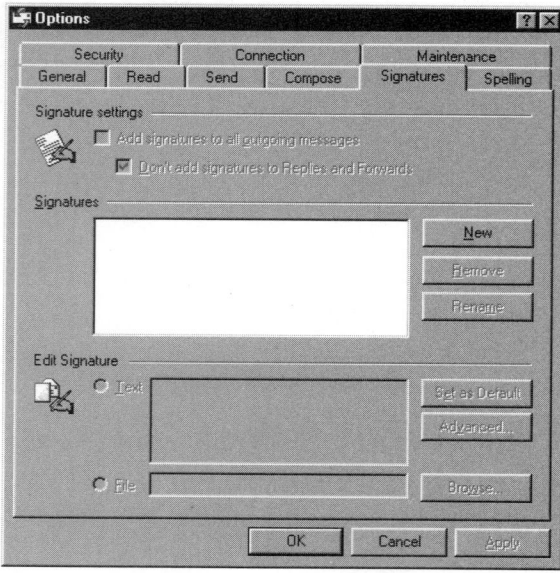

3 Click the New button.

The signature options become available.

4 In the Signatures Settings section, click the Add Signatures To All Outgoing Messages check box.

The signature will appear on all messages you send.

5 Click the Rename button, and type **Main Signature**.

6 In the Edit Signature section, click in the Text text box, type your name, and press Enter.

Your name is added to the signature.

7 Type your e-mail address.

Your e-mail address is added to the signature.

8 Click OK.

The Options dialog box closes.

9 Click the New Mail button.

A New Message window opens with the signature information in the body of the message.

10 On the File menu, click Close.

The New Message window closes.

11 On the Tools menu, click Options, and then click the Signatures tab.

12 In the Signatures section, click the Main Signature entry, and then click Remove.

The signature is removed.

13 Click OK.

The Options dialog box closes.

Attach a file to a message

In this exercise, you attach a Microsoft Word document to an e-mail message.

1 On the toolbar, click the New Mail button.

A New Message window opens.

2 In the To text box, type your e-mail address.

3 In the Subject text box, type **Test**.

You can attach more than one file to an e-mail message.

4 In the message box, type **Please look at the attached file**.

5 On the toolbar, click the Attach button.

The Insert Attachment dialog box appears.

6 In the Insert Attachment dialog box, use the Look In drop-down list to navigate to the Lesson 7 folder in the Internet Explorer 5 SBS Practice folder on your hard disk drive.

You can also add an attachment to an e-mail message by dragging a file icon from a folder or your desktop onto the e-mail message.

7 Click Letter, and click the Attach button.

The Letter filename appears in the Attach text box.

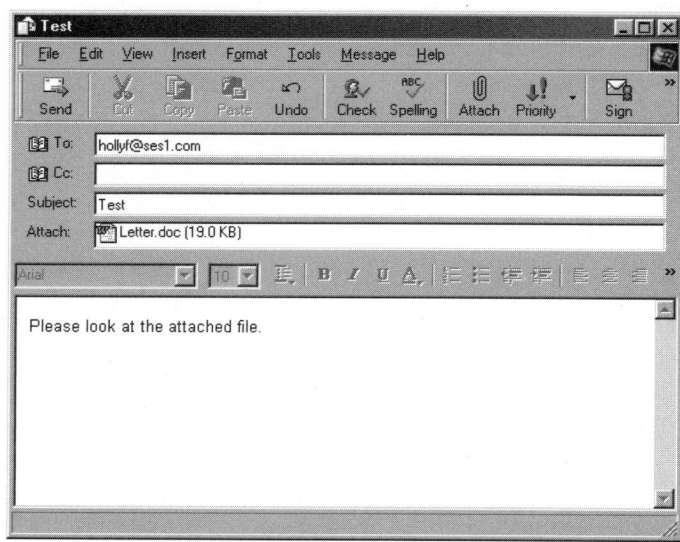

8 On the toolbar, click the Send button.

The window closes, and the message is sent to you.

Receiving Messages

By default, Outlook Express checks for messages every 30 minutes. If you prefer, you can manually check for e-mail messages by clicking the Send/Recv button on the Outlook Express toolbar. When you click the Send/Recv button, all messages stored in your Outbox are sent and you receive all messages that are waiting for you on your Internet service provider's mail server.

When you receive a message, Outlook Express identifies the new message by displaying the message's header in boldface in your Inbox and accompanying the message header with a closed envelope icon. A message header is the line of text that appears in the message list of the Outlook Express window, directly above the preview pane. The message list identifies each e-mail message's sender, subject line, and date.

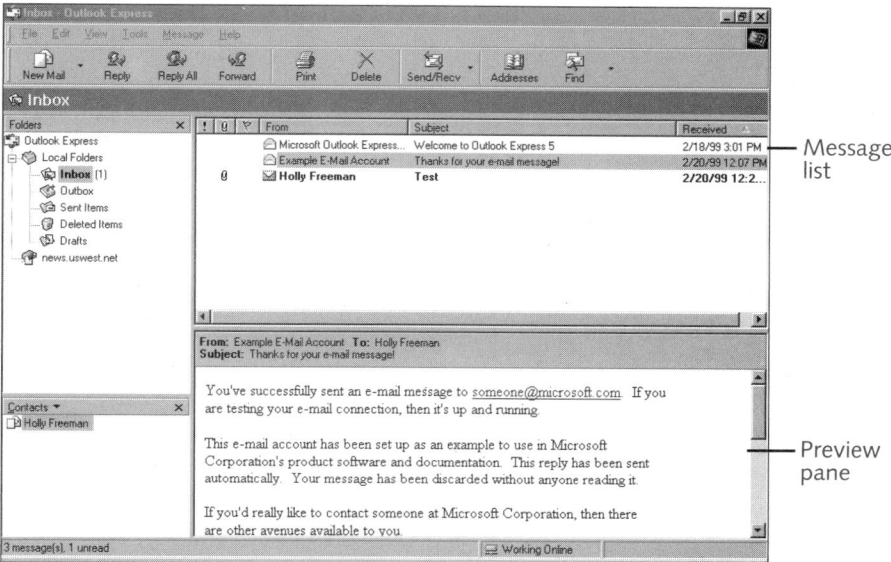

Message list

Preview pane

You can control where to store messages by using Outlook Express' message rules. Message rules enable you to automatically move, or *filter*, e-mail messages into specified folders. You can use message rules to move all of the e-mail messages that you receive from your boss into a separate mail folder named Boss. Finally, you can use message rules to block messages from particular senders. You might want to block a sender if you constantly receive unwanted marketing messages from the same sales representative. When you block a sender, messages from the sender are automatically placed in your Deleted Items folder.

After you receive e-mail messages, the next step is to open and read the messages. To open a message, you click the message header to show the message content in the preview pane or double-click the message header to open the message in a separate window. Messages with attachments are accompanied by a paper clip icon.

Paper Clip

Create message rules to handle incoming e-mail

In this exercise, you create a message rule to filter incoming e-mail messages from Microsoft into a new mail folder.

1 If necessary, start Outlook Express.

2 On the Tools menu, point to Message Rules, and then click Mail.

The New Mail Rule dialog box appears.

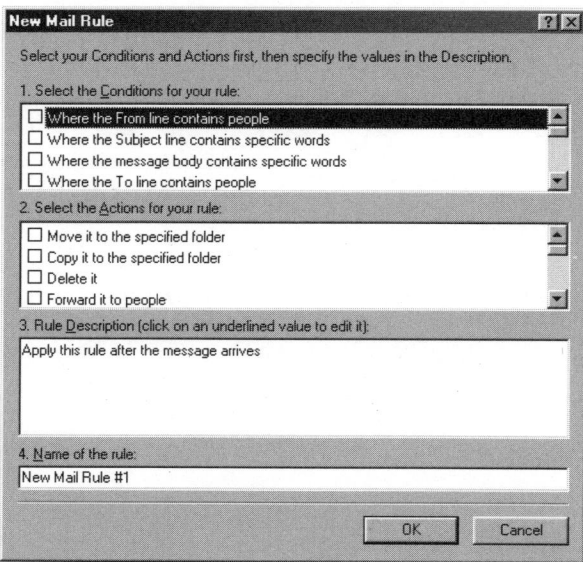

❸ In section 1 of the New Mail Rule dialog box, click the Where The From Line Contains People check box.

E-mail messages will be identified by sender.

❹ In section 2, click the Move It To The Specified Folder check box.

Specified messages will be moved into a separate folder.

❺ In section 3, click the Contains People link.

The Select People dialog box appears.

❻ In the Select People dialog box, type **someone@microsoft.com** in the first text box, click Add, and click OK.

The People Contains link changes to *someone@microsoft.com.*

❼ In section 3, click the Specified link.

The Move dialog box opens.

❽ In the Move dialog box, click the New Folder button.

The New Folder dialog box opens.

❾ In the Folder Name text box, type **Testing E-mail**, and then click OK.

A New Folder named Testing E-mail is added to the Outlook Express Folders list.

❿ In the Move dialog box, click OK.

The Specified link is changed to Testing E-mail, and the rule will now place all messages received from *someone@microsoft.com* into the Testing E-mail folder.

⓫ In section 4 of the New Mail Rule dialog box, select the text in the Name Of The Rule text box, type **Testing E-mail**, and click OK.

The rule is named Testing E-mail, and the rule appears on the Mail Rules tab in the Message Rules dialog box.

⓬ Verify that the Testing E-mail rule is selected, click Remove, and click Yes.

The Testing E-mail rule is deleted.

⓭ In the Message Rules dialog box, click OK.

The Message Rules dialog box closes.

Manage your blocked senders list

In this exercise, you add and remove an e-mail address from your blocked senders list.

❶ On the Tools menu, point to Message Rules, and click Block Senders List.

The Block Senders tab appears in the Message Rules dialog box.

New!

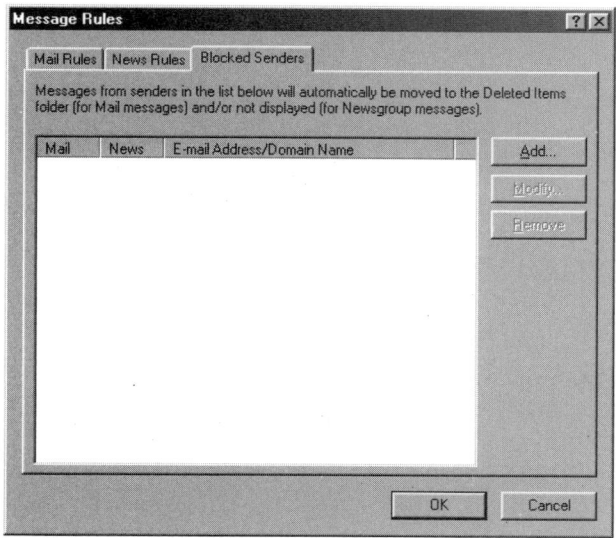

2   On the Block Senders tab, click Add.

The Add Sender dialog box opens.

3   Type **someone@microsoft.com** in the Address text box, and click OK.

The address *someone@microsoft.com* is added to the list.

tip

To quickly add a sender to your blocked senders list, select a message header from the message list, click Block Sender on the Message menu, and specify whether you want to remove all messages from the sender from the current folder.

4   Select *someone@microsoft.com*, click Remove, and click Yes.

The address *someone@microsoft.com* is removed from the list.

5   In the Message Rules dialog box, click OK.

The Message Rules dialog box closes.

Check for messages and open new e-mail

In this exercise, you check for new messages and open a new e-mail message.

This exercise assumes that you've sent an e-mail message to yourself. If you have not, follow the steps in the exercise "Attach a File to a Message" earlier in this lesson.

1   On the toolbar, click the Send/Recv button.

An Outlook Express dialog box appears, showing the status of your e-mail.

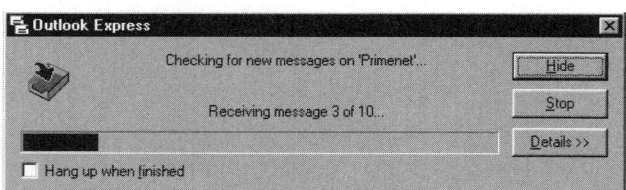

Unread messages appear in the message list with bold text and a closed-envelope icon.

2   If necessary, in the Folders list, click the Inbox folder.

The content of the Inbox appears in the message list and the preview pane.

3   In the message list, click the Test message header.

The message content appears in the preview pane.

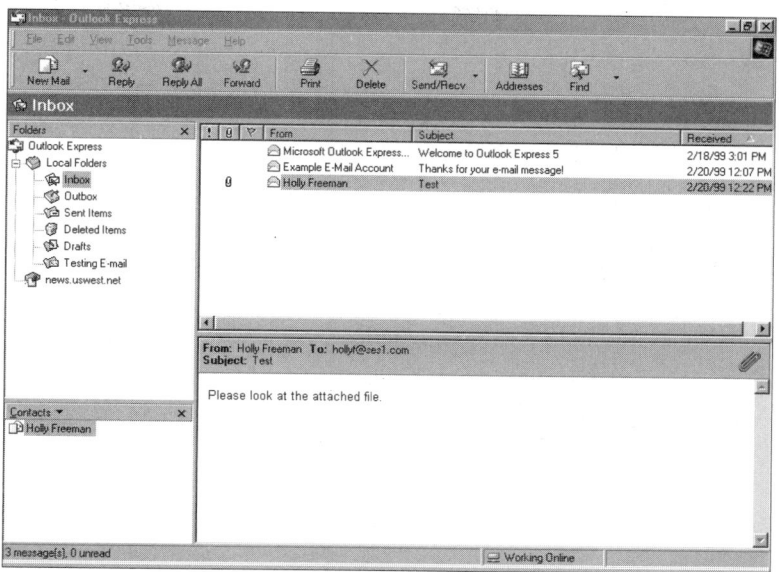

❹ Double-click the Test message header.

The message content appears in a separate window.

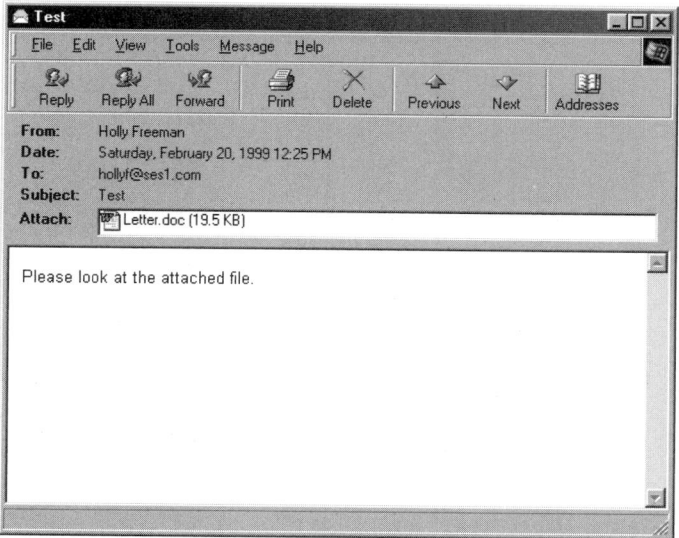

❺ In the Test window, click Close on the File menu.

The Test window closes.

View an attachment

In this exercise, you open a file attached to an e-mail message.

Messages that have attachments appear in the Inbox with a paper clip icon next to the message header.

1 If necessary, click the Test message header.

The message's content appears in the preview pane.

2 In the preview pane, click the paper clip icon.

A shortcut menu appears.

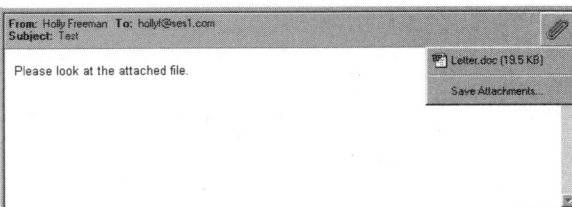

```
From: Holly Freeman  To: hollyf@ses1.com
Subject: Test

Please look at the attached file.          Letter.doc (19.5 KB)
                                           Save Attachments...
```

New!

3 On the shortcut menu, click Letter.doc.

The attachment opens.

important

In some cases, when you open attached files such as pictures or Web page URLs, you will see the Open Attachment Warning dialog box. The Open Attachment Warning dialog box enables you to open the attached file or save the attached file to your hard disk drive. In most cases, you should save the file to your hard disk drive (thereby giving your virus checker software a chance to check the file for viruses) and then open the file from your hard disk drive. If the attachment is from a highly trusted source, and you don't want to save the file, you might choose to open the file without saving it to your hard disk drive.

Close

4 Click the Close button in the top-right corner of the Letter attachment.

The attachment closes.

Forwarding and Responding to Messages

You can forward and reply to a message that someone has sent to you. Outlook Express makes this easy by providing convenient toolbar buttons. When you forward a message, the original message appears in a new message window and you must indicate the person(s) to whom you want to send a copy of the message.

When you reply to an e-mail message, a new message window opens with the e-mail address inserted into the To text box and the content of the original message copied into the message window. In both cases, you can add text to the new message, delete content from the copy of the original message, and add attachments to the e-mail message.

Reply to a message

This exercise assumes that you've sent an e-mail message to Microsoft. If you have not, follow the steps in the exercise "Create and Send a Message" earlier in this lesson.

In this exercise, you respond to a message in your Inbox.

1　If necessary, start Outlook Express, and display the contents of the Inbox folder.

important

You may have to wait until Microsoft sends you a message. If you don't want to wait for a response, use the Test e-mail message you created in the exercise "Attach a File to a Message" earlier in this lesson.

2　In the message list, click the Example E-mail Account message header.

The message is selected, and its content appears in the preview pane.

3　On the toolbar, click the Reply button.

A new message window opens (as shown on the following page), containing the recipient's e-mail address in the To text box and a copy of the original message in the message window.

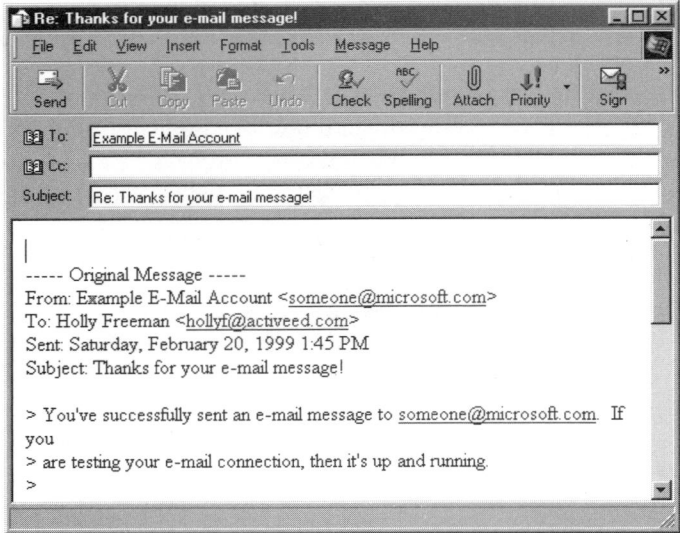

When you reply to a message, the reply message uses the same text format as the original message by default.

❹   Type **Testing** in the message box, and click the Send button on the toolbar.

The reply is sent to Microsoft.

Replying to Everyone Involved

In addition to replying to the sender of an e-mail message, you can also respond to all of the recipients of the original message, whether their addresses appear in the To text box or in the Cc text box. To reply to everyone involved with a message, click the Reply All button on the toolbar.

Forward a message

This exercise assumes that you've sent an e-mail message to yourself. If you have not, follow the steps in the exercise "Attach a File to a Message" earlier in this lesson.

In this exercise, you forward a test message to Microsoft.

❶   In the message list, click the Test message header.

The message is selected, and its content appears in the preview pane.

❷   On the toolbar, click the Forward button.

A new message window opens, containing the content of the original message, including any attachments.

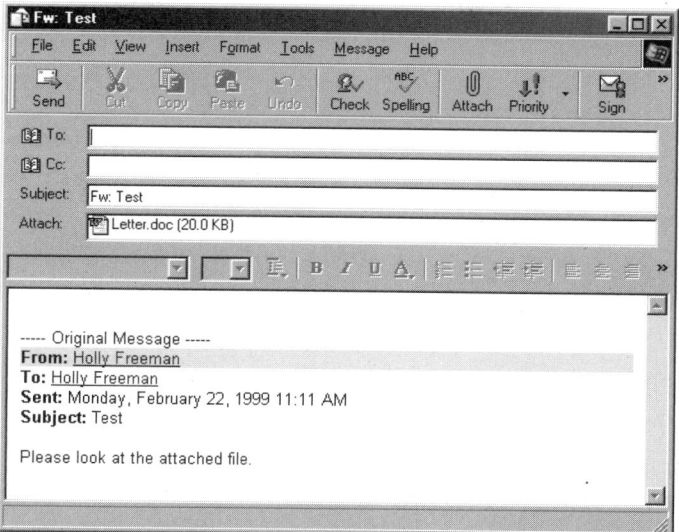

3 Type **someone@microsoft.com** in the To text box, and click the Send button.

The message is forwarded to Microsoft.

Printing Messages

Print

There will be times when you'll need a hard copy of an e-mail message. You can easily print a message by selecting a message in the Outlook Express Inbox and then clicking the Print button on the toolbar. Or you can double-click a message header and then click the Print button on the message window's toolbar.

You will find that printed e-mail messages are often laid out differently than they appear on screen. Most often, this is because e-mail message windows are resizable, so information shifts to fit the window size. Paper, on the other hand, is a fixed size, so information is printed with the default paper size settings. Also, be aware that any attachments that are displayed in an e-mail's message window, such as a graphic, will be printed along with the e-mail message. Attachments that do not appear in the message window, such as Microsoft Word documents or Microsoft Excel spreadsheets, will not be printed along with the e-mail message.

Print an e-mail message

*This exercise
assumes that
you've sent an
e-mail to
yourself. If
you have not,
follow the
steps in the
exercise
"Attach a File
to a Message"
earlier in this
lesson.*

In this exercise, you print the content of an e-mail message.

1 If necessary, start Outlook Express, and display the contents of the Inbox folder.

2 In the message list, click the Test message header.

The message is selected, and its content appears in the preview pane.

3 On the toolbar, click the Print button.

The Print dialog box appears.

4 Click OK.

The selected message is printed.

Print

Managing Your Address Book

The Outlook Express Address Book works much like a typical address book. It stores e-mail addresses, phone numbers, addresses, and other data about coworkers, friends, family members, organizations, and other contacts. The illustration shows two Address Book entries containing e-mail addresses.

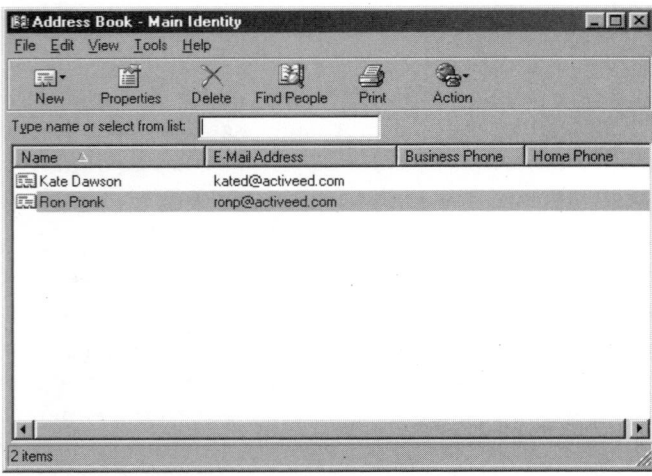

You can add entries to your Address Book manually by filling in the text boxes of the Properties dialog box, or you can create Address Book entries from messages appearing in your Inbox. Also, by default, Outlook Express automatically creates Address Book entries every time you reply to an e-mail message.

> ## tip
> You can turn off Outlook Express' default setting that creates an Address Book entry each time you reply to an e-mail message. To turn this feature off, on the Tools menu, click Options, and then click the Send tab. Clear the Automatically Put People I Reply To In My Address Book check box, and then click OK.

In addition to storing information, you can use the Address Book to automatically insert e-mail addresses into messages. Not only does this save you from having to retype information, but it greatly reduces the risk of mistyping e-mail addresses.

To help you send messages to groups of people without having to add each individual e-mail address to a message, you can create Address Book entries that contain multiple contacts. For example, you can create an Address Book entry entitled Family that contains all your family members' e-mail addresses.

When you use a group Address Book entry, you can address an e-mail message with the Address Book entry and then have Outlook Express automatically send the message to each person included in the group's member list. For example, you could use your Family Address Book entry to send an announcement to your family that you've just bought a fully refurbished Victorian house, and that everyone's welcome to visit for the holidays.

Finally, just like any address book, the Outlook Express Address Book is only as useful as you make it. You need to keep the information up to date, and old entries should be deleted to keep your Address Book from becoming cluttered and unwieldy. You delete Address Book entries by opening your Address Book, selecting an entry, and then clicking the Delete button on the Address Book toolbar.

Managing Your E-mail 7

Create a new Address Book entry

This exercise assumes that you've sent an e-mail to yourself. If you have not, follow the steps in the exercise "Attach a File to a Message." You must be connected to a printer to do this exercise.

In this exercise, you add an Address Book entry for Hogarth Moore, an advertising contact.

1   If necessary, start Outlook Express.

2   On the toolbar, click the Addresses button.

   The Address Book opens.

3   On the Address Book's toolbar, click the New button, and click New Contact on the drop-down menu.

   The Properties dialog box appears.

4   In the First text box, type **Hogarth**.

5   In the Last text box, and type **Moore**.

6   In the E-mail Addresses text box, type **hmoore@semson.com**.

7   Click the Add button, and then click OK.

   The Properties dialog box closes, and an entry for Hogarth Moore is added to the Address Book.

8   Click the Close button in the top-right corner of the Address Book window.

   The Address Book closes.

Close

Add an Address Book entry from an e-mail message

This exercise assumes that you've sent an e-mail to yourself. If you have not, follow the steps in the exercise "Attach a File to a Message" earlier in this lesson.

In this exercise, you create an Address book entry from a message in your Inbox.

1   If necessary, display the content of the Inbox folder.

2   In the message list, click the Test message header.

   The message is selected, and its content appears in the preview pane.

important

If you receive an alert box telling you that the contact is already in your Address Book, right-click your name in the Contacts list, click Delete, click Yes in the alert box, and repeat steps 1 and 2.

❸ Right-click the selected message, and click Add Sender To Address Book.

The sender's information is automatically added to the Address Book.

❹ On the toolbar, click the Addresses button.

The Address Book opens and shows the newly created Address Book entry.

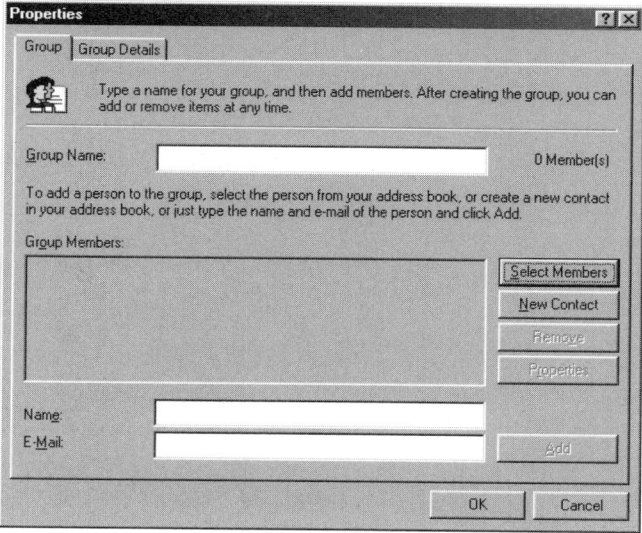

❺ Click the Close button in the top-right corner of the Address Book window.

The Address Book closes.

Close

Create a group

In this exercise, you group three e-mail addresses into a single Address Book entry.

❶ On the toolbar, click the Addresses button.

The Address Book opens.

❷ On the Address Book's toolbar, click the New button, and click New Group on the drop-down menu.

The Properties dialog box opens.

You can create new Address Book entries while creating a group by clicking the New Contact button on the Group tab.

❸ Type **New Contacts** in the Group Name text box.

The group is named New Contacts.

❹ Click the Select Members button.

The Select Group Members dialog box opens.

❺ Click Hogarth Moore, and click Select.

Hogarth Moore is added to the Members list.

❻ Click your name, and click Select.

Your name is added to the Members list.

❼ Click OK.

The Select Group Members dialog box closes, and the Address Book entries appear in the Group Members list on the Group tab.

❽ On the Group tab, click the Name text box, type **Microsoft**, press Tab, type **someone@microsoft.com**, and click Add.

Microsoft is added to the Group Members list.

❾ Click OK.

Group

The Properties dialog box closes, and the New Contacts Address Book entry is created, accompanied by a group icon.

❿ Click the Close button in the top-right corner of the Address Book window.

Close

The Address Book closes.

Use your Address Book when creating messages

In this exercise, you use the Address Book to enter an e-mail address into a new message.

You can open a pread-dressed New Message window by double-click-ing a contact's name in the Contacts list.

❶ On the toolbar, click the New Mail button.

A New Message window opens.

❷ In the New Message window, click the To button.

The Select Recipients dialog box appears.

❸ In the Select Recipients dialog box, click Hogarth Moore in the Name list box.

❹ Click the To button.

The Hogarth Moore entry (and possibly other entries) appears in the Message Recipients list.

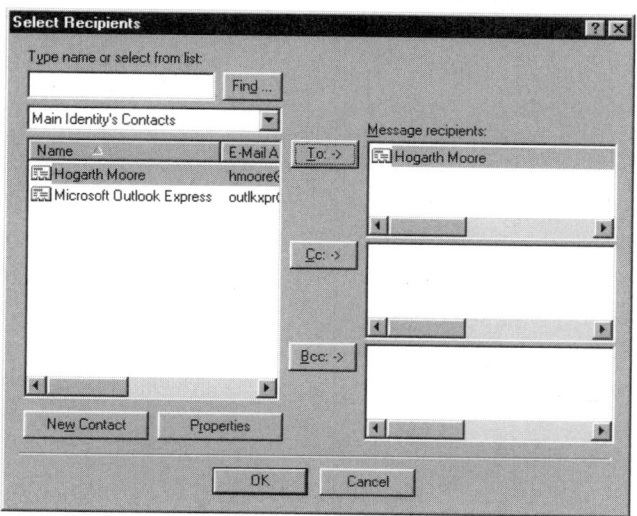

5 Click OK.

The Hogarth Moore entry appears in the To text box in the New Message window.

Close

6 Without saving changes, click the Close button in the top-right corner of the New Message window.

The New Message window closes.

Delete an Address Book entry

In this exercise, you remove the Hogarth Moore entry from your Address Book.

1 On the toolbar, click the Addresses button.

The Address Book opens.

2 In the Address Book, click the Hogarth Moore Address Book entry.

3 On the Address Book toolbar, click Delete.

An alert box appears, asking if you are sure you want to permanently delete the entry.

4 Click Yes.

The Hogarth Moore entry is deleted.

Close

5 Click the Close button in the top-right corner of the Address Book window.

The Address Book closes.

Managing Your E-mail

Using Electronic Business Cards

The easiest way to exchange contact information with people over the Internet is to attach an electronic business card, or *vCard*, to e-mail messages. Basically, an electronic business card contains your name, phone number, e-mail address, and other information stored in an entry in your Address Book that you've created for yourself. Therefore, you must have your information stored in your Address Book before you can create a business card.

You can use the Compose tab of the Options dialog box to create an electronic business card. Simply click the Mail check box and use the drop-down arrow to the right of it to select your name. After you create a business card, you can attach the card to any e-mail message that you create by turning on the My Business Card option on the Insert menu.

Create an electronic business card

This exercise assumes that you've created an Address Book entry for yourself. If you have not, follow the steps in the exercise "Add an Address Book Entry from an E-mail Message" earlier in this lesson.

In this exercise, you create an electronic business card.

1 If necessary, start Outlook Express.

2 On the Tools menu, click Options.

The Options dialog box appears.

3 Click the Compose tab.

4 In the Business Cards section, click the Mail check box.

The drop-down list becomes available.

5 Click the drop-down arrow to the right of the Mail check box, click your name, and click OK.

Your electronic business card is created, and the Options dialog box closes.

Add your business card to an e-mail message

In this exercise, you insert your business card into an e-mail message, send the message to yourself, and then view the business card.

1 On the toolbar, click the New Mail button.

A New Message window opens.

2 Type your e-mail address in the To text box, type **Business card**, in the Subject text box, and type **Testing electronic business card.** in the message box.

3 On the Insert menu, verify that My Business Card is selected.

Your business card is added to the e-mail message.

➍   On the toolbar, click the Send button.

The message is sent to you.

➎   On the toolbar, click the Send/Recv button.

An Outlook Express dialog box appears, showing the status of your e-mail, and the Business Card message header appears in the message list.

➏   Click the Business Card message header.

A business card icon appears in the right corner of the preview pane.

*Electronic
Business Card*

➐   Click the electronic business card icon.

The Open Attachment dialog box appears.

➑   Click Open It, and click OK.

The Properties dialog box appears, showing your electronic business card information.

➒   Click Cancel.

The Properties dialog box closes.

Finding E-mail
Addresses on the Internet

You might have noticed that as the world grows smaller, phonebooks grow bigger. The Internet provides the largest "phonebook" of all, which is called the *e-mail directory services,* and you'll frequently need to use e-mail directory services to find e-mail addresses and other contact information. Outlook Express makes searching Internet directories easy by including links to popular e-mail directory services. Instead of visiting each e-mail directory service Web page when you need to find information about a person, Outlook Express consolidates the search services in the Find People dialog box.

Opening the Find People Dialog Box

You can access the Find People dialog box in a variety of ways:

- In the Address Book, click the Find People button on the toolbar.
- In Outlook Express, click the drop-down arrow on the Find button, and click People.
- In Outlook Express, on the Edit menu, point to Find, and click People.
- On the Windows taskbar, click the Start button, point to Find, and click People.
- Click anywhere in the Outlook Express window, and press Ctrl+E.

The Find People dialog box enables you to specify who you want to search for and which directory service you want to use. If one service doesn't return the desired results, you can search another directory service using the same search techniques. To change the directory service, you click the Look In drop-down arrow, select a service in the list, and click the Find Now button. Keep in mind that some directory services require people to voluntarily submit their information to the service. To add your information, visit the service's home page on the Web.

tip

You can visit a directory service's Web site from the Find People dialog box. Verify that you are connected to the Internet, open the Find People dialog box, display the directory service name in the Look In drop-down list, and then click the Web Site button.

Use the Find People feature

In this exercise, you use Outlook Express' Find People feature to search for your name on the Internet.

1 If necessary, start Outlook Express.

2 On the toolbar, click the Addresses button.

The Address Book opens.

3 On the Address Book toolbar, click the Find People button.

The Find People dialog box opens.

④ Click the Look In drop-down arrow, and then click Yahoo! People Search.

⑤ Type your name in the Name text box.

⑥ In the Find People dialog box, click the Find Now button.

The search is conducted, and the results appear in the Find People dialog box.

⑦ In the Find People dialog box, click the Close button.

The Find People dialog box closes.

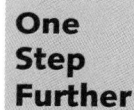

Close

⑧ Click the Close button at the top-right corner of the Address Book.

The Address Book closes.

One Step Further **Using Digital IDs**

Digital IDs (also called personal certificates) help you to verify that the person or company with whom you are exchanging information on the Internet is legitimately the person or company that you want to contact. As electronic transactions become more common, e-mail security issues grow increasingly important. Internet users need a way to protect sensitive information and verify that sensitive information hasn't been tampered with (or changed along its route across the Internet). To ensure the legitimacy of information exchanged on the Internet, you can use digital IDs to help prove your identity to others on the Internet, just as you might show your passport or driver's license in real life. In turn, others can send digital IDs to you to prove their identity.

You can also use digital IDs to *encrypt* (or code) messages that you send so that if someone intercepts the message, he or she won't be able to read it. Before you can send an encrypted message, you must obtain the recipient's digital ID and add it to your Address Book (see the "Adding Digital IDs to Your Address Book" sidebar on the following page). For more information about digital IDs, encryption, and Internet security issues in general, visit Microsoft's Security Advisor Web page, at *www.microsoft.com/security*.

Managing Your E-mail

Adding Digital IDs to Your Address Book

When a contact sends you a digital ID, you can add the ID to your Address Book. Adding a digital ID to your Address Book will enable you and the contact to exchange encrypted messages with each other. To add a digital ID that you receive from a contact to your Address Book, follow these steps:

1 Start Outlook Express, display the Inbox, and select the digitally signed message.

2 On the File menu, click Properties.

3 In the Digital Id dialog box, click the Security tab, and then click Add To Address Book.

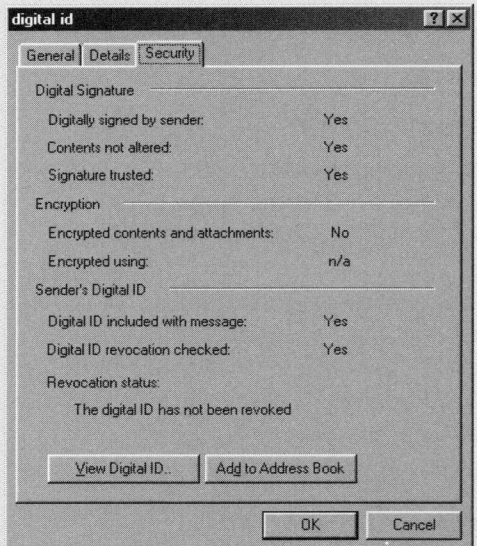

4 Click OK to close the message box, and then click OK to close the Digital Id dialog box.

The process of sending digital IDs in Outlook Express involves obtaining a digital ID for yourself on the Internet. After you have a digital ID, you must configure your Outlook Express mail account to use the digital ID. Finally, you digitally sign an e-mail message by turning on the digital ID option in the message window after you create an e-mail message.

Obtain a digital ID

In this exercise, you sign up for a digital ID.

❶ If necessary, start Outlook Express.

❷ On the Tools menu, click Accounts.

The Internet Accounts dialog box opens.

❸ In the Internet Accounts dialog box, click the account you want to send secure mail from, and then click the Properties button.

The mail account Properties dialog box opens.

❹ In the mail account Properties dialog box, click the Security tab.

❺ Click the Get Digital ID button.

The Outlook Express Features Web page opens in Internet Explorer.

❻ On the Outlook Express Features Web page, select a digital ID provider, and follow the Web page's instructions for obtaining a digital ID.

Assign a digital ID to your mail account

In this exercise, you add a digital ID to your mail account properties.

❶ If necessary, start Outlook Express.

❷ On the Tools menu, click Accounts.

The Internet Accounts dialog box opens.

❸ In the Internet Accounts dialog box, click your mail account name, and then click the Properties button.

The mail account Properties dialog box opens.

❹ In the Properties dialog box, click the Security tab.

❺ If necessary, in the S/MIME Secure E-mail section, click the Use A Digital ID When Sending Secure Messages From check box.

The digital ID option is turned on.

❻ On the Security tab, click the Digital ID button.

The Select Certificate dialog box appears.

7

Managing Your E-mail

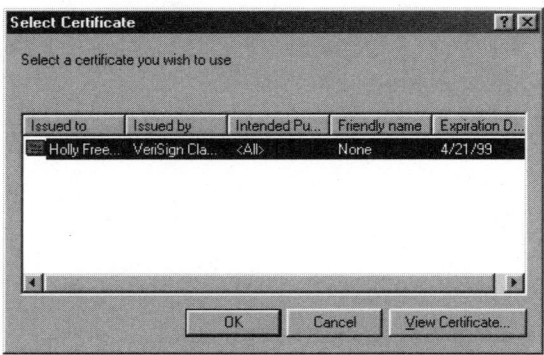

7 Click a digital ID, and then click OK.

The Select Certificate dialog box closes.

8 Click OK.

The Properties dialog box closes.

9 Click Close.

The Internet Accounts dialog box closes.

Digitally sign an e-mail message

In this exercise, you create a new message that uses a digital signature.

1 On the toolbar, click the New Mail button.

The New Message window opens.

2 Type your e-mail address in the Address text box, type **Digital Id** in the Subject text box, and type **Testing Digital Id.** in the message box.

3 On the toolbar, click the Sign button.

The digital ID is added to the message.

4 On the toolbar, click the Send button.

The message is sent to you.

5 On the toolbar, click the Send/Recv button.

An Outlook Express dialog box appears, showing the status of your e-mail, and the Digital Id message header appears in the message list. Notice that to the left of your name, the envelope icon is accompanied by a ribbon. This indicates that the message is digitally signed.

Digitally Signed Message

Finish the lesson

1 Right-click the New Contacts folder in the Contacts list, click Delete, and click Yes.

The New Contacts folder is deleted.

2 On the Tools menu, click Accounts, click Properties, click the Security tab, and clear the Use Digital ID When Sending Secure Messages From check box. Click OK, and click Close.

The digital ID option is turned off.

3 Quit Outlook Express.

4 If necessary, quit Internet Explorer.

Lesson 7 Quick Reference

To	Do this
Start Outlook Express	On the Windows taskbar, click Start, point to Programs, and click Outlook Express.
Modify Outlook Express' layout	Click Layout on the View menu, and change the options in the Window Layout Properties dialog box. Click the Apply button, and click OK.
View your send options	Click Options on the Tools menu, view the send options on the General and Send tabs, and click OK.
Create and send a message	Click the New Mail button on the toolbar, enter an e-mail address in the To text box, enter a subject line in the Subject text box, and type a message in the message box. Click the Send button on the toolbar.
Create a message using stationery	Click the New Mail button's drop-down arrow on the toolbar, click Select Stationery, click a stationery style in the Select Stationery dialog box, and click OK.

Managing Your E-mail

7

Lesson 7 Quick Reference

To	Do this	Icon
Create a signature	Click Options on the Tools menu, and click the Signatures tab. Click the New button, click the Add Signatures To All Outgoing Messages check box, click the Rename button, and type a name. Type your name and any other information that you want to include in your signature in the Text text box, pressing Enter after each item you add, and then click OK.	
Attach a file to an e-mail message	Create a message, click the Attach button, navigate to the document that you want to attach, click it, and then click the Attach button in the Insert Attachment dialog box.	
Create message rules to handle incoming mail	On the Tools menu, point to Message Rules, and then click Mail. Complete the four sections in the New Mail Rule dialog box, click OK, and click OK again.	
Mange your blocked senders list	On the Tools menu, point to Message Rules, click Block Senders List, and then click Add. Enter an e-mail address in the Address text box, click OK, and click OK.	
Manually check for new mail	Click the Send/Recv button on the toolbar.	
Open new mail	Click the Inbox folder in the Folders list, and click or double-click an unread message.	
View an attachment	Click the Inbox folder in the Folders list, click a message that contains an attachment, click the paper clip icon in the upper-right corner of the preview pane, and click the filename.	

Lesson 7 Quick Reference

To	Do this	Button
Reply to a message	Click the Inbox folder in the Folders list, click a message header, and then click the Reply button. Write a message, and click the Send button.	
Forward a message	Click the Inbox folder in the Folders list, click a message header, and then click the Forward button. Type an e-mail address in the To text box. If desired, write a message, and click the Send button.	
Print an e-mail message	Click the Inbox folder in the Folders list, click a message header, click the Print button, and click OK.	
Create a new Address Book entry	Click the Addresses button on the toolbar, click the New button, click New Contact, enter contact information in the Properties dialog box, click the Add button, and click OK.	
Add an Address Book entry from an e-mail message	Click the Inbox folder in the Folders list, click a message header, right-click the selected message, and click Add Sender To Address Book.	
Create a group	Click the Addresses button on the toolbar. Click the New Button, click New Group, type a name in the Group Name text box, click Select Members, click a name in the list, click Select, add other group members if desired, click OK twice, and then click the Close button.	
Use your Address Book when creating mesages	Click the New Mail button on the toolbar, click the To button, click a contact entry, click the To button, and click OK.	

Lesson 7 Quick Reference

To	Do this
Delete an Address Book entry	Click the Addresses button on the toolbar, click a contact entry, click Delete, click Yes, and click the Close button.
Create an electronic business card	Click Options on the Tools menu. Click the Compose tab. Click the Mail check box in the Business Cards section. Click the drop-down arrow to the right of the Mail check box, and click your name. Click OK.
Use the Find People feature	Click the Addresses button on the toolbar, and click Find People. Click the Look In drop-down arrow, select a directory service, type a name in the Name text box, and click Find Now.
Obtain a digital ID	Click Accounts on the Tools menu, click your account name, and then click the Properties button. Click the Security tab, click Get Digital ID, and then complete the Web page instructions to obtain a digital ID.
Assign a digital ID to your mail account	Click Accounts on the Tools menu, click your mail account name, and click the Properties button. Click the Security tab, click the Use A Digital ID When Sending Secure Messages From check box. Click the Digital ID button, click a digital ID, and click OK. Click OK, and then click Close.
Digitally sign an e-mail message	Click the New Mail button on the toolbar, create a message, click the Sign button, and click the Send button on the toolbar.

8

Participating in Newsgroups

In this lesson you will learn how to:

✔ *Subscribe to newsgroups.*

✔ *View newsgroup messages.*

✔ *Access newsgroups offline.*

✔ *Post messages.*

✔ *Print messages.*

✔ *Clean up your Outlook Express folders.*

ESTIMATED TIME 20 min.

As an account executive at Impact Public Relations, you try to keep careful track of popular opinion. For the Lakewood Mountains Resort account, you especially want to know what people are looking for in resorts, vacation spots, and business convention facilities. You read professional journals, reports, polls, newspapers, and magazines to learn the latest trends and statistics, but you would also like to talk directly to travelers. You can easily talk to an international collection of people via *newsgroups* on the Internet using Microsoft Outlook Express. A newsgroup contains messages sent by individuals interested in discussing a specific topic.

In this lesson, you will subscribe to newsgroups, view newsgroup messages, access newsgroups offline, and post and print messages. Finally, you will take a few minutes to clean up your Outlook Express folders.

Getting Acquainted with Newsgroups

One of the Internet's major attractions is that it provides an easy way to communicate with people around the world. For this reason, newsgroups have proven to be a popular means of communication among Internet users. A newsgroup consists of a collection of messages, or *posts*, sent by individuals who have access to a *news server*. A news server is a computer that is maintained by a company, group, or individual and is configured to accept news messages from the news network (called *Usenet*). Most often, Internet service providers maintain a news server for their customers.

News servers can host tens of thousands of newsgroups. Typically, newsgroup messages expire and are deleted after a few weeks. (The news group's administrator determines how long messages are stored.)

When you post a message to a newsgroup, you are in effect broadcasting your message to every news server configured to allow access to the newsgroup. In contrast, when you send an e-mail message, you send the message to a specific server and e-mail recipient on the Internet.

Because of administrators' preferences, not all news servers offer the same newsgroups.

If you are using a dial-up connection, your Internet service provider probably also provides newsgroup capabilities. You must configure your news account settings in Outlook Express before you can access a news server. Setting up your news account is similar to setting up your e-mail account. You must supply the information Outlook Express needs to contact your provider's news server. (See Appendix A, "Installation and Setup Procedures," for information about configuring your news account.) After your news account is set up, you can read and post messages on any newsgroup supported by your Internet service provider's news server.

tip

In newsgroup terminology, the word *post* can mean a message (noun) or the act of sending a message (verb).

When you want to access a newsgroup, you connect to your Internet service provider's news server, select a newsgroup, and view and send messages using a *newsreader*. A newsreader is an application that enables you to send and receive newsgroup messages.

Outlook Express comes equipped with a built-in newsreader. When you use Outlook Express' newsreader, sending and receiving newsgroup messages are similar to sending and receiving e-mail messages, but newsgroup messages are decidedly different from e-mail messages.

First, unlike your Inbox, which can contain personal messages from your grandmother along with corporate memos from your boss, newsgroups contain messages that are topical. Newsgroups are like clubs or special interest groups. If you're interested in gardening, you can visit a gardening newsgroup, and you'll find a wide variety of posts that include questions, hints, and observations related to gardening. There are even more specific gardening newsgroups that talk simply about edible gardens, soil conditioning, roses, tulips, tomatoes, and so forth. Many people turn to newsgroups for advice and to hear about people's experiences in a particular area. The illustration shows a gardening newsgroup.

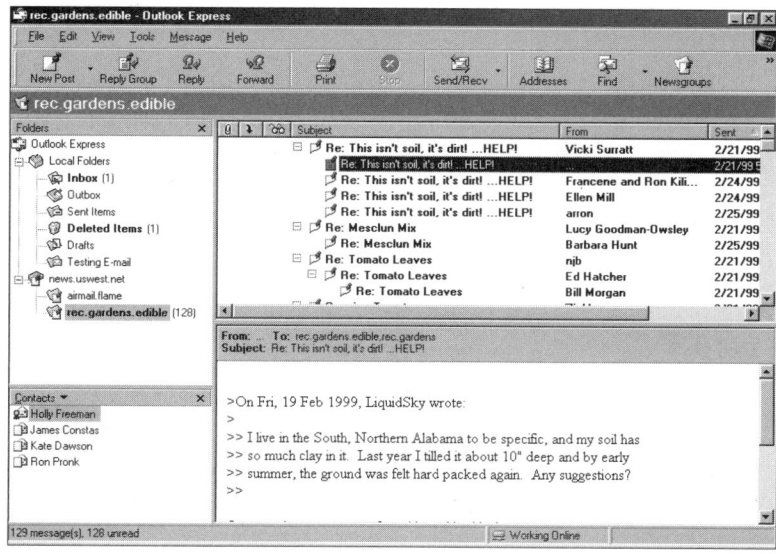

Newsgroups are often much more active than e-mail accounts. It's not unusual for some newsgroups to receive 100 to 200 posts in a single day, and some of the most popular newsgroups can receive upwards of a thousand posts per day. Fortunately, Outlook Express provides features to help you manage newsgroup information. But before you start sifting through messages, you must find a newsgroup.

You can also search for newsgroups on the Web by using news-group search engines, such as Dejanews at www. dejanews.com.

To find a newsgroup, you must first access your Internet service provider's news server. When you log on to the news server, you can instruct Outlook Express to list the available newsgroups in the Newsgroup Subscriptions dialog box. The dialog box lets you enter keywords for Outlook Express to use to search for specific newsgroups. For example, you can instruct Outlook Express to list only newsgroup names that contain the word *garden*. Newsgroup names look similar to *rec.gardens.edible*. A newsgroup's name usually gives you a fair indication of the newsgroup's subject.

Newsgroup Classifications

Abbreviation	Description	Example
alt	Alternative topics that are divided into major categories such as television, music, or sports	alt.tv.er, alt.music.u2 alt.sports.radio
comp	Information about computer science, hardware, and software	comp.ai.edu
humanities	General topics in arts and humanities	humanities.misc
misc	General information about a specific topic	misc.consumers
news	News about newsgroups	news.answers
rec	Discussions about arts, hobbies, and other recreational activities	rec.sport.tennis
sci	Information about scientific topics and research	sci.answers
soc	Discussions of social issues	soc.culture
talk	Debate-oriented discussions	talk.environment

important

Your Internet service provider's news server might not offer certain newsgroups because the subject matter may be considered objectionable.

Subscribing to Newsgroups

To view the subject headers of recent newsgroup messages, click a newsgroup in the Newsgroup Subscriptions dialog box, and then click the Go To button. If you find that the newsgroup is a group you'd like to return to in the future, you can *subscribe* to the newsgroup.

For a demonstration of how to find and subscribe to a newsgroup, in the Multimedia folder in the Microsoft Internet Explorer 5 Step by Step CD-ROM, double-click the News icon.

In Outlook Express, to subscribe means to add a newsgroup's name to the Folders list. After you subscribe to a newsgroup, you can click the newsgroup name in the Folders list to view the content of the newsgroup. Basically, subscribing makes it easier for you to return to a newsgroup that interests you. It's like having a Little Black Book of newsgroup addresses.

Note that subscribing to a newsgroup does not cause the newsgroups' messages to be stored on your computer. Instead, the messages are stored on the news server. As mentioned earlier, newsgroups can get hundreds of messages a day; therefore, it is more efficient for newsgroup messages to be stored on a server instead of on your computer's hard disk drive.

Over time, if you find that you rarely visit a newsgroup you've subscribed to, you can easily unsubscribe from the newsgroup and remove its name from your Folders list.

Find newsgroups

In this exercise, you find a newsgroup where members discuss topics relating to resorts.

❶   Start Outlook Express.

❷   In the Folders list, click the news server's name.

If an alert box appears, asking if you want Outlook Express to be your default news client, click Yes.

An alert box appears, stating that you are not subscribed to any newsgroups and asking if you would like to view a list of newsgroups.

8

Participating in Newsgroups

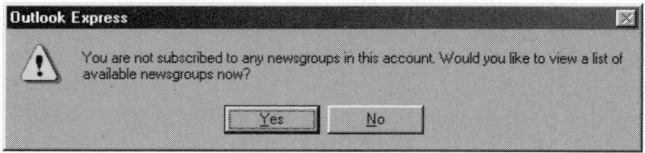

3 Click Yes.

The Newsgroup Subscriptions dialog box opens.

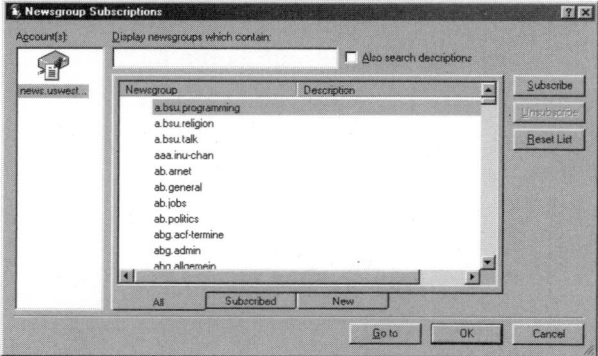

4 In the Display Newsgroups Which Contain text box, type **resort.**

After a few seconds, the Newsgroup Subscriptions dialog box shows all newsgroup titles that contain the word *resort*. The results should look similar to those shown in the illustration.

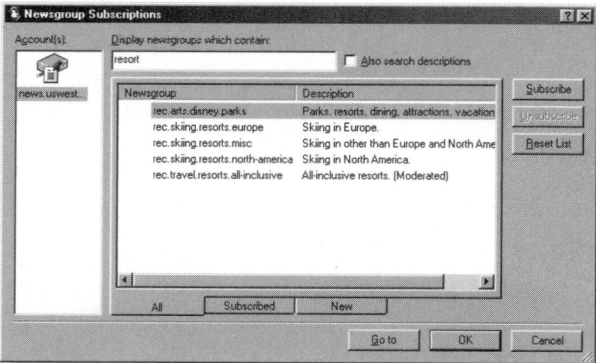

If you get an alert box stating that you need to download descriptions before you search by description, click Yes to activate this feature.

tip

When you search for newsgroups by topic, you can search for a keyword that appears in newsgroups' descriptions. To search both names and descriptions, display the Newsgroup Subscriptions dialog box, click the Also Search Descriptions check box, and then type a keyword in the Display Newsgroups Which Contain text box.

5   In the Newsgroup Subscriptions dialog box, scroll (if necessary), and click *rec.travel.resorts.all-inclusive.*

The newsgroup you want to view is selected.

6   Click the Go To button.

It might take a few moments for the message headers to appear in the message list.

Outlook Express shows the newsgroup's name in the Folders list with a grayed-out icon, and the headers for the most recent messages sent to the newsgroup appear in the message list.

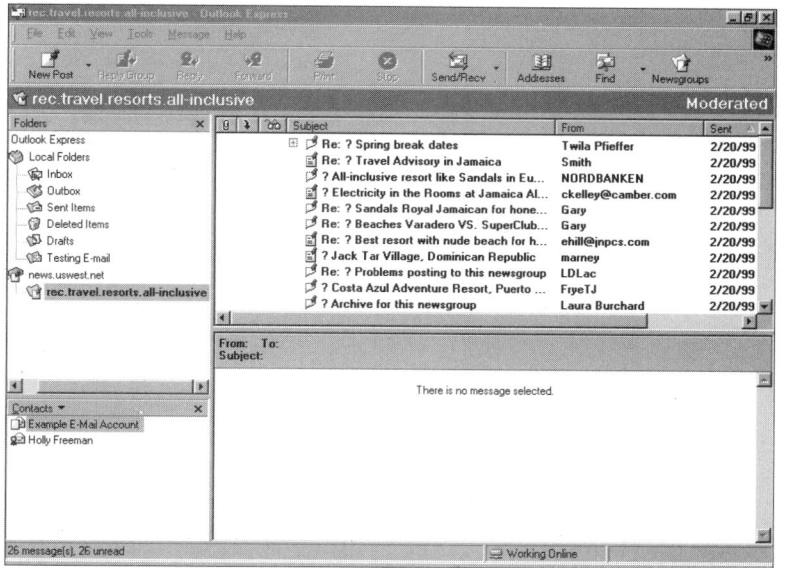

7   On the File menu, click Exit.

An alert box appears, asking if you want to subscribe to the currently displayed newsgroup.

8   Click No.

Outlook Express closes. You are not subscribed to the newsgroup.

Subscribe to a newsgroup

In this exercise, you subscribe to a music newsgroup.

❶   Start Outlook Express.

❷   In the Folders list, click the news server's name.

An alert box appears, stating that you are not subscribed to any newsgroups and asking if you'd like to view a list of newsgroups.

❸   Click Yes.

The Newsgroup Subscriptions dialog box opens.

❹   In the Display Newsgroups Which Contain text box, type **rec.music.folk**.

After a few seconds, *rec.music.folk* is selected.

❺   Click Subscribe.

The newsgroup listing is accompanied by a subscription icon as shown in the illustration.

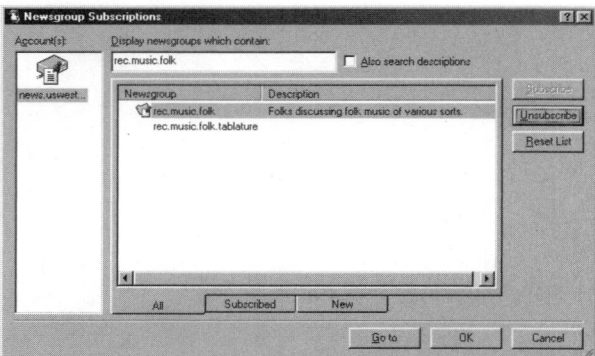

tip

You can subscribe to a newsgroup after it appears in the Folders list by right-clicking the newsgroup name and clicking Subscribe on the shortcut menu.

❻   Click OK.

The newsgroup is listed in the Folders list and the newsgroup window.

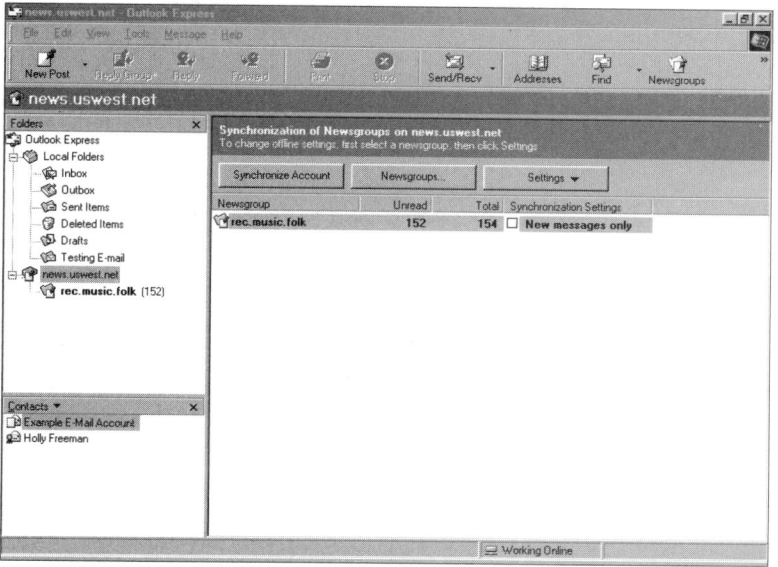

Unsubscribe from a newsgroup

In this exercise, you unsubscribe from the music newsgroup.

1   In the newsgroup window, right-click *rec.music.folk,* and then click Unsubscribe.

     An alert box opens, asking if you are sure that you want to unsubscribe from the newsgroup.

2   Click OK.

     The alert box closes, and the newsgroup listing is removed from the newsgroup window and the Folders list.

Viewing Newsgroup Messages

Viewing newsgroup messages is similar to viewing e-mail messages. By default, Outlook Express displays the message headers in the message list and message content of selected messages in the preview pane. You can quickly identify unread messages, because the headers for unread messages appear in bold. You can also view message content in a new window by double-clicking a message header. Finally, you can organize messages into *threads*. A thread is made up of a new newsgroup message followed by the replies to that message.

When many people participate in a newsgroup, the replies can be difficult to track. Therefore, Outlook Express automatically groups replies under their original messages. Outlook Express also lets you list messages in the order in which they were sent. This is helpful if you want to quickly see how old a post is.

Think of a newsgroup as a type of party. Everyone's in the same room, but various people are involved in different conversations. Each conversation is made up of comments, replies, opinions, and so forth relating to a particular topic. These exchanges are like threads. In Outlook Express, threads are denoted by plus and minus signs appearing next to the header of the originating message. Clicking a plus sign expands the thread, and clicking a minus sign collapses the thread. When you expand a thread, message replies are indented below the original message, as shown in the illustration.

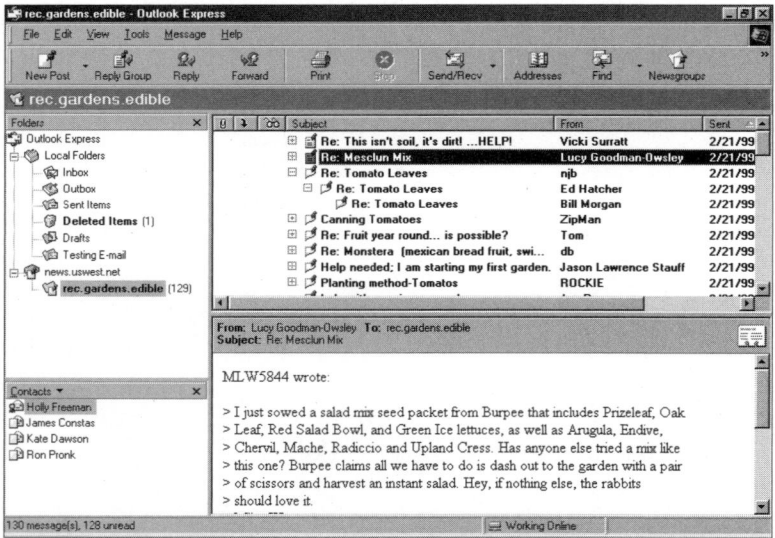

When you configure Outlook Express to show threads, they appear collapsed by default. If you prefer, you can configure Outlook Express to expand threads automatically by clicking Options on the Tools menu and then clicking the Read tab.

Read messages in a newsgroup

In this exercise, you view a newsgroup message.

1 If necessary, start Outlook Express.

2 In the Folders list, click the news server's name.

An alert box appears, asking if you want to view a list of newsgroups.

3 Click No.

4 In the newsgroup window, click the Newsgroups button.

The Newsgroup Subscriptions dialog box opens.

5 In the Display Newsgroups Which Contain text box, type **rec.music.folk**.

After a few seconds, the Newsgroup Subscriptions dialog box selects *rec.music.folk*.

6 Click the Go To button.

The Folders list shows the newsgroup, and the most recent messages sent to the newsgroup appear in the message list.

7 Click a message header.

The content of the message appears in the preview pane, as shown in the illustration.

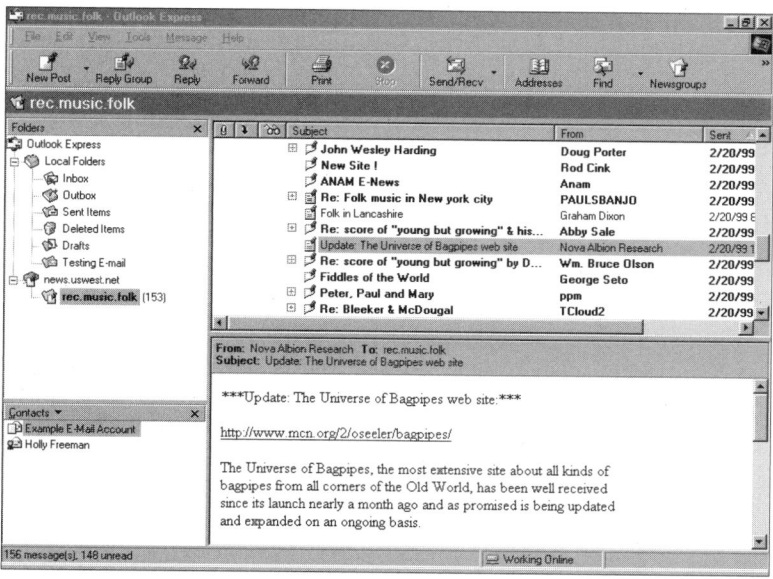

Open a message in a new window

In this exercise, you open a news post in a separate window.

1   In the message list, double-click a message header.

The news post opens in a separate window.

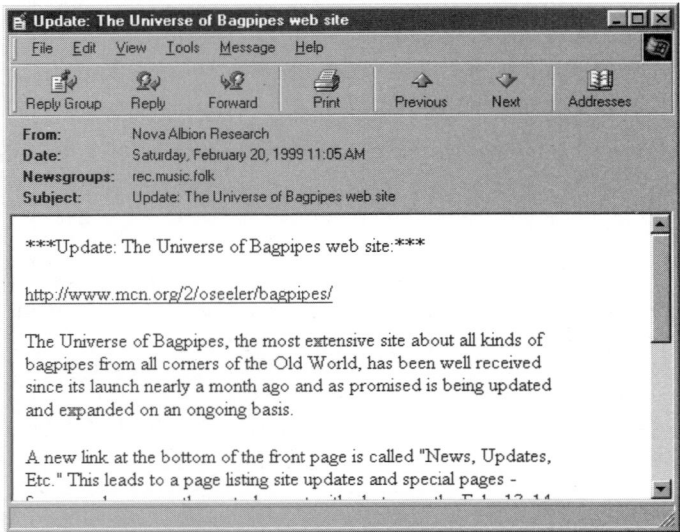

Close

2   Click the Close button in the top-right corner of the news post's window.

The news post's window closes.

Disable and enable the thread feature

In this exercise, you turn off and on the thread feature to see how threading affects the message list.

1   On the View menu, point to Current View, and clear Group Messages By Conversation.

The message headers are listed in the order in which they were sent.

2   On the View menu, point to Current View, and click Group Messages By Conversation.

The messages are organized into threads. (The replies are grouped under original messages.)

Expand and collapse news threads

In this exercise, you expand a thread to view the responses of a news post and then collapse the thread to hide the responses.

❶ In the message list, click a plus sign to the left of a message header.

The thread expands and shows all posts sent in response to the original post. Notice that the responses to the messages are in the order in which they were sent.

You might have to expand a newsgroup before you can collapse it.

❷ In the message list, click a minus sign to the left of a message header.

The thread collapses and then hides all news posts sent in response to the original post.

Automatically expand threads

In this exercise, you configure Outlook Express to automatically expand message threads.

❶ On the Tools menu, click Options.

The Options dialog box opens.

❷ Click the Read tab.

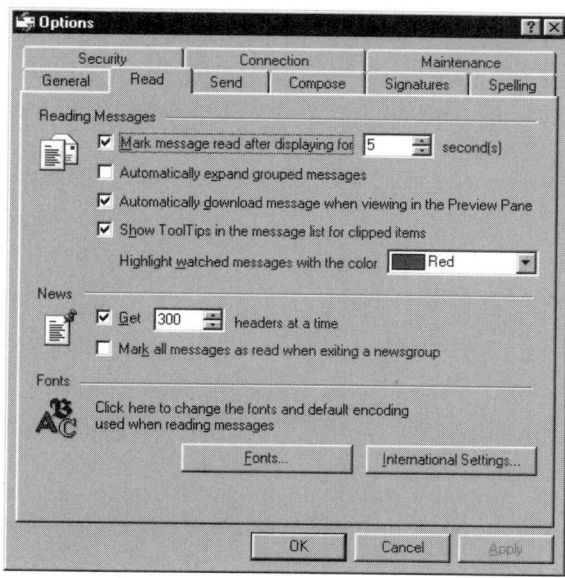

tip

Notice that the Read tab of the Options dialog box includes a News section. In the News section, you can specify how many headers to download at one time. By default, the newsreader is set to retrieve 300 headers at a time. Therefore, when you click the Go To button in the Newsgroup Subscriptions dialog box, or when you open a newsgroup that you are subscribed to, the newsreader will download up to 300 message headers. You can change this option to any number you wish.

❸ Click the Automatically Expand Grouped Messages check box.

❹ Click OK.

The Options dialog box closes and all of the threads have been expanded.

❺ In the Folders list, right-click *rec.music.folk*.

A shortcut menu appears.

❻ Click Subscribe.

You are now subscribed to *rec.music.folk*.

Accessing Newsgroups Offline

Accessing newsgroups offline means that you download, or *synchronize*, a newsgroup's message headers or content from the news server to your hard disk drive. Synchronizing newsgroups is similar to synchronizing Web pages. In both instances, you download files from the Internet onto your hard disk drive so you can view the information later without having to be online. For more information about working offline, see Lesson 5, "Working Offline."

To synchronize a newsgroup's messages, you must first subscribe to the newsgroup. Then you can specify whether you want to synchronize all messages, new messages, or just message headers.

important

Keep in mind that, because Usenet regularly deletes old messages from news groups, you will not be able to access older messages. If you mark to download a message, but you don't synchronize the message before it expires, you will be unable to view its content.

Synchronize a newsgroup for offline viewing

This exercise assumes that you have subscribed to rec. music.folk. If you have not, follow the steps in the exercise "Subscribe to a Newsgroup" earlier in this lesson.

In this exercise, you specify to download all messages for a newsgroup each time you synchronize newsgroups.

important

This exercise assumes that you use a dial-up connection to connect to the Internet. If you are not using a dial-up connection, skip this exercise.

You can also open the newsgroup window in Internet Explorer. Click the Mail button on the toolbar, and click Read News.

1 If necessary, start Outlook Express.

2 In the Folders list, click the news server's name.

The newsgroup window opens.

3 In the newsgroup window, click the *rec.music.folk* newsgroup.

The newsgroup is selected.

4 In the newsgroup window, click the Settings button.

The Settings drop-down list appears.

5 Click All Messages.

The content for all message headers will be downloaded when you synchronize newsgroups for offline viewing.

For a review of disconnecting from the Internet, read the section "Viewing Offline Web Pages" in Lesson 5, "Working Offline."

6 Disconnect from the Internet.

7 In the newsgroup window, double-click the *rec.music.folk* newsgroup.

The message headers appear in the message list.

8 In the message list, click an unread message header (a header that appears in bold).

The Dial-up Connection dialog box opens.

tip

If you are offline and you choose to view a message you've recently read while online, you might be able to access the content of the message. This is because the message's content will be stored in your computer's temporary cache. After you clear the cache in Internet Explorer (click Internet Options on the Tools menu, click Delete Files on the General tab, and click OK), the message's content will no longer be available for offline viewing.

Participating in Newsgroups   8

9 Click Cancel.

The Dial-up Connection dialog box closes, and a message appears in the preview pane stating that the content of the selected message is unavailable while you are offline.

You can click the Here hyperlink in the Message Unavailable While Offline message to open the Dial-up Connection dialog box.

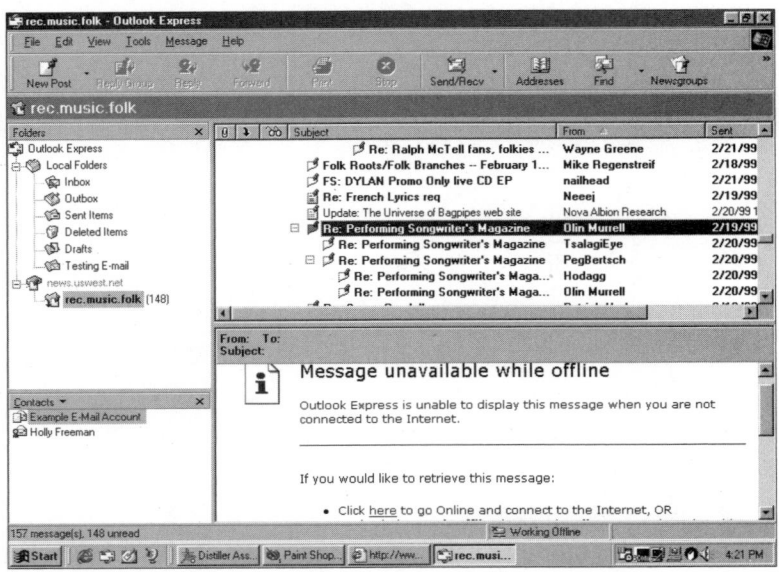

10 Connect to the Internet.

11 In the Folders list, click the news server's name.

The newsgroup window opens.

You can also click Synchronize Newsgroup on the Tools menu to synchronize newsgroup messages.

12 In the newsgroup window, click the Synchronize Account button.

The newsgroup messages are downloaded to your hard disk drive.

13 Disconnect from the Internet.

14 Double-click the *rec.music.folk* newsgroup.

15 In the message list, click an unread message header.

The message content appears in the preview pane.

Posting Messages

The great appeal of newsgroups is that anyone can post messages for other newsgroup readers to view. Some newsgroups are moderated, which means that a person or group of people reviews posts sent to the newsgroup to make sure the content adheres to the newsgroup's rules and topic guidelines. Other groups are not moderated, which means any content can appear within the newsgroup.

tip

Many unmoderated newsgroups are often awash in *spam*. Spam is an Internet term for junk mail. (Junk mail can be classified as irrelevant or inappropriate messages sent in bulk quantities to a large number of newsgroup or e-mail recipients.)

You can post a newsgroup message in three ways:

- You can reply to an existing post in a newsgroup, making your message available to everyone who accesses the newsgroup.
- You can reply only to the author of a newsgroup message, which means that your message will be sent as an e-mail message to the person who posted the original message.
- You can create and post a new message.

Before you start posting messages to a newsgroup, you should view the newsgroup for a week or so to get a feel for the type of information shared in the newsgroup. Furthermore, you should read the newsgroup's *FAQ* (Frequently Asked Questions). Most newsgroups provide an FAQ for new members in order to avoid having to answer common questions repeatedly. You can find many newsgroups' FAQs at *www.dejanews.com*. If you can't find a newsgroup's FAQ on the Web, consider asking where you can find the newsgroup's FAQ in your first post to the newsgroup.

tip

You should usually avoid posting advertisements. If you aren't sure what constitutes an advertisement, check out the newsgroup's FAQ for more specific rules.

Switching Your Identity

You can store multiple *identities* (names for yourself or others). You might want to use a different identity if you have more than one e-mail account (such as one for work and one for leisure) or if more than one person uses the same computer. To create multiple identities, on the File menu, point to Identities, and then click Add New Identity. Type your identity in the New Identity dialog box, and click OK. To switch between identities, on the File menu, click Switch Identity, click the identity you want to use, and then click OK. When you switch identities, you will have to set up a mail account and specify a news server for your new identity.

Reply to a newsgroup

This exercise assumes that you have subscribed to rec. music.folk. If you have not, follow the steps in the exercise "Subscribe to a Newsgroup" earlier in this lesson.

In this exercise, you reply to a newsgroup message.

1 Connect to the Internet, if necessary, and start Outlook Express.

2 In the Folders list, click the *rec.music.folk* newsgroup.

The message list opens.

3 In the message list, click a message header.

4 On the toolbar, click the Reply Group button.

A new message window opens (Newsgroups and Subject are filled in).

If you don't need to include the original message's text in your response, you should delete some or all of the message in your post to help keep the newsgroup uncluttered.

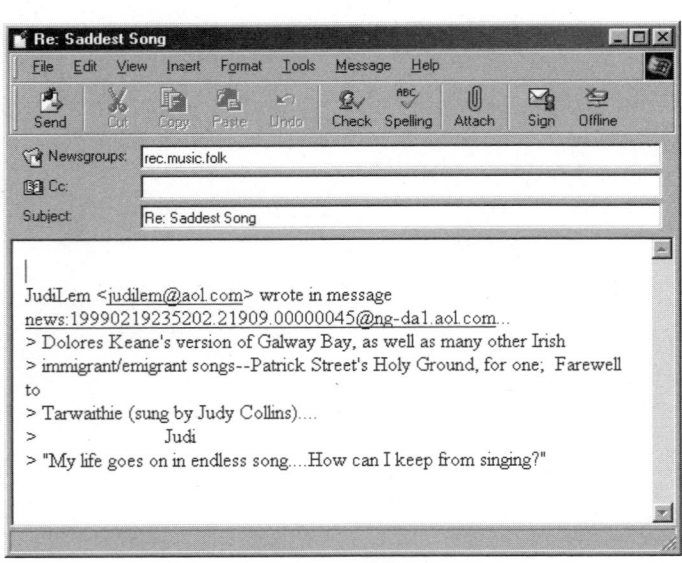

If you've deselected the Send Messages Immediately check box in the Options dialog box, the message will be stored in your Outbox until you send and receive your messages.

5 Write a response in the message box.

6 Click the Send button.

The Post News alert box appears, informing you that your response might not appear immediately.

7 Click OK.

The reply is sent to the newsgroup, and the message's header should appear in the newsgroup within a few minutes.

important

If you prefer not to send a message to the newsgroup, close the new message window without saving changes.

Reply to a message sender

In this exercise, you reply only to the sender of a message.

1 In the message list, click a message header of a message that you want to reply to.

2 On the toolbar, click the Reply button.

A new message window opens with the To text box and the Subject text box filled in.

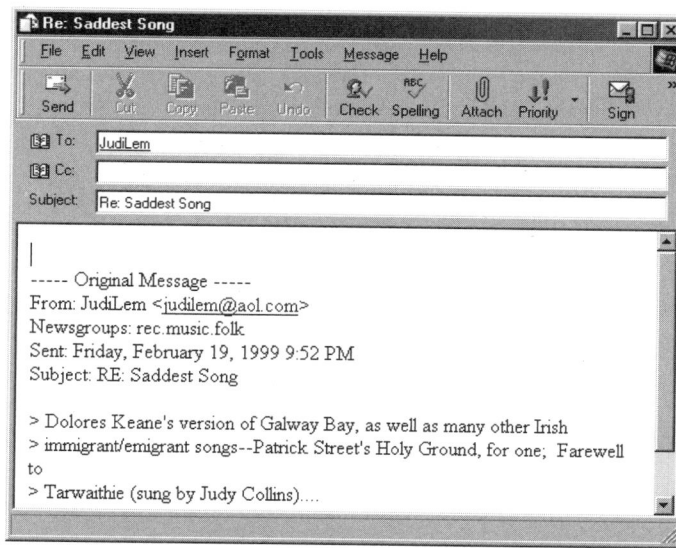

3 Write a reply in the message box.

4 Click the Send button.

The reply is sent to the message sender's Inbox.

important

If you prefer not to send a message to the sender, close the new message window without saving changes.

Post a new message to a newsgroup

In this exercise, you create a message and send it to a newsgroup.

1 On the toolbar, click the New Post button (but not the drop-down arrow next to it).

A new message window opens with the newsgroup's address in the Newsgroups text box.

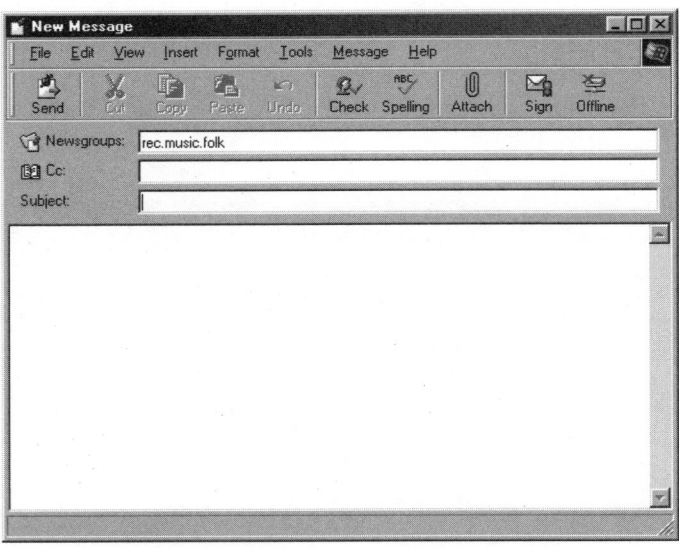

Before sending a post, you should always check the spelling in your message by clicking the Spelling button on the toolbar.

2 Type **Newbie** in the Subject text box.

3 Type **Could someone please tell me where I can find an FAQ for this newsgroup? Thanks.** in the message box.

④   Click the Send button.

The Post News alert box appears, informing you that your post might not appear immediately.

⑤   Click OK.

The message is sent to the newsgroup, and the message's header should appear in the newsgroup within a few minutes.

> # important
>
> If you prefer not to send a message to the newsgroup, close the new message window without saving changes.

Printing Messages

At times, you might want to print a newsgroup message. For example, maybe someone's advice is so detailed that you want to print a hard copy for reference, or possibly you want to share information with another person who is not online. Printing messages is simply a matter of displaying the message and then clicking the Print button on the toolbar.

Print

This exercise assumes that you have subscribed to rec. music.folk. If you have not, follow the steps in the exercise "Subscribe to a Newsgroup" earlier in this lesson.

Print a newsgroup message

In this exercise, you print a hard copy of a newsgroup message.

①   If necessary, start Outlook Express.

②   In the Folders list, click the *rec.music.folk* newsgroup.

③   In the message list, click a message header.

The message you want to print is selected.

④   On the toolbar, click the Print button.

The Print dialog box opens.

⑤   In the Print dialog box, click OK.

The selected message is printed.

One Step Further   Cleaning Up Your Outlook Express Folders

Outlook Express messages—both newsreader messages and e-mail messages—can pile up quickly on your hard disk drive. Therefore, you should regularly clean up your hard disk drive by purging old information and compacting your folders to free up wasted space. Outlook Express provides three ways to maintain your folders and free up hard disk drive space:

- Empty your Deleted Items folder.
- Compact Outlook Express folders.
- Purge newsgroup headers and message content.

When you delete e-mail and newsgroup messages, they are sent to the Deleted Items folder. You must then permanently delete items in the Deleted Items folder to regain the disk space. Outlook Express provides a menu command to make emptying the Deleted Items folder quick and easy.

Compacting folders involves removing wasted space within your Outlook Express folders. You can easily compact all your Outlook Express folders at once using the Compact All Folders command from the File menu.

Finally, purging newsgroup headers and message bodies involves deleting newsgroup information that is stored on your hard disk drive. You can choose to delete just message content or both message headers and message content.

Empty the Deleted Items folder

In this exercise, you create an item to be deleted and then you permanently delete the item in the Deleted Items folder.

1. If necessary, start Outlook Express.
2. In the Folders list, click the news server's name, and click the New Post button on the toolbar.

   A new message window appears.
3. In the Subject text box, type **Delete this post**, and click close on the File menu.

   An alert box appears, asking if you want to save your changes to the message.

The Drafts folder stores saved messages.

4 Click Yes.

The Saved Message information box appears, telling you that your message has been saved to your Drafts folder.

5 Click OK.

The new message window closes.

6 In the Folders list, click Drafts.

The content of the Drafts folder appears in the message list.

7 Click the header that has Delete This Post for a subject, and then click the Delete button on the toolbar.

The Delete This Post message is moved to the Deleted Items folder.

8 On the Edit menu, click Empty 'Deleted Items' Folder.

An alert box appears, asking if you are sure that you want to permanently delete the items in the Deleted Items folder.

9 Click Yes.

The Deleted Items folder is emptied.

tip

You can configure Outlook Express to automatically delete items from the Deleted Items folder each time you quit Outlook Express. To configure this setting, click Options on the Tools menu, and then click the Maintenance tab. On the Maintenance tab, click the Empty Messages From The 'Deleted Items' Folder On Exit check box, and then click OK.

Compact Outlook Express folders

In this exercise, you compact all the Outlook Express folders.

● On the File menu, point to Folder, and click Compact All Folders.

A progress bar appears as the folders are compacted.

Delete newsgroup messages

In this exercise, you delete newsgroup headers and message bodies that are stored on your hard disk drive.

1 On the Tools menu, click Options.

The Options dialog box opens.

Participating in Newsgroups

8

2   In the Options dialog box, click the Maintenance tab.

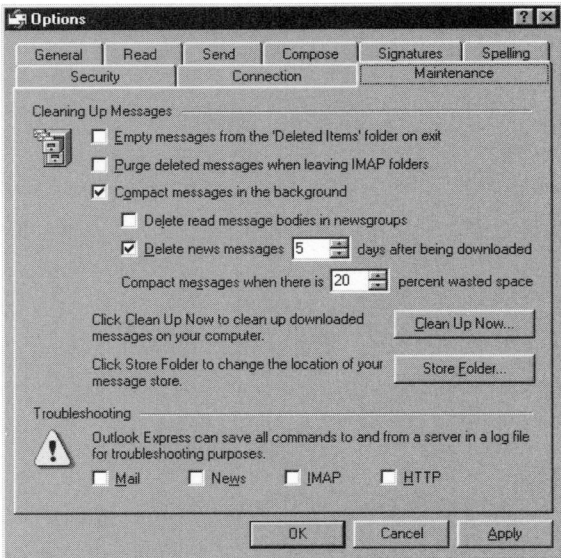

New!

3   In the Cleaning Up Messages section, click the Clean Up Now button. The Local File Clean Up dialog box opens.

The Local File Clean Up dialog box also includes a Compact button. You can use the Compact button to reduce the size of your Outlook Express folders.

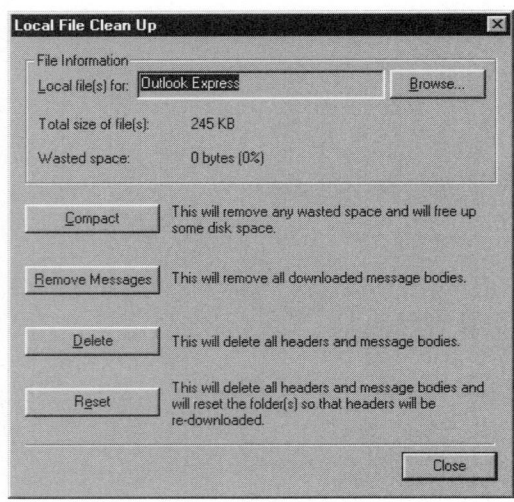

④ In the Local File Clean Up dialog box, click Delete.

An alert box appears, asking if you are sure that you want to delete all locally cached messages from all folders.

tip

You can delete newsgroup headers and message content for selected newsgroups instead of deleting information for all newsgroups. In the Local File Clean Up dialog box, click the Browse button next to the Local File(s) For text box, and then double-click the newsgroup that you want to clean up. The newsgroup name will appear in the Local File(s) For text box in place of Outlook Express (the default setting). When you click the Compact, Remove Messages, Delete, or Reset button in the Local File Clean Up dialog box, the action will apply only to the newsgroup appearing in the Local File(s) For text box. Remember to then reset the Local File(s) For text box to Outlook Express to perform maintenance on all Outlook Express folders.

⑤ Click Yes.

A progress bar appears while messages are removed from your hard disk drive.

⑥ Click Close.

The Local File Clean Up dialog box closes.

⑦ Click OK.

The Options dialog box closes.

Finish the lesson

① In the Folders list, right-click *rec.music.folk*, click Unsubscribe, and click OK in the alert box.

You are no longer subscribed to *rec.music.folk*.

② If Outlook Express displays an alert box asking if you want to view a list of available newsgroups, click No.

③ Quit Outlook Express.

④ If necessary, quit Internet Explorer.

Lesson 8 Quick Reference

To	Do this
Find a newsgroup	Click the news server's name in the Folders list, click Yes, and type a keyword in the Display Newsgroups Which Contain text box. Click a newsgroup name, and then click Go To.
Subscribe to a newsgroup	Click the news server's name in the Folders list, click Yes, and type a keyword in the Display Newsgroups Which Contain text box. Click a newsgroup name, click Subscribe, and click OK.
Unsubscribe from a newsgroup	Right-click a newsgroup in the Folders list or the newsgroup window, click Unsubscribe, and click OK.
Read messages in a newsgroup	Click a newsgroup in the Folders list, and click a message header in the message list.
Open messages in a new window	Click a newsgroup in the Folders list, and then double-click a message header in the message list.
Disable and enable the thread feature	Click a newsgroup in the Folders list. On the View menu, point to Current View, and click Group Messages By Conversation.
Expand news threads	Click a newsgroup in the Folders list, and click the plus sign next to a message header in the message list.
Collapse news threads	Click a newsgroup in the Folders list, and click the minus sign next to a message header in the message list.
Automatically expand threads	Click a newsgroup in the Folders list, click Options on the Tools menu, click the Read tab, click the Automatically Expand Grouped Messages check box, and click OK.
Synchronize newsgroups	If necessary, subscribe to a newsgroup. Click the news server's name, click a newsgroup in the newsgroup window, click the Settings button in the newsgroup window, and then select an option in the Settings drop-down list. Click the Synchronize Account button in the newsgroup window.

Lesson 8 Quick Reference

To	Do this	Button
Reply to a newsgroup	Click a newsgroup in the Folders list, and click a message header in the message list. Click the Reply Group button on the toolbar, write a response in the message box, click the Send button, and click OK.	
Reply to a message sender	Click a newsgroup in the Folders list, and click a message header in the message list. Click the Reply button on the toolbar, write a response in the message box, and click the Send button.	
Post a new message to a newsgroup	Click a newsgroup in the Folders list, click the New Post button on the toolbar, type a subject in the Subject text box, write a message in the message box, click the Send button, and click OK.	
Print a newsgroup message	Click a newsgroup in the Folders list, and click a message header in the message list. Click the Print button on the toolbar, and click OK.	
Empty the Deleted Items folder	Click Empty 'Deleted Items' Folder on the Edit menu, and click Yes.	
Compact Outlook Express folders	On the File menu, point to Folder, and click Compact All Folders.	
Delete newsgroup messages	Click Options on the Tools menu, click the Maintenance tab, click Clean Up Now, click Delete, click Yes, click Close, and then click OK.	

9

Collaborating on the Internet with NetMeeting

**ESTIMATED TIME
30 min.**

NetMeeting

In this lesson you will learn how to:

✔ *Start NetMeeting.*

✔ *Call meeting participants.*

✔ *Use audio and video capabilities.*

✔ *Use the Chat window.*

✔ *Draw on the Whiteboard.*

✔ *Share applications and files.*

✔ *Use Microsoft's Online Support.*

You're planning to attend the International Resorts Conference in Perth, Australia. You think it would be beneficial if some of Impact Public Relations' key clients attended the conference, as well. You would like to speak with each client in person about attending the international event, but there isn't room in your schedule for the extra travel. You decide to use Microsoft NetMeeting to contact and share information with your clients about the International Resorts Conference. NetMeeting is a Microsoft Internet Explorer add-on component that can be used to conduct meetings across networks, including the Internet.

In this lesson, you will start NetMeeting, call meeting participants, and then use NetMeeting's audio and video capabilities.

You will also send text-based messages using the Chat window and share information by using the Whiteboard. In addition, you will share applications and files using NetMeeting's sharing and collaboration features. Finally, you will access the wealth of information supplied by Microsoft's Personal Support Center Web site.

important

The exercises in this lesson assume that you've configured NetMeeting. Appendix A, "Installation and Setup Procedures," provides steps to configure NetMeeting if you need assistance. In addition, the exercises assume you have speakers, a microphone, and a video camera installed on your computer. If you don't have this hardware, you can still work through many of the exercises by using the keyboard instead.

Starting NetMeeting

The goal of NetMeeting is to enable you to meet with people anywhere in the world by conducting multimedia conferences. You can converse with participants using a microphone and speakers. In addition, you can send and receive video for "face-to-face" interaction. NetMeeting also enables you to type messages back and forth in a Chat window, use a *Whiteboard* (a blank screen that simulates marker boards used in offices and classrooms), and share files and applications.

NetMeeting is installed automatically if you perform a complete installation of Internet Explorer, but it is considered to be an add-on component. If NetMeeting isn't installed on your computer, use Internet Explorer's automatic update feature (as described in Lesson 4, "Activating Security and Personal Information Settings," in the section "One Step Further: Adding a Component") to add NetMeeting to your computer.

You can access NetMeeting from within Internet Explorer as well as from the Windows taskbar. Regardless of how you start NetMeeting, the application will always open in its own window, as shown in the following illustration.

Directory
server
category

Microphone
volume

Speaker
volume

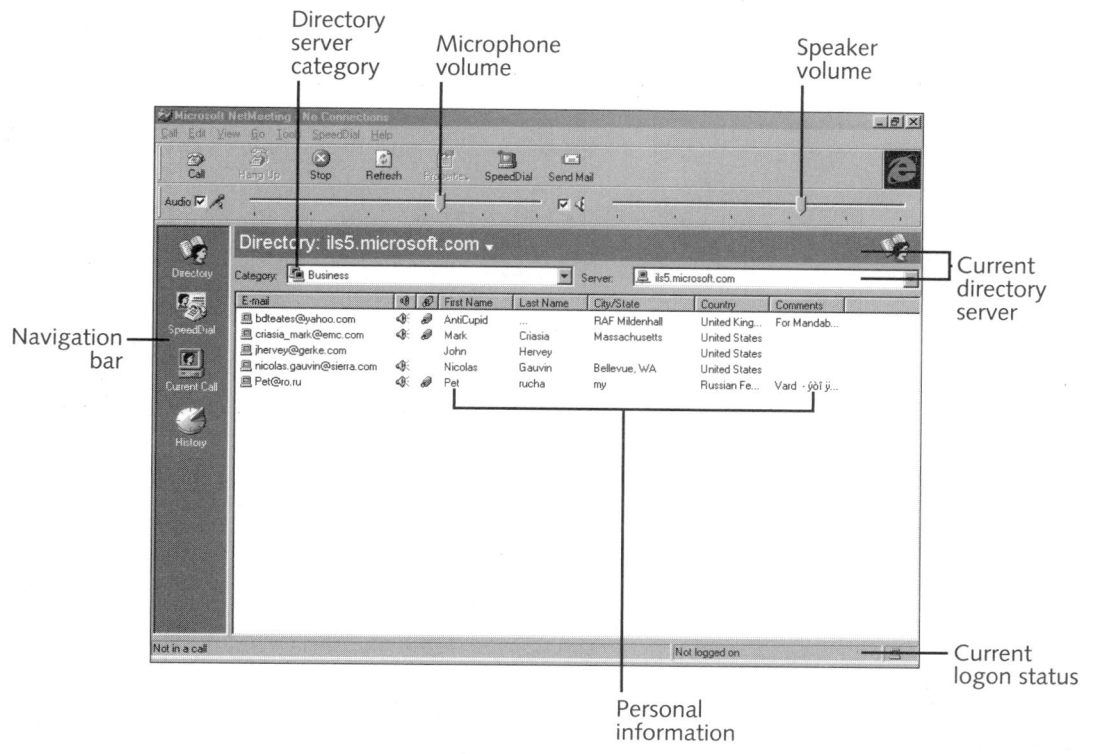

Navigation
bar

Current
directory
server

Current
logon status

Personal
information

The table below shows NetMeeting's easy-to-recognize icons that provide quick information about NetMeeting users.

Icon	Description
🖥	Indicates that user is currently in a call.
🎙	Indicates that user has a microphone and speakers.
📷	Indicates that user has a video camera.

Start NetMeeting

To open NetMeeting from the Windows taskbar, click the Start button, point to Programs, point to Internet Explorer, and then click Microsoft NetMeeting.

In this exercise, you start NetMeeting from within the Internet Explorer window.

1 Start Internet Explorer.

NetMeeting

9

tip

Occasionally, you might receive an alert box when you start NetMeeting that states that there was a problem connecting to the directory server. The directory server is the default server your computer logs on to when you start NetMeeting. Generally, receiving this alert box means that the directory server is busy. Click OK to close the alert box, and then click the Refresh button on the toolbar. Eventually, the directory list will appear, but you will not be logged on to the directory server. For more information about logging on to a directory server, see the following section, "Calling Meeting Participants."

②   On the File menu, point to New, and click Internet Call.
       The NetMeeting window opens.

important

If you have not installed and configured NetMeeting as described in Appendix A, "Installation and Setup Procedures," you will see a series of setup dialog boxes when you click Internet Call on the File menu. If you see the dialog boxes, turn to Appendix A, "Installation and Setup Procedures," for further instructions.

③   On the Call menu, click Exit.
       The NetMeeting window closes.

Calling Meeting Participants

The NetMeeting window provides a wealth of tools and information. Most notably, NetMeeting displays the content of your default *Internet Locator Service (ILS) directory*. An ILS directory lists users who are currently connected, or *logged on*, to a particular computer that serves as a contact point for NetMeeting participants. ILS directory lists are designed to help you find and contact the people with whom you want to collaborate.

When you set up NetMeeting, you choose an ILS directory. Then, by default, NetMeeting logs on to the specified ILS directory each time you start NetMeeting. As you work with NetMeeting, you'll find that some ILS directories are busier than others, and you might want to change your default ILS directory.

You can change your default ILS directory by clicking Options on the Tools menu and then clicking the Calling tab. The Calling tab provides a drop-down list that enables you to select a different ILS directory. You can also use the Calling tab to turn off the setting to automatically log on to the default ILS server. When you turn off the setting to automatically log on, you will be able to view who is logged on to the directory server, but you won't be logged on. Choosing to not automatically log on can be a time-saver, especially if you are using a modem, because you won't always have to log on to an ILS directory to place a NetMeeting call. Further, you can choose to log on at anytime by click-ing the Log On option on the Call menu.

The first step to using NetMeeting is to place a call. When you call a *remote* user (the person at a distance with whom you want to converse), the user must be running NetMeeting. You can call remote users in two ways. You can call the remote user directly, by entering the user's IP (Internet Protocol) address in NetMeeting's New Call dialog box, or you can double-click the remote user's name in an ILS directory.

When you call remote users, the users receive a pop-up message stating that they are receiving an incoming call from you. In addition, if their speakers are turned on, they'll hear a telephone ringing sound to alert them that they have a call. The illustration shows an incoming call dialog box.

To begin the call, the remote user clicks the Accept button. Then, to view the details regarding the current call, you click the Current Call icon on the Naviga-tion bar.

More About IP Addresses

Each time you connect to the Internet, your computer is assigned an IP address. An IP address uses numbers and dots to identify your computer on the network. Your IP address changes each time you log on to the Internet. You can place NetMeeting calls to remote users by using their IP addresses (or remote users can call you by using your IP address). Your contact will need to connect to the Internet and then tell you his or her IP address, or you will need to notify the remote user of your IP address. In either case, the IP address information will need to be swapped by either e-mail or phone each time you participate in a NetMeeting call.

important

If your NetMeeting is limited to a local area network (LAN), you must enter an IP address to connect to a contact. In this situation, your meeting is not being conducted on the Internet, so the ILS directories will not be used.

Using IP addresses to connect to remote users can save you time if you are having difficulty connecting to an ILS directory. Instead of waiting for the ILS directory server's traffic to lighten, you can bypass the server and place your NetMeeting call directly to your contact. Further, by using IP addresses, you avoid having to show your personal information in an ILS directory list. When your personal information appears in the directory list, anyone can double-click your entry in an attempt to establish a NetMeeting connection. Every time someone double-clicks your entry in the directory list, a dialog box will pop up on your monitor notifying you that someone is trying to call you. You might not want to have these interruptions.

Uncovering Your IP Address

To find your computer's IP address, connect to the Internet, click the Start button, point to Programs, click MS-DOS Prompt, type **ipconfig**, and press Enter. Your IP address will be listed in the first Ethernet Adapter section to the right of the words *IP Address*. (If you are on a LAN, the address will be listed in the second Ethernet Adapter section.)

View the NetMeeting options

In this exercise, you view the NetMeeting options that enable you to configure personal information and ILS directory settings. By default, you initially configure your personal information when you configure NetMeeting, as described in Appendix A, "Installation and Setup Procedures."

1   Start NetMeeting.

2   On the Tools menu, click Options.
       The Options dialog box appears.

3   In the Options dialog box, click the My Information tab.
       The My Information tab lets you change your personal information settings, as shown in the illustration.

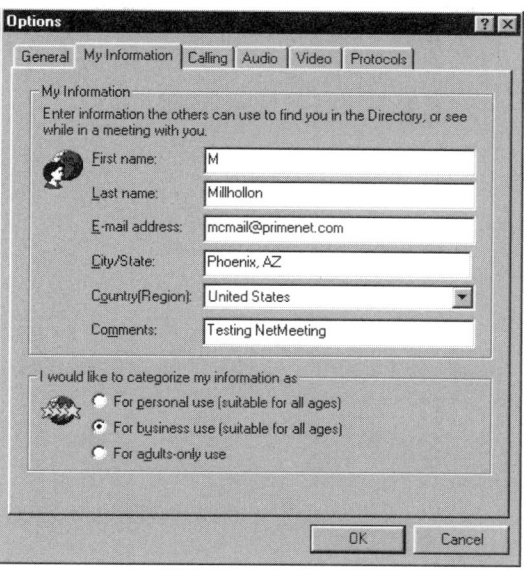

④ In the Options dialog box, click the Calling tab.

The Calling tab lets you change your calling settings and change your default directory server setting.

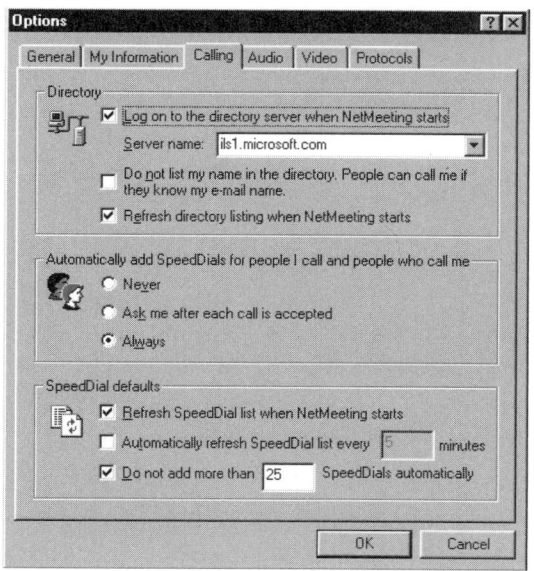

⑤ Click OK.

The Options dialog box closes.

Place a direct call

In this exercise, you call a contact using the contact's IP address.

> ## important
> This exercise assumes that you have a coworker or contact who is running NetMeeting.

1   If necessary, obtain your contact's current IP address information.

> ## tip
> The best way to swap the current session's IP address information is to call your contact on the telephone or send an e-mail message. Remember, if you are using a modem, your IP address will probably change each time you connect to the Internet.

2   On the toolbar, click the Call button.

   The New Call dialog box opens.

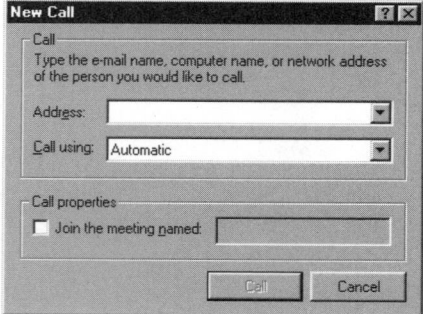

3   Type your contact's IP address in the Address text box.

4   Click the Call Using drop-down arrow, and click Network (TCP/IP).

5   Click the Call button. (Your contact will have to accept the call.)

   NetMeeting connects to the computer of the person you are calling, and the Current Call window opens.

Notice that the Current Call window has different toolbar buttons from the first window you see when you start NetMeeting.

To turn on the video display, click the Play button in the My Video window. See "Using Audio and Video Capabilities" later in this lesson for more information.

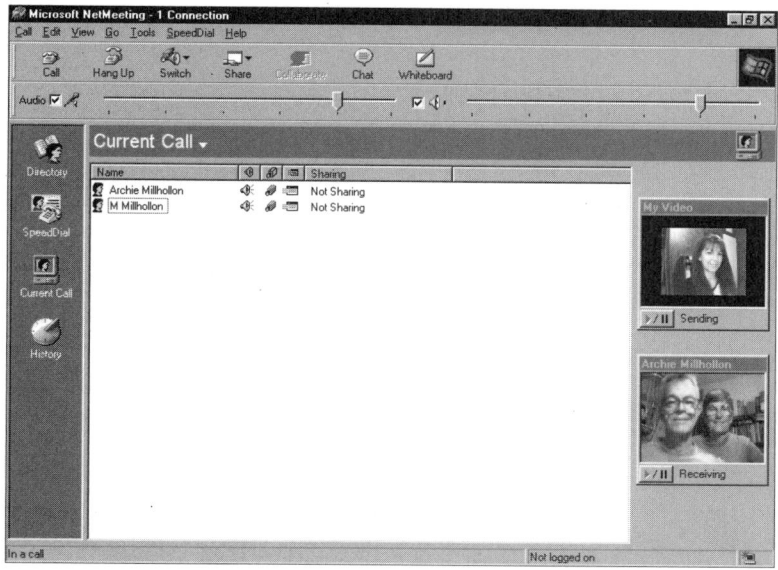

⑥   Click the Hang Up button on the Current Call toolbar.

The call is disconnected.

tip

NetMeeting helps you to quickly create an e-mail message containing your IP address. First, find your IP address. On the SpeedDial menu, click Add SpeedDial to open the Add SpeedDial dialog box. In the Address text box, type your current IP address. In the Call Using drop-down list, click Network (TCP/IP). In the After Creating The SpeedDial section, click the Send To Mail Recipient option, and click OK. If necessary, select a profile in the Choose Profile dialog box, and click OK. A New Message window opens with a link to your IP address embedded in the window. Insert your contact's e-mail address and send the message. The recipient of the message can double-click the IP address icon to establish a NetMeeting call with your computer.

9

NetMeeting

Use a directory server to place a call

In this exercise, you double-click a name in a directory server to establish an Internet call.

important

This exercise assumes that you have a coworker or contact who is running NetMeeting, and is logged on to a directory server. You will not be able to do this exercise if you are on a local area network that uses a proxy server to connect to the Internet.

❶ If necessary, ask your contact which directory server he or she is logged on to.

The Directory drop-down arrow appears above the Category list box in the NetMeeting window.

❷ In the Directory window, click the Directory drop-down arrow, and click the name of the directory server your contact is logged on to.

You can click any column header in the Directory window to sort column entries. For example, click the First Name header to sort all entries in alphabetical order by first name.

The list of users currently logged on to the selected directory server is shown in the Directory window.

❸ Double-click your contact's name.

NetMeeting connects to the computer of the person you are calling.

❹ On the Navigation bar, click the Current Call icon.

The Current Call window opens.

tip

When you call a contact, the contact is automatically added to your *SpeedDial list*. The SpeedDial list enables you to quickly call a contact that you've called in the past without having to find the contact in an ILS directory list. To open your SpeedDial list, click the SpeedDial icon on the Navigation bar. To call a contact using your SpeedDial list, double-click a contact's entry. Keep in mind that the SpeedDial entry will work only if the contact is logged on to the same ILS directory that was used when the SpeedDial entry was created. (To check which ILS directory a SpeedDial entry references, right-click a SpeedDial entry, and click Properties.)

5 On the Current Call toolbar, click the Hang Up button.

The call is disconnected.

Using Audio and Video Capabilities

After you establish a NetMeeting call, you'll want to use NetMeeting's communication tools. Audio and video are two of the most technologically advanced tools for communicating over the Internet. When you use NetMeeting, you can talk to, listen to, and view a contact anywhere in the world for the price of your Internet connection.

The audio controls for NetMeeting appear below the toolbar.

You can click the Audio toolbar's microphone and speakers check boxes to turn the components off and on. A check mark next to the component means that it is turned on. Further, you can adjust the microphone and speaker volumes by dragging the sliders to the left to lower the volume and to the right to increase the volume.

tip

Often a computer's microphone is plugged into the system's modem card. NetMeeting works only with sound cards, so you should verify that your microphone is plugged directly into your computer's sound card.

To control video transmission, you use the buttons that appear in NetMeeting's video windows. You can start to send or receive video by clicking the Play button. To pause a transmission, you click the Pause button (the Play button changes to a Pause button when a video is transmitting).

tip

If transmission times seem delayed (particularly if you are using a modem), consider turning off the video feature after you make initial introductions. Video transmissions take up a lot of your computer's processing capabilities as well as your Internet connection's capability to download information. This can make your computer run slowly. You can always restart the video transmission if the need arises.

At times, you might want to move a video window from its default location. (Perhaps you prefer your video window to appear along the bottom or left side of the window.) NetMeeting enables you to move and detach a video window from its default position. To detach a video window, you simply drag it upward. By default, a detached window always remains on top, regardless of which application is active on your desktop. This is helpful if you are conferencing with a contact and you want to view a different application. You will be able to open the application on your desktop without hiding Net-Meeting's video window. To reattach a video window to the NetMeeting window, click the Close button in the top-right corner of the video window.

Face to Face with Audio and Video

While audio and video represent a giant leap forward in Internet communication, you can use audio and video features with only one meeting participant at a time. Fortunately, you can switch from participant to participant during a meeting, and several pairs of meeting participants can use audio and video simultaneously (as long as the participants don't try to contact someone who is already using audio and video with another meeting participant). Think of it like a tennis tournament. Everyone's participating in the same tournament, but there are various sets of people playing matches at the same time.

important

The next two exercises assume that you have a coworker or contact who is running NetMeeting.

Use audio

In this exercise, you use your microphone and speakers to talk to a contact.

1   If necessary, start NetMeeting, and call your contact.

2   Speak into your microphone.

   Your contact should hear your voice.

3   On the Audio toolbar, clear the check box next to the microphone icon, and then speak to your contact.

   The microphone is turned off, and your contact will not hear your voice.

4   On the Audio toolbar, click the check box next to the microphone icon.

   The microphone is turned on.

5   Tell your contact to speak to you.

   You should hear your contact's voice.

6   On the Audio toolbar, clear the check box next to the speaker icon, and then tell your contact to speak to you.

   The speaker is turned off, and you will not hear your contact's voice.

7   On the Audio toolbar, click the check box next to the speaker icon, and then tell your contact to speak to you.

   The speaker is turned on, and you will hear your contact's voice.

Use video

In this exercise, you send and receive video transmissions.

1   On the Tools menu, point to Video, and click Send.

   A check mark appears next to the Send option, and you see your image in the My Video window.

Pause

2   In the My Video window, click the Pause button.

   The video in the My Video window stops transmitting.

Pause

Play

❸ In the remote video window, click the Pause button.

Your computer stops receiving a video transmission from the remote computer.

❹ In the My Video window, click the Play button.

The video in the My Video window starts transmitting.

❺ In the remote video window, click the Play button.

Your computer receives a video transmission from the remote computer.

tip

You can preview how you will look in your video transmission before placing a call. On the Navigation bar, click the Current Call icon. In the My Video window, click the Play button. Your camera will start to record as if you are sending a video transmission in a meeting, as shown in the illustration. You can adjust your video options, such as the video's size and speed of transmission, by clicking Options on the Tools menu, and then clicking the Video tab.

Video size ⎯⎯⎯

Video speed ⎯⎯⎯

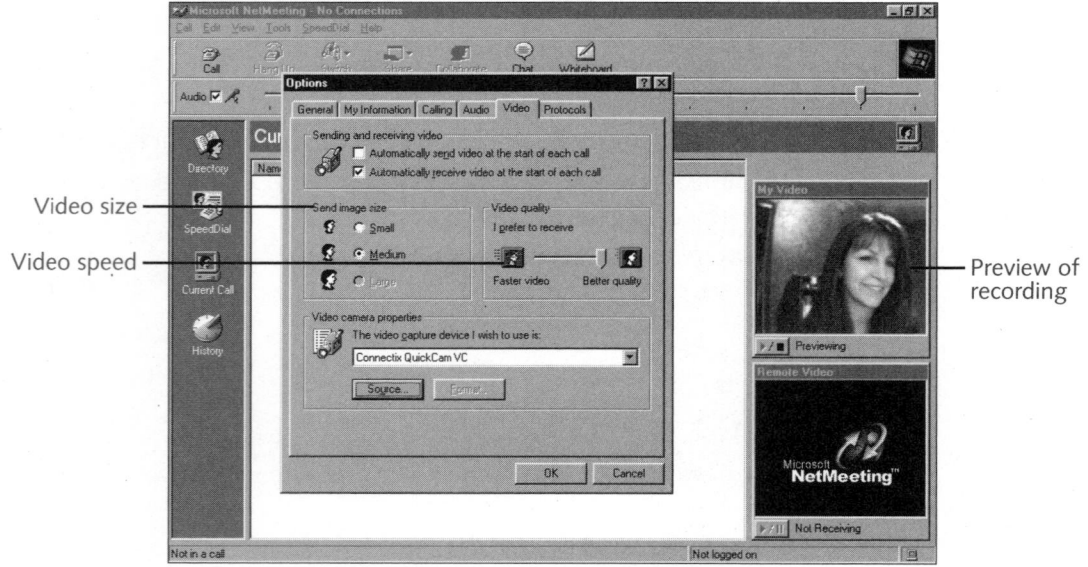

Preview of recording

Arrange a video window

In this exercise, you detach a video window from NetMeeting's default location.

1 Click the video window, and drag it upward.

The video window is detached from the NetMeeting window.

Minimize

2 Click the Minimize button at the top-right corner of the NetMeeting window.

NetMeeting is minimized, and the video window remains on your desktop.

Close

3 Click the Close button at the top-right corner of the video window.

The video window is removed from your desktop.

4 Restore the NetMeeting window.

NetMeeting appears, and the video window appears in its default location.

tip
You can change the location of the attached video windows to the left side by dragging a video window slightly past the left edge of the list of current call participants.

Switching Audio and Video Partners

To switch audio and video connections from one meeting participant to another, click the Switch button on the Current Call toolbar. A list of meeting participants appears, and a check mark appears next to the person with whom you are currently exchanging audio and video. Click another meeting participant's name to change your audio and video communication to that participant. The other participant will also need to agree to communicate with you.

NetMeeting

Using the Chat Window

The Chat window provides a way for everyone in a meeting to communicate. When you use the Chat window, you exchange typed messages among meeting participants almost instantaneously. Just type a message, press Enter, and then all other meeting participants can view your message in the Chat window.

Often, the Chat window serves as a good way to record topics addressed during the meeting (which comes in handy when typing the minutes). In addition, the Chat window is a convenient means of sending lists, URLs, phone numbers, and instructions. Finally, the Chat window doesn't require any extra hardware, such as microphones or video cameras, so everyone in the meeting can participate in this mode of communication.

When one person opens the Chat window, the window automatically opens on all other meeting participants' desktops. As meeting participants send messages, each person's Chat window is updated automatically. The illustration shows the Chat window with a few messages.

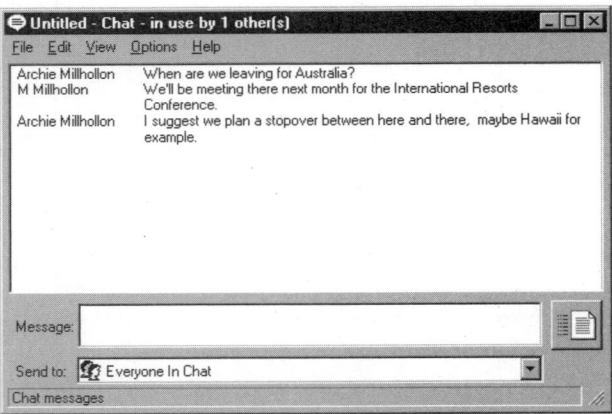

To open the Chat window, click the Chat button on the toolbar in the Current Call window. Of course, if another meeting participant has already opened the Chat window, there's rarely a need for you to open a second window. When you are ready to send a message, type a message in the Chat window's Message text box, and then click the Send button (or press Enter). As long as you're participating in a meeting and the Chat window is open, you'll automatically receive messages sent by other users.

Send

tip

You can also send a private message to a particular meeting participant. For example, maybe one of the meeting participants lives near you, and you want to know if he or she would like to meet for lunch. To send a private message, click the Send To drop-down arrow in the Chat window, and click the person's name. Then type your message in the Message text box, and press Enter. Only the person selected in the Send To list will receive your message. When you want everyone to see your messages again, click the Send To drop-down arrow, and select Everyone In Chat before you send your message.

Open and close the Chat window

In this exercise, you use the Chat button to open the Chat window and then you close the Chat window.

When you open a Chat window during a meeting, the Chat window automatically appears on all participants' desktops.

1 If necessary, start NetMeeting.

2 On the Navigation bar, click the Current Call icon.

The Current Call window appears.

3 On the Current Call toolbar, click the Chat button.

An Untitled - Chat window opens.

4 In the Untitled - Chat window, click Exit on the File menu.

The Chat window closes.

Send and receive Chat messages

In this exercise, you use the Chat window to exchange messages with a meeting participant.

You can also press Enter at the end of your comment to send it.

1 If necessary, call your contact.

2 On the Current Call toolbar, click the Chat button.

An Untitled - Chat window opens on your desktop as well as on that of the other meeting participant(s).

3 In the Message text box, type a message, and click the Send button.

Your comment appears in the Chat window, and then after your contact responds, your contact's comment appears in the Chat window.

NetMeeting

Print a Chat session

In this exercise, you print the messages appearing in a Chat window.

important

This exercise assumes that your computer is connected to a printer, and that the printer is ready to print.

1 In the Untitled - Chat window, click Print on the File menu.

The Print dialog box appears.

2 Click OK.

The Untitled - Chat window's content is printed.

Save a Chat session

In this exercise, you save the content of the Chat window.

1 In the Untitled - Chat window, click Save As on the File menu.

The Save As dialog box appears.

2 In the Save As dialog box, click the drop-down arrow next to the Save In text box, and click Desktop.

The Chat messages will be saved as a text document on your desktop.

3 Click the File Name text box, type **Chat Message,** and then click Save.

The content of the Untitled - Chat window is saved on your desktop in a file named Chat Message.

4 On the File menu, click Exit.

The Chat window closes.

5 On the Current Call toolbar, click the Hang Up button.

The call is disconnected.

Drawing on the Whiteboard

The Whiteboard is NetMeeting's marker board. Similar to the Chat window, the Whiteboard can be viewed by all meeting participants simultaneously. When one participant opens the Whiteboard, the Whiteboard automatically opens on all other participants' desktops.

To open the Whiteboard, click the Whiteboard button on the toolbar in the Current Call window. As you can see in the illustration, the Whiteboard simulates a scaled-down version of a typical paint program.

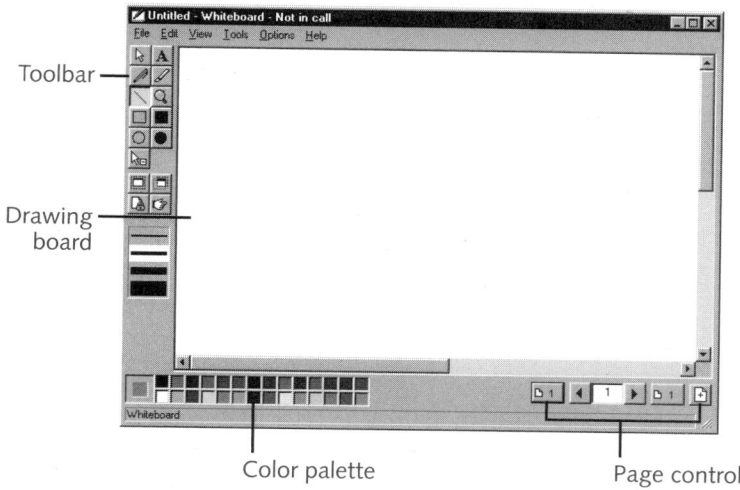

Toolbar

Drawing board

Color palette   Page controls

For a demonstration of how to draw on the Whiteboard, in the Multimedia folder on the Microsoft Internet Explorer 5 Step by Step CD-ROM, double-click the Draw icon.

You can draw, type, and paste pictures onto the Whiteboard using the toolbar, color palette, drawing board, and page controls. By default, every object placed or drawn on the Whiteboard can be moved around or deleted by any meeting participant. If you prefer, you can lock the Whiteboard while you work on it by clicking the Lock Contents tool. When you lock the Whiteboard, you are the only one who can manipulate the Whiteboard's content. The other meeting participants can alter the content of the Whiteboard only after you unlock it.

As users work on the Whiteboard, meeting participants can watch the progress of the drawing. For example, if you draw a circle, meeting participants will first see a mark as you place the tool on the Whiteboard, and then see the path as you drag the tool to form a circle. Watching someone draw on the Whiteboard is similar to watching the smoke trail from a skywriter. If you like, you can create and save your Whiteboards before establishing a NetMeeting call. This enables you to draw at your leisure (and saves you from possible artistic embarrassment). When you are finished, you can print the Whiteboard's content.

9

NetMeeting

Whiteboard Toolbar Buttons

Button	Tool name	Use this tool to
	Selector	Select items and move them by dragging the mouse pointer.
	Text	Type text on the Whiteboard.
	Pen	Write or draw using the color selected on the color palette.
	Highlighter	Paint a light shade of the color selected on the color palette over Whiteboard elements (similar to using a marker to emphasize text on a page).
	Line	Draw lines using the color selected on the color palette.
	Zoom	Toggle between a double-size view and a normal-size view.
	Unfilled Rectangle	Draw rectangles using the color selected on the color palette.
	Filled Rectangle	Draw rectangles that are filled with the color selected on the color palette.
	Unfilled Ellipse	Draw ellipses using the color selected on the color palette.
	Filled Ellipse	Draw ellipses that are filled with the color selected on the color palette.
	Eraser	Delete elements.
	Select Window	Paste a copy of a window onto the Whiteboard.
	Select Area	Paste an area of a screen onto the Whiteboard.
	Lock Contents	Prevent other users from altering the Whiteboard's content.
	Remote Pointer On	Point to items on the Whiteboard (each participant has a different color pointer).

Use the Whiteboard

In this exercise, you copy a map onto the Whiteboard and use the toolbar to draw on the map and add text.

1 If necessary, start NetMeeting, and call your contact.

2 Click the Start button on the Windows taskbar, point to Programs, and click Microsoft Word.

3 On the File menu, click Open, and then use the Look In drop-down list to navigate to the Lesson 9 folder in the Internet Explorer 5 SBS Practice folder on your hard disk drive.

4 Double-click the World file.

A Microsoft Word document containing an image of a world map opens.

5 If necessary, click the Maximize button at the top-right corner of the Microsoft Word window.

Maximize

6 Click NetMeeting on the Windows taskbar.

NetMeeting becomes the active window.

7 On the Navigation bar, click the Current Call icon.

The Current Call window appears.

8 On the Current Call toolbar, click the Whiteboard button.

The Whiteboard opens.

Restore

Minimize

Select Area

9 Click the Restore button so that you can see the NetMeeting window behind the Whiteboard (if necessary), and click the Minimize button in the top-right corner of the NetMeeting window.

10 On the Whiteboard toolbar, click the Select Area button.

The Whiteboard Select Area dialog box appears. You are prompted to select an area of the screen to paste onto the Whiteboard.

Not only can you select tools on the Whiteboard toolbar, you can also select tools from the Tools menu.

11 Click OK.

The dialog box closes, the mouse pointer changes to a crosshairs pointer, and the Whiteboard is removed from view.

12 In the World document, click the upper-left corner of the map image, drag to the lower-right corner of the image, and then release the mouse button.

The Whiteboard reappears with the map displayed on the drawing board, as shown in the following illustration.

NetMeeting

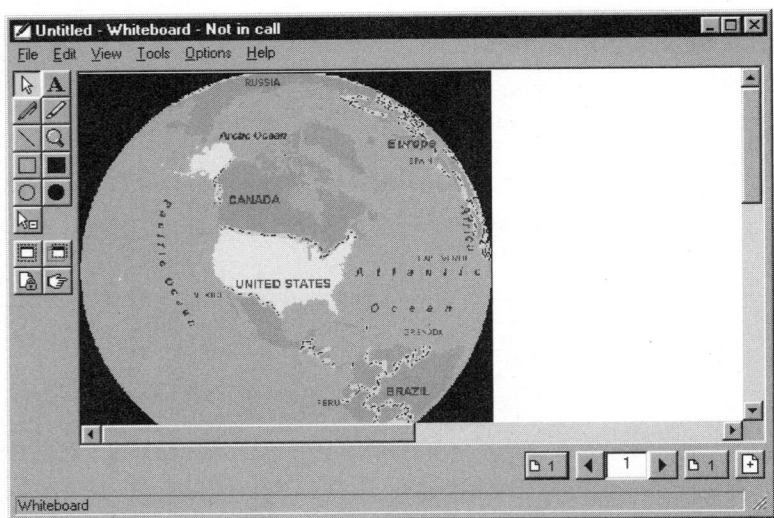

You can also copy and paste images onto the Whiteboard. For example, you can select an image, copy it, open the White- board, and click Paste on the Edit menu.

Text

Selector

Unfilled Ellipse

13 On the Whiteboard toolbar, click the Text button, and click Canada on the map.

A text box appears.

14 Type **LMR**.

Text appears on the map.

15 On the Whiteboard toolbar, click the Selector button.

The mouse pointer appears, and you can select items in the Whiteboard window.

16 On the map, click the LMR text, and drag it to the United States.

17 On the Whiteboard toolbar, click the Unfilled Ellipse button, and then click a red color square on the color palette.

The Whiteboard is set up to draw red ellipses.

18 On the map, click the Pacific Ocean near the United States's West Coast, and then draw an oval around the west coast.

19 On the Whiteboard toolbar, click the Remote Pointer On button.

A pointing hand appears on the Whiteboard.

Remote Pointer On

20 Click the hand, and drag it so that it points to Florida.

The Remote Pointer points to Florida, as shown in the illustration.

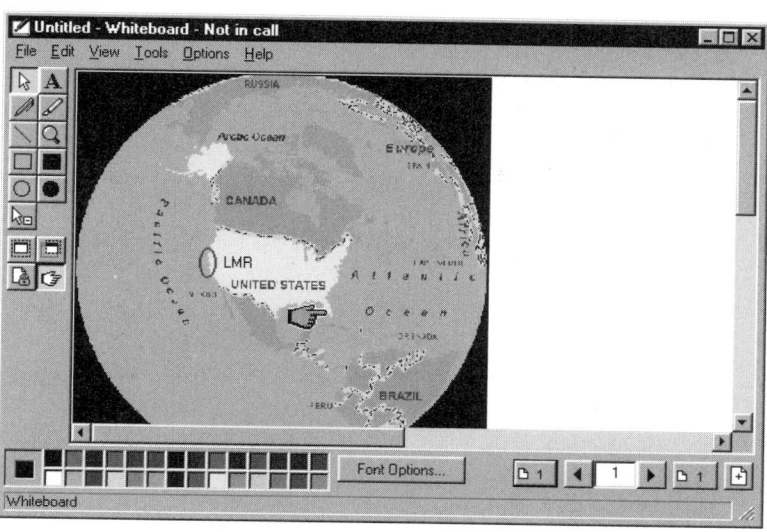

Lock the Whiteboard

In this exercise, you lock the Whiteboard so that no other meeting participants can move, delete, or add elements to the Whiteboard.

*Lock
Contents*

① On the Whiteboard toolbar, click the Lock Contents button.

The Whiteboard is locked. Notice that the title bar changes to LOCKED BY: *Your Name*.

② On the Whiteboard toolbar, click the Lock Contents button again.

The Whiteboard is unlocked, and the title bar reverts to Untitled - Whiteboard - Not In Call.

③ On the File menu, click Exit.

A Whiteboard alert box opens, asking if you want to save the Whiteboard.

④ Click No.

The Whiteboard closes.

Print the Whiteboard

In this exercise, you draw on the Whiteboard and print the content of the Whiteboard.

① Click NetMeeting on the Windows taskbar.

The Current Call window opens.

2 On the Current Call toolbar, click the Whiteboard button.

The Whiteboard opens.

3 On the Whiteboard toolbar, click the Pen button, and choose a color on the color palette.

Pen

4 Create a simple line drawing on the Whiteboard (such as a smiley face).

5 On the Whiteboard toolbar, click the Filled Rectangle tool, and click a color on the color palette.

Filled Rectangle

6 Click the drawing board, and drag the crosshairs pointer to form a rectangle.

A color-filled rectangle is drawn.

7 On the File menu, click Print.

The Print dialog box appears.

8 In the Print dialog box, click OK.

Your drawing is printed.

Save the Whiteboard

In this exercise, you save the content of the Whiteboard on your desktop.

1 On the File menu, click Save As.

The Save As dialog box opens.

2 In the Save As dialog box, click the Save In drop-down arrow, and click Desktop.

The Whiteboard messages will be saved on your desktop.

3 In the File Name text box, type **Whiteboard Art**, and then click Save.

The content of the Untitled - Whiteboard window is saved on your desktop in a file named Whiteboard Art, and the Untitled - Whiteboard window is renamed Whiteboard Art - Whiteboard.

4 On the File menu, click Exit.

The Whiteboard closes.

5 On the Current Call toolbar, click the Hang up button.

Your call is disconnected.

Sharing Files and Applications

A meeting wouldn't be a meeting if there weren't at least a couple of handouts floating around. While NetMeeting doesn't literally pass papers around the table, it can be used to share and collaborate on documents. NetMeeting enables you to share documents in three ways:

- You can send files to meeting participants.

- You can show, or *share*, a document.

- You can open a document or application and enable meeting participants to work (or *collaborate*) on the document or application.

Sending a file to meeting participants is similar to sending an e-mail attachment to each participant. Each person receives a copy of the document on his or her computer. Sending files requires that you use NetMeeting menu commands. When other meeting participants send you a file, you see a dialog box stating that a meeting participant has sent you a file.

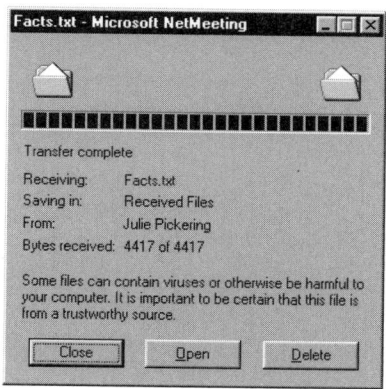

To view the file, you click Open in the dialog box. By default, NetMeeting places transferred files in the Program Files/NetMeeting/Received Files folder on your hard disk drive.

When you share a document, you show a document to meeting participants without copying the document to their computers—the document resides on your computer and only you can change it. You can tell when a window is shared, because a tab appears along the top of the window identifying which meeting participant is sharing the window, as shown in the illustration.

NetMeeting

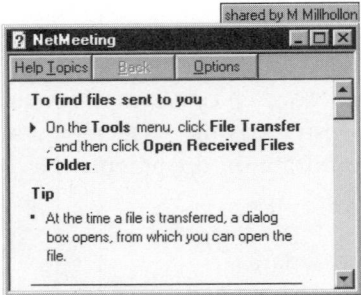

Finally, when you collaborate with meeting participants, you are essentially enabling other users to make changes to documents or use applications that are stored on your computer. In other words, meeting participants can make changes to files and run applications stored on your computer. If you want meeting participants to have a copy of a document on which you've collaborated, you will have to send the file to the meeting participants after you are finished.

Keep in mind that when someone else is in control of a shared application, you will not have the use of your mouse pointer—not only in the shared application, but for any other purpose. If you move your mouse when someone else is in control of a shared application, you will see a pop-up message stating that you will need to click to regain control of the mouse pointer.

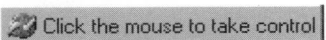

tip
To stop collaborating on a shared document, press the Esc key. Pressing Esc stops collaboration with everyone in the meeting, although the others will be able to watch you work in the application.

FTP: Transferring Documents Within Internet Explorer

You don't need to place a NetMeeting call just to transfer documents to other people on a network or the Internet. You can use Internet Explorer's FTP (File Transfer Protocol) capabilities to transfer files. FTP enables you to download files from an FTP server to your computer, transfer files from your computer to an FTP server, and enables others to download your files to their computer. Transferring documents using FTP is quicker than e-mailing documents (especially for modem users).

Internet Explorer's FTP interface uses the familiar Windows file and folder interface. To log on to an FTP server, start Internet Explorer, and type the FTP address in the Address bar. (You can obtain FTP addresses from your contacts or from Web pages.) For example, type **ftp://ftp.microsoft.com** and press Enter. You will see Microsoft's public FTP site, as shown in the illustration.

New!

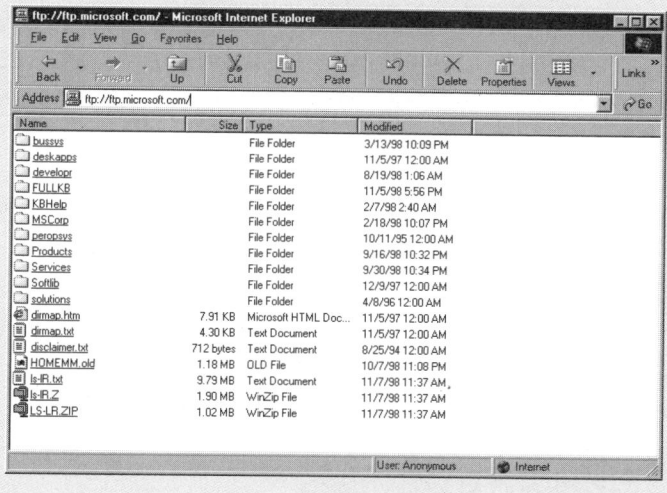

You can double-click folders to open them and double-click files to download them to your computer. If you have permission, you can also copy files from your computer to the FTP server. Copying files to an FTP server generally requires you to use a user name and password to access the FTP site. To log on to an FTP server that requires a user name and password, you use the following addressing format in Internet Explorer's Address bar: *ftp://username:password@ftp.domain.com*.

Send files

If your contact still has the Chat window open, the Chat window will appear after you make your call. If necessary, close the Chat window.

In this exercise, you send the Facts.txt file to a contact.

1 Start NetMeeting, and call your contact.

2 On the Tools menu, point to File Transfer, and click Send File.

The Select A File To Send dialog box opens, as shown in the illustration.

You can also click Ctrl+F to open the Select A File To Send dialog box.

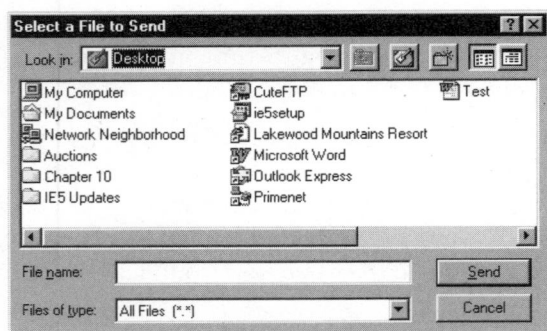

3 In the Select A File To Send dialog box, use the Look In drop-down list to navigate to the Lesson 9 folder in the Internet Explorer 5 SBS Practice folder located on your hard disk drive.

4 Click the Facts file, and then click Send.

The file is sent to each computer participating in the NetMeeting call, and an alert box appears, stating that the transmission was successful.

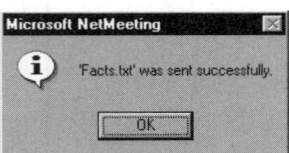

5 In the alert box, click OK.

The alert box closes.

Share applications

In this exercise, you share a NetMeeting Help file window with a contact.

1 On the Help menu, click Help Topics.

The Help Topics: NetMeeting window opens.

2 Make sure the Index tab is selected.

3 In the text box under section 1, type **sharing files.**

The sharing files help topic is selected in the help topic list window.

4 Click Display.

The Topics Found dialog box opens.

5 In the Topics Found dialog box, click Display.

The NetMeeting help window opens.

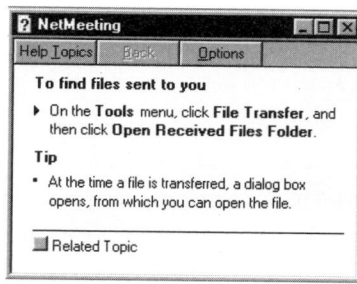

6 On the Current Call toolbar, click the Share button.

The Share drop-down list opens and reveals the applications and documents that are currently open on your computer.

7 In the Share drop-down list, click NetMeeting (as shown below). If an alert box appears, click OK.

Notice that the words Not Collaborating appear in the Sharing column next to meeting participant names.

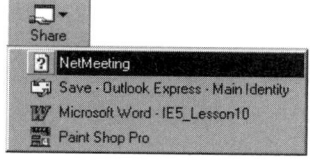

The words *shared by (your name)* appear above the NetMeeting help application. The application is now shared, and call participants can view the file (but they can't alter it).

Notice that the words Not Sharing appear in the Sharing column next to meeting participant names.

8 On the Current Call toolbar, click Share, and then click NetMeeting in the Share drop-down list.

The help topic is no longer shared.

9 Close the NetMeeting help file window.

Collaborate on documents

In this exercise, you collaborate on a game of Solitaire with a contact.

If your computer does not have Solitaire, you can open any other application or document to complete this exercise.

1 Open a game of Solitaire on your computer (click Start, point to Programs, point to Accessories, point to Games, and click Solitaire), and move the Solitaire window down so that you can see the Current Call toolbar.

2 On the Current Call toolbar, click Share, and click Solitaire in the Share drop-down list.

The Solitaire game is shared.

3 On the Current Call toolbar, click the Collaborate button.

The Solitaire game is shared, and the words *In Control* appear next to your name in the Current Call window.

If you are using the Chat window, move the window down so that you can see your name in the Current Call window.

4 Using either the microphone or the Chat window, tell your contact that you are going to take turns playing Solitaire. Ask your contact to click the Collaborate button in his or her window.

The word *Collaborating* appears next to your name in the Current Call window.

important

When you are collaborating with another user and the other user has control of the mouse pointer, you cannot access any application on your computer without regaining control of the mouse pointer. If you move your mouse while another user has control of the mouse pointer, you will receive a pop-up message stating that you need to click your mouse to regain control of the mouse pointer.

5 Click your mouse to take control, click Solitaire on the Window's taskbar, and tell your contact to do the same.

6 Take turns moving cards in the card game.

7 On the NetMeeting toolbar, click the Collaborate button, and then click OK.

The Solitaire game can no longer be played by other meeting participants.

8 On the Current Call toolbar, click the Share button, and then click Solitaire in the Share drop-down menu.

The Solitaire game is no longer shared.

9 On the Current Call toolbar, click the Hang Up button.

The call is disconnected.

important

Be careful when granting meeting participants access to your computer. For example, if you allow other users to access your Exploring window, they will be able to open and change any document on your hard disk drive.

One Step Further

Using Microsoft's Online Support

Microsoft's Personal Support Center Web site provides a wealth of information about Microsoft products such as Internet Explorer, Outlook Express, and NetMeeting. The Web site features hundreds of articles that help you solve problems. It might be helpful to think of Microsoft's help documentation as a set of car manuals. The help files stored on your computer are like the smaller car manuals that you get when you buy a car—the basic information is there, like how to change your oil, but the manual doesn't get overly detailed. In contrast, the Personal Support Center Web site offers you the commercial car manuals—the books that you buy at an auto parts store that show you how to replace an alternator or change a timing belt. When you have a software problem that requires more in-depth information than your local help files can handle, you should turn to Microsoft's comprehensive Personal Support Center Web site.

You can usually access Microsoft's Personal Support Center Web site by clicking Online Support on the Help menu of most Microsoft applications. You can access the Personal Support Center Web site from within Internet Explorer, Outlook Express, the Outlook Express newsreader, and NetMeeting. The search page for the Personal Support Center Web site appears in the illustration on the following page.

9

NetMeeting

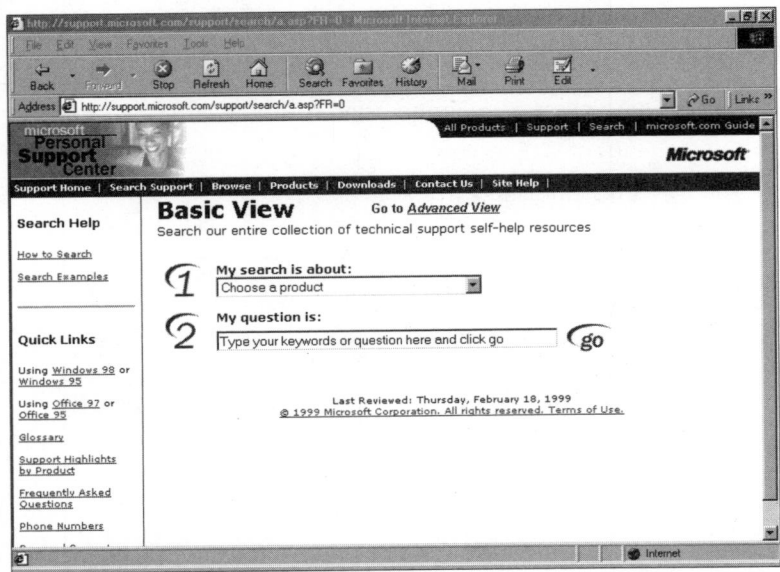

After you open the Personal Support Center Web site, you can determine how you want to search through the articles that make up the Web site's data (for example, you can search through articles by keyword, article ID number, and so forth). Next you specify the words you want to include in your search. As you will see, searching the Personal Support Center Web site is similar to using a search engine, as described in Lesson 2, "Finding and Managing Information."

Access Microsoft's Personal Support Center Web site

In this exercise, you access Microsoft's Personal Support Center Web site from within the NetMeeting window.

❶   If necessary, start NetMeeting.

❷   On the Help menu, click Online Support.

The Personal Support Center Web page is displayed.

❸   If an alert box appears, click Yes.

❹   Click the Search Support hyperlink (located on the blue bar at the top of the Web page).

The search page appears.

Search for answers

In this exercise, you search for information about video capabilities.

1 If you are on the Advanced View page, click the Basic View hyperlink (located below the blue bar at the top of the Web page).

2 On the Basic View page, in section 1, click the drop-down arrow, and select NetMeeting.

3 In section 2, type **NetMeeting and video** in the My Question Is text box, and click the Go hyperlink.

4 If any alert boxes appear, click Yes.

The search is conducted, and a page of links to related articles appears.

If you click a hyperlink that doesn't solve your problem, click Internet Explorer's Back button to return to your search's list of hyperlinks. (You might have to click the Refresh button after clicking Back to view the hyperlinks.)

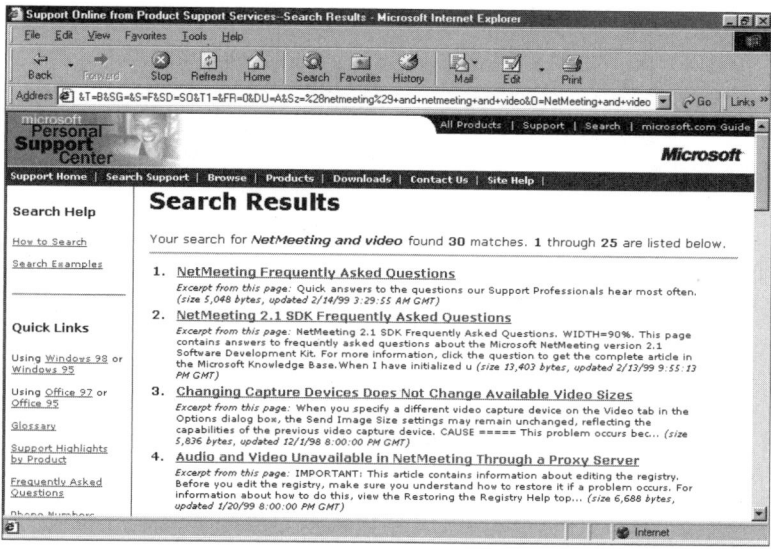

5 Click a hyperlink to read an article.

Finish the lesson

1 Quit Internet Explorer.

2 Quit NetMeeting.

3 Quit the Solitaire game.

4 Quit Microsoft Word.

5 On your desktop, right-click the Chat Message file, click Delete, and then click Yes.

The Chat Message file is deleted.

6 On your desktop, right-click the Whiteboard Art file, click Delete, and then click Yes.

The Whiteboard Art file is deleted.

Lesson 9 Quick Reference

To	Do this	Button
Start NetMeeting	Start Internet Explorer, point to New on the File menu, and click Internet Call.	
View the NetMeeting options	Click Options on the Tools menu.	
Place a direct call	Obtain your contact's IP address. Click the Call button on the toolbar, and enter your contact's IP address in the Address text box. Click the Call Using drop-down arrow, click Network (TCP/IP), and then click Call.	
Use a directory server to place a call	Click the Directory drop-down arrow, click the directory server your contact is logged on to, and double-click your contact's name.	
Disconnect a call	Click the Hang Up button on the Current Call toolbar.	
Use audio	Call your contact, and speak into your microphone.	
Use video	Call your contact, point to Video on the Tools menu, and click Send.	
Arrange a video window	Click the Current Call icon on the Navigation bar, click a video window, and drag it to a new location.	
Open the Chat window	Click the Current Call icon on the Navigation bar, and click the Chat button on the Current Call toolbar.	
Close the Chat window	In the Chat window, click Exit on the File menu.	
Send and receive Chat messages	Call a contact, open the Chat window, type a messages in the Message text box, and then click the Send button.	

Lesson 9 Quick Reference

To	Do this	Button
Print a Chat session	In the Chat window, click Print on the File menu, and click OK.	
Save a Chat session	In the Chat window, click Save As on the File menu, provide a location and filename, and click Save.	
Use the Whiteboard	Click the Current Call icon on the Navigation bar, click the Whiteboard button, and then use the Whiteboard toolbar tools to add content.	
Lock the Whiteboard	In the Whiteboard, click the Lock Contents button on the Whiteboard toolbar.	
Print the Whiteboard	In the Whiteboard, click Print on the File menu, and click OK.	
Save the Whiteboard	In the Whiteboard, click Save As on the File menu, provide a location and filename, and click Save.	
Send files	Call your contact, point to File Transfer on the Tools menu, click Send File, navigate to a file in the Select A File To Send dialog box, click the file to send, click Send, and click OK.	
Share applications	Open the file or application you want to share, start NetMeeting, and call your contact. Click the Share button on the Current Call toolbar, and click the file or application you want to share in the Share drop-down menu.	

9

NetMeeting

Lesson 9 Quick Reference

To	Do this
Collaborate on documents	Open the file or application on which you want collaborate, start NetMeeting, and call your contact. Click the Share button on the Current Call toolbar, and click the file or application you want to share in the Share drop-down menu. Click the Collaborate button on the Current Call toolbar. Instruct your contact to click the Collaborate button. Click your mouse button to take control, open the shared file, and tell your contact to do the same.
Access Microsoft's Personal Support Center Web site	Click Online Support on the Help menu.
Search for answers on Microsoft's Personal Support Center Web Site	Access the Personal Support Center Web site. Click the Search Support hyperlink. If necessary, click the Basic View hyperlink. Select an application in the section 1 text box, enter search terms in section 2, and click the Go hyperlink. If necessary, click Yes. Click a hyperlink to read an article.

Review & Practice

**ESTIMATED
TIME
20 min.**

You will review and practice how to:

✔ *Create e-mail messages.*

✔ *Add entries to the Address Book.*

✔ *Use Outlook Express' newsreader to participate in newsgroups.*

✔ *Conduct an online conference using Microsoft NetMeeting.*

Before you complete this book, you can practice the skills you learned in Part 3 by working through this Review & Practice. In this section, you will use Outlook Express' e-mail and newsreader features, as well as conduct an online conference using NetMeeting.

Scenario

A major gourmet magazine has contacted you. Its editors would like to feature Lakewood Mountains Resort in the magazine's annual fine dining edition. You're thrilled at the prospect, and you believe that the article will provide some positive exposure for the resort—if everything goes well. The magazine's writer and photographer will be visiting the resort next month, so you have some time to plan for the event.

Step 1:   Use E-mail to Touch Base with Contacts

You want to quickly involve the resort's key personnel to prepare for the interview. You would like to contact the general managers, food and beverage manager, event coordinator, and landscaper (after all, the resort has recently become a regional arboretum) as soon as possible. You decide that the quickest and most efficient way to contact all the key staff simultaneously is to send a formal announcement via e-mail.

1 Start Outlook Express.

2 Use the New Mail button's drop-down arrow to create an e-mail message using one of the standard stationery designs.

3 Click the Addresses button on the toolbar, add e-mail addresses for the resort's key personnel to your Address Book, and then include the addresses in a group called *Lakewood Contacts*.

important

You can create fictional e-mail addresses for this exercise, such as *CEO@Lakewood.com* and *landscaper@Lakewood.com*.

4 Enter text into the body of an e-mail message stating that the magazine will be featuring the resort in a future edition.

5 Add a signature to the message.

6 Send the e-mail message using the Lakewood Contacts Address Book entry.

For more information about	See
Starting Outlook Express	Lesson 7
Using stationery in e-mail messages	Lesson 7
Creating entries in your Address Book	Lesson 7
Grouping Address Book contacts	Lesson 7
Creating e-mail messages	Lesson 7
Creating signatures for e-mail messages	Lesson 7

Step 2: **Visit Newsgroups to Gather Opinions**

The staff at Lakewood Mountains Resort is busy preparing to welcome the gourmet magazine's staff. In the meantime, you decide to research what people are saying about fine dining. So you visit a newsgroup that discusses restaurants.

1 Open Outlook Express' newsreader.

2 Use the Newsgroup Subscriptions dialog box to find a newsgroup containing the word *restaurant*.

3 View the content of a restaurant-related newsgroup.

4 Subscribe to the newsgroup, and reply to one of the messages, making your reply available to everyone who accesses the newsgroup.

5 Post a message to the newsgroup.

For more information about	See
Opening Outlook Express' newsreader	Lesson 8
Finding a newsgroup	Lesson 8
Viewing the content of a newsgroup	Lesson 8
Subscribing to newsgroups	Lesson 8
Replying to a newsgroup	Lesson 8
Posting a message to a newsgroup	Lesson 8

Step 3: **Conduct an Online Conference Using NetMeeting**

For three weeks, you've been planning for the arrival of the reporters from the gourmet magazine. They will be arriving next Monday, and you would like to ensure that the resort's preparations are running smoothly. You decide to use NetMeeting to hold a conference with key personnel at Lakewood Mountains Resort.

important

This exercise assumes that you have a coworker or contact who is running NetMeeting.

1 Start NetMeeting.

2 Instruct your contact to e-mail his or her IP address to you.

3 Click the Call button on the toolbar, and place a direct NetMeeting call to your contact using his or her address.

4 Use the audio and video features.

5 Send and receive messages in the Chat window.

6 Create a simple drawing on the Whiteboard.

7 Open a Microsoft Word document, and enable your contact to work on the document.

For more information about	See
Starting NetMeeting	Lesson 9
Receiving e-mail messages	Lesson 7
Placing a direct call to a contact	Lesson 9
Using NetMeeting's audio and video features	Lesson 9
Exchanging information in the Chat window	Lesson 9
Drawing on the Whiteboard	Lesson 9
Sharing and collaborating on documents in NetMeeting	Lesson 9

Finish the Review & Practice

1 Delete the fictional entries and group you created in your Address Book.

2 Unsubscribe to the restaurant-related newsgroup.

3 Quit Outlook Express.

4 Close NetMeeting without saving changes to the Chat window or Whiteboard.

5 Close the Microsoft Word document without saving changes.

6 Quit Internet Explorer.

Installation and Setup Procedures

Installing Microsoft Internet Explorer 5 is a fairly straightforward process. Internet Explorer's ability to run a variety of Web and Internet technologies ensures that you do not need to install and configure a number of ancillary applications—you just need to install the Internet Explorer software and configure your Internet, mail, news, and conferencing settings.

If you're using a dial-up connection, you'll need to configure a connection to your Internet service provider (ISP). (If your computer is part of a network or intranet, your network administrator will probably manage your Internet connection.) An ISP acts as your gateway to the Internet. You connect to your service provider, and your service provider connects to the Internet. Each time you want to visit the Internet, you must connect to your Internet service provider. If you are upgrading Internet Explorer or currently using another browser, your Internet connection is probably already established.

If you're planning to use Internet Explorer's mail, newsreader, and conferencing features, you'll need to provide Internet Explorer with the appropriate information. Fortunately, Internet Explorer's wizards and dialog boxes help you to easily configure mail, news, and conferencing accounts.

This appendix points the way to the wizards and dialog boxes you can use to install and set up Internet Explorer and its added features.

If you have recently subscribed to an ISP and have received a setup disk that includes Internet Explorer (version 4 or 5), the installation program will perform most of the setup procedures described in this appendix. You will probably need to supply only your e-mail address and password.

Installing Internet Explorer

You can install Internet Explore in two ways. You can install the application from a CD-ROM (such as the Microsoft Office 2000 suite), or you can download Internet Explorer from the Internet. Each installation process has its benefits. Installing Internet Explorer from a CD-ROM is much quicker than downloading the application from the Internet. (On average, downloading a typical installation of Internet Explorer requires at least one hour to complete using a 56 Kbps modem, while CD-ROM installation requires less than a half hour.) On the other hand, downloading Internet Explorer means that you are assured of installing the latest upgrades and bug fixes incorporated into the software. (Of course, to download Internet Explorer 5, you will need to use a previous version of Internet Explorer or another Web browser.)

Hardware Minimum Requirements

Before you install Internet Explorer, verify that your computer fulfills the following minimum system requirements:

- 486 with a 66 MHz processor (Pentium processor recommended)
- 16 MB of RAM
- Mouse
- Modem
- CD-ROM drive (if installation is done from a CD-ROM)
- 9.8 MB of hard disk space for a typical install and 6 through 45 MB for a custom install

tip

Whether you install Internet Explorer from a CD-ROM or from the Internet, the installation process copies all setup files to your hard disk drive. This allows you to reinstall Internet Explorer more quickly, if necessary. If you want to reclaim the disk space (about 958 K), you can delete the folder containing the setup files. To remove the Internet Explorer 5 setup files, click Start on the Windows taskbar, point to Settings, and then click Control Panel. Next double-click the Add/Remove Programs icon in the Control Panel, click Internet Explorer 5 And Internet Tools, and then click Add/Remove. In the Internet Explorer 5 And Internet Tools dialog box, click the Advanced button, click the Remove The Folder Containing Windows Update Setup Files option, and then click OK.

Install Internet Explorer from a CD-ROM

In this exercise, you install Internet Explorer from a CD-ROM.

① Insert the CD-ROM containing Microsoft Internet Explorer 5.

> ### important
> In some instances, the Internet Explorer CD-ROM might open a setup window when you place the disk in the CD-ROM disk drive. If this occurs, follow the window's installation directions instead of using the Run dialog box as described in this exercise.

② On the Windows taskbar, click the Start button, and click Run.

The Run dialog box opens.

③ In the Run dialog box, click Browse.

The Browse window opens.

④ In the Browse window, navigate to the CD contents, find the file named ie5setup, click ie5setup, and then click Open.

The ie5setup program name is shown in the Run dialog box.

⑤ In the Run dialog box, click OK.

The Windows Update window opens and shows the Internet Explorer 5 license agreement.

⑥ Read the End User License Agreement, click the I Accept The Agreement option (if you agree), and click Next.

The Windows Update window provides the option to complete a typical installation or a custom installation.

By default, a typical installation of Internet Explorer installs the browser, Outlook Express, Windows Media Player, and other components in the C:\Program Files\ Internet Explorer folder, which the setup program will create if it does not already exist.

⑦ In the Windows Update window, click the Install Now – Typical Set Of Components option, and click Next.

After a few seconds, the installation process begins.

⑧ After the installation and optimization processes are complete, save and close all other files that are open on your computer, and then click Finish in the Windows Update window.

Your computer automatically restarts and shows a progress bar as the installation is completed.

tip

If your computer stalls while restarting, verify that you do not have a disk in your floppy drive. If that's not the cause of the stalled restart, press your computer's reset button to restart your computer.

Download Internet Explorer from the Internet

In this exercise, you connect to the Internet, and then download and install Internet Explorer by using an existing browser on your computer.

1 Connect to the Internet, and open the browser you're currently using.

2 Open *www.microsoft.com/windows/ie/ie5/default.asp*.

The Microsoft Windows Technologies Internet Explorer page opens.

3 Click the Download Today hyperlink.

4 Click the name of your operating system to expand a list of items to download, and then click Internet Explorer 5 And Internet Tools.

5 If a Security Warning dialog box appears, click Yes.

An alert box appears, asking if the program may determine which components are installed on your computer.

6 Click Yes.

The program determines which components are already installed on your computer, and the Windows Update page appears.

7 Scroll until you see the Internet Explorer 5 And Internet Tools check box, and click the check box.

The Download Checklist page opens.

8 In section 3, click the Start Download button.

A progress bar appears as Internet Explorer 5 downloads, and then the Internet Explorer 5 license agreement appears.

9 Read the license rules, click the I Accept The Agreement option, and click Next.

After a few seconds, the Windows Update window provides the option to complete a typical installation or a custom installation.

⑩ Verify that the Install Now - Typical Set Of Components - 17.2MB option is selected, and then click Next.

After a few seconds, the Windows Update window appears and shows the progress of the download process, as shown in the illustration.

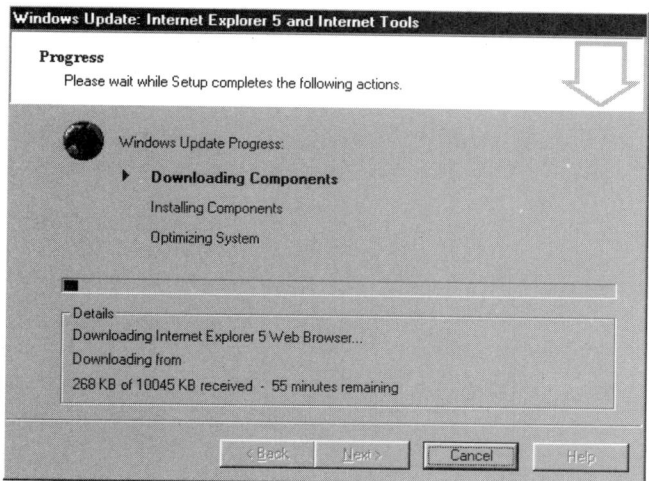

⑪ After the installation and optimization processes are complete, save and close all other files that are open on your computer, and then click Finish in the Windows Update window.

An alert box opens, indicating that you must restart your computer.

⑫ Click OK.

Your computer restarts and shows a progress bar as the installation completes.

Connecting to the Internet

After you install Internet Explorer, you must connect to the Internet. If you are currently surfing the Internet with an older version of Internet Explorer or another browser altogether, you already have an Internet connection, so you do not need to perform the steps in this section. If you installed Internet Explorer from a CD-ROM, you can use Internet Explorer's Connection Wizard to set up your Internet connection.

When you sign up with an ISP, the provider will probably give you a CD-ROM or a disk that you can use to set up an Internet connection, so you will not need to use the Connection Wizard. If you do not receive a CD-ROM or a disk from your ISP, your provider will at least give you the information you need to set up an Internet connection. After you receive the information, you can use the Internet Connection Wizard to create a dial-up connection. A dial-up connection contains the information your computer needs to connect to the Internet.

ISP Information

You will need to obtain the following information from your ISP before you can create a dial-up connection:

- The ISP's phone number
- Your user name
- Your password
- Your ISP's domain name server (DNS) addresses
- Optionally, the IP address and Subnet Mask assigned to you

After you create a dial-up connection, you can connect manually to the Internet by clicking the dial-up connection icon in your My Computer window. Also, you can connect to the Internet when you open Internet Explorer or Outlook Express. By default, when you open Internet Explorer or Outlook Express, the program will show a Dial-up Connection dialog box that prompts you to connect to the Internet, as shown in the illustration.

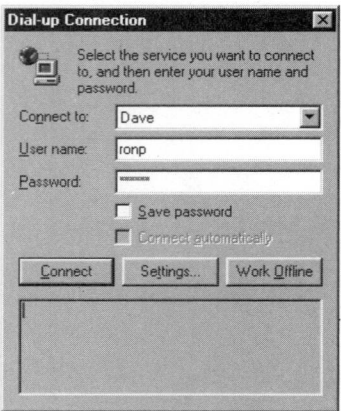

Use the Connection Wizard

In this exercise, you create a dial-up connection using the Connection Wizard.

On some installations, you might find the Connection Wizard shortcut by clicking Start, pointing to Programs, pointing to Internet Explorer, and clicking Connection Wizard.

1 On the Windows taskbar, click Start, point to Programs, point to Accessories, point to Communications, and then click Internet Connection Wizard.

The first Internet Connection Wizard dialog box opens.

2 Click the I Want To Set Up My Internet Connection Manually, Or I Connect Through A Local Area Network (LAN) option, and then click Next.

The Setting Up Your Internet Connection dialog box opens.

3 Click the I Connect Through A Phone Line And A Modem option, and then click Next.

The Choose Modem dialog box opens.

4 Use the drop-down list to select the modem you will use to connect to the Internet, and then click Next.

The Step 1 Of 3: Internet Account Connection Information dialog box opens.

5 Enter the phone number you will use to connect to your ISP, verify that the country setting is correct, verify that the Dial Using The Area Code And Country Code option is selected, and click Next.

The Step 2 Of 3: Internet Account Logon Information dialog box opens.

6 In the User Name text box, enter the user name your ISP assigned to you, and press Tab.

The user name is entered.

7 In the Password text box, enter the password your ISP assigned to you, and click Next.

The password is entered, and the Step 3 Of 3: Configuring Your Computer dialog box opens.

8 In the Connection dialog box, enter a name for the dial-up connection, and click Next.

The Set Up Your Internet Mail Account dialog box opens.

You can click Yes in the Set Up Your Internet Mail Account dialog box to present dialog boxes that enable you to configure your e-mail and news accounts.

9 Click No, and then click Next.

The Congratulations! dialog box appears and indicates that you have successfully set up a dial-up connection.

10 Click Finish.

tip
Most ISPs will walk you through the steps of setting up your Internet connection. If necessary, call your ISP's customer service telephone number for assistance.

Use your modem to connect to the Internet

In this exercise, you use your dial-up connection to connect to the Internet without opening Internet Explorer or Outlook Express.

❶   On your desktop, double-click the My Computer icon.

The My Computer window opens.

❷   Click the Dial-Up Networking folder icon.

The contents of the Dial-Up Networking folder appear.

❸   Right-click the name of your Internet connection.

❹   On the shortcut menu, click Properties.

The My Connection dialog box appears.

important
The next seven steps are examples and will vary depending upon the information your ISP has given you.

❺   Click the Server Types tab.

❻   Make sure the TCP/IP check box is selected, and click the TCP/IP Settings button.

The TCP/IP Settings dialog box appears.

❼   Click the Specify Name Server Addresses option.

❽   In the Primary DNS text box, type in the first DNS Address given to you by your ISP.

❾   In the Secondary DNS text box, type in the second DNS Address given to you by your ISP.

❿   Click OK.

The TCP/IP Settings dialog box closes.

⓫   Click OK.

The My Connection dialog box closes.

⓬ Double-click the dial-up connection icon for your Internet account.
The Connect To dialog box opens, as shown in the illustration.

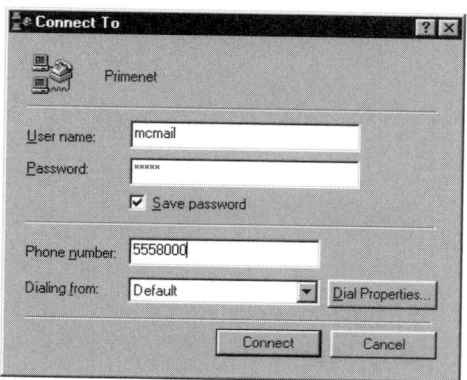

⓭ Click the Connect button.
The connecting dialog box appears until the connection is established, the window is minimized, and the Dial-Up icon appears on the Windows taskbar.

Disconnect your modem from the Internet

In this exercise, you disconnect from your ISP.

❶ On the Windows taskbar, right-click the Dial-Up icon.
A shortcut menu appears.

❷ On the shortcut menu, click Disconnect.
Your computer is disconnected from your ISP, and you cannot access the Internet without re-establishing a connection.

Setting Up Your E-mail and News Accounts

You must configure mail and news accounts within Outlook Express before you can use Outlook Express' e-mail and newsreader applications. The mail and news accounts provide the information necessary for Outlook Express to transfer and receive e-mail messages and news posts. Your ISP should provide the information necessary for you to configure the mail and news accounts. The first time you start Outlook Express, it will display a wizard prompting you for e-mail account information. You can also enter or change e-mail account information (or add new e-mail accounts) at a later time if you wish. The procedures described next (except steps 2 through 4) are the same for both first-time and later account setup.

E-mail Account Information

You will need to obtain the following information from your ISP before you can set up an e-mail account:

- Your e-mail address
- Your POP3 server name
- Your SMTP server name
- Your user name
- Your password

News Account Information

You will need to obtain the following information from your ISP before you can set up a news account:

- Your e-mail address
- Your NNTP server name
- Your user name
- Your password

Set up your e-mail account

In this exercise, you set up an e-mail account from within Outlook Express.

1 On the Windows taskbar, click the Start button, point to Programs, and click Outlook Express.

The Outlook Express window opens.

important

It is not necessary for you to connect to the Internet to configure your e-mail account.

② On the Tools menu, click Accounts.

The Internet Accounts dialog box appears.

③ Click the Add button.

A shortcut menu appears.

④ On the shortcut menu, click Mail.

The Internet Connection Wizard dialog box opens.

⑤ In the Display Name text box, type your name (if necessary), and then click Next.

The Internet E-mail Address dialog box opens.

⑥ In the E-mail Address text box, enter your e-mail address (if necessary), and click Next.

The E-mail Server Names dialog box opens.

⑦ Type the POP3 server name provided by your ISP, and then press Tab.

The insertion point moves to the Outgoing Mail (SMTP) Server text box.

⑧ Type the SMTP server name provided by your ISP, and then click Next.

The Internet Mail Logon dialog box appears.

⑨ Verify that the Logon Using Secure Password Authentication (SPA) option is selected, click the Account Name text box, type the user name your ISP assigned to you, and press Tab.

The cursor moves to the Password text box.

⑩ Type the password your ISP assigned to you, click Next, and click Finish.

The Internet Connection Wizard dialog box closes, and the Internet Accounts dialog box appears with the new mail account, as shown in the illustration.

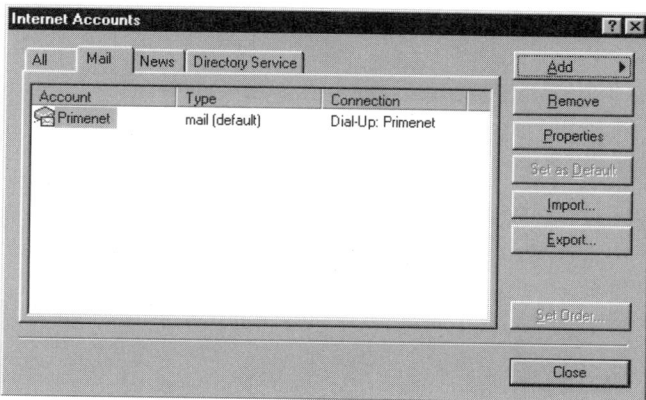

⑪ Close the Internet Accounts dialog box.

Set up your news account

In this exercise, you set up a news account from within the Outlook Express window.

1 If necessary, on the Windows taskbar, click the Start button, point to Programs, and click Outlook Express.

The Outlook Express window opens.

important

It is not necessary for you to connect to the Internet to configure your news account.

2 On the Tools menu, click Accounts.

The Internet Accounts dialog box opens.

3 Click the Add button.

A shortcut menu appears.

4 Click News.

The Internet Connection Wizard dialog box opens.

5 In the Display Name text box, type your name (if necessary), and then click Next.

The Internet News E-mail Address dialog box opens.

6 In the E-mail Address text box, type your e-mail address (if necessary), and click Next.

The Internet News Server Name dialog box opens.

7 In the News (NNTP) Server text box, type the news server name provided by your ISP, click Next, and then click Finish.

The Internet Connection Wizard dialog box closes, and the Internet Accounts dialog box appears with the new news account.

8 Close the Internet Accounts dialog box.

An alert box appears, asking if you want to download newsgroups from the news server.

9 Click Yes.

If you have a 56 Kbps modem or slower, this process will take 10 minutes or longer; however, you will have to do this only once.

Specifying Default E-mail and Newsreader Applications

You can configure Internet Explorer to use any newsreader or e-mail application installed on your computer. Selecting a default e-mail application means that whenever you click an e-mail link while on a Web page or choose a Mail command in Internet Explorer or in a newsreader, the default e-mail application opens. Similarly, setting a default newsreader means that when you click a newsgroup link on a Web page or choose a News command in Internet Explorer, the default newsreader application opens.

Specify Outlook Express as the default e-mail application and newsreader

In this exercise, you configure Internet Explorer to use Outlook Express by default whenever a procedure involves using an e-mail application or newsreader.

1️⃣   Start Internet Explorer.

2️⃣   On the Tools menu, click Internet Options.

       The Internet Options dialog box opens.

3️⃣   Click the Programs tab.

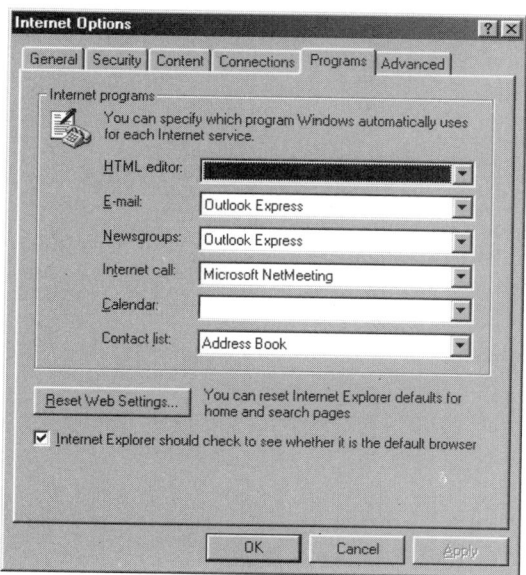

④ If necessary, click the E-mail drop-down arrow, and click Outlook Express.

Outlook Express is selected to be your default e-mail application.

⑤ If necessary, click the Newsgroups drop-down arrow, and click Outlook Express.

Outlook Express is selected to be your default newsreader application.

⑥ Click OK.

The Internet Options dialog box closes.

⑦ Quit Internet Explorer.

Configuring NetMeeting

NetMeeting is Internet Explorer's multimedia conferencing application. NetMeeting enables you to use your speakers, microphone, video camera, keyboard, and mouse to communicate with others on the Internet in real-time. To use these features, you must configure NetMeeting to work with your communication hardware. If NetMeeting is your default conferencing program, the NetMeeting Wizard runs automatically the first time you place an Internet call.

Recommended Hardware Requirements

To gain optimal performance from NetMeeting, your computer should meet the following requirements:

- 16 MB RAM
- 90 MHz Pentium processor or better (133 MHz is best if you're using video)
- Sound card
- Video card
- Speakers
- Video camera
- Microphone

important

NetMeeting is an Internet Explorer add-on component. To learn how to incorporate add-on components with your Internet Explorer setup, see the "One Step Further: Adding Components" section in Lesson 4.

Configure NetMeeting

In this exercise, you configure NetMeeting by working with the Microsoft NetMeeting Wizard.

important

It is not necessary for you to connect to the Internet to configure your NetMeeting settings.

❶ Start Internet Explorer.

❷ On the File menu, point to New, and click Internet Call.

The Microsoft NetMeeting Wizard opens, as shown in the illustration.

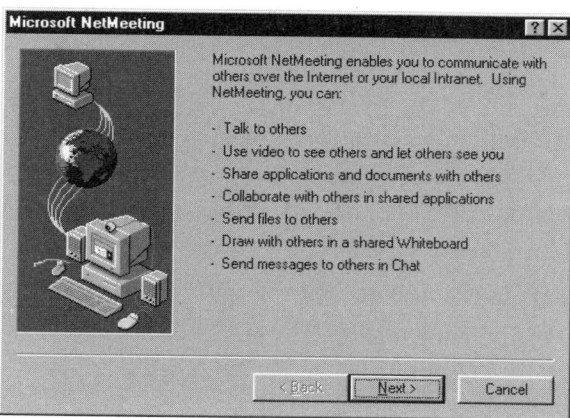

❸ Click Next.

The next Microsoft NetMeeting Wizard dialog box appears.

❹ Specify whether you want to log on to the directory server when NetMeeting starts.

If you have a slow Internet connection, you might not choose to automatically log on to a directory server. Directory servers are often busy and can sometimes be difficult to log on to. Further, if the person you are calling is logged on to a server, you do not need to log on.

5 Use the drop-down arrow to select a default directory server, and click Next.

A default directory server is selected, and the next wizard dialog box appears.

6 Enter your personal information in the first three fields and in any other fields, if desired.

The City/State, Country, and Comments sections are not essential. Keep in mind that the information provided in this dialog box appears to others whenever you log on to a directory server.

7 Click Next.

The next wizard dialog box opens.

8 Click the option representing the speed of your Internet connection, and click Next.

The Audio Tuning Wizard opens, indicating that you are about to tune your audio settings.

9 Click Next.

The next wizard dialog box opens.

10 If you want, select Recording and Play Back settings, and click the Next button.

11 Click the Test button.

A sound clip is played, and the Test button changes to a Stop button.

If you can't hear the sound test, make sure your speaker volume controls are turned up.

12 Adjust the dialog box's audio control by dragging the volume slider left or right, click Stop, and then click Next.

The speaker test is completed, and the next wizard dialog box opens.

13 Read the test statement into your microphone, adjust the volume control if necessary, and then click Next.

The microphone test is completed, and the final wizard dialog box appears.

If the microphone test is unsuccessful, make sure your microphone is plugged into your sound card and not your voice modem.

14 Click Finish.

NetMeeting starts automatically.

15 Quit NetMeeting, and then quit Internet Explorer.

Using a Configuration Script

If you will be connecting to the Internet via your organization's local area network, your network administrator will probably perform all or most of the Internet Explorer and Outlook Express setup procedures for you. However, you might be asked to specify a *configuration script* when you first use Internet Explorer. A configuration script is much like the setup program that an ISP supplies to new subscribers. The script file is located on a network server or on your hard disk drive and supplies Internet Explorer with all of the network settings required to pass you through the network server and out to the Internet. You need to supply the address of the computer that contains the configuration script (or the filename) only if the script is located on your computer. This address should be supplied to you by your network administrator and will be a URL or an IP address.

Specify the address of a configuration script

In this exercise, you specify the address of a configuration script that will provide the Internet Explorer settings required to pass you from the network server out to the Internet.

1 On your desktop, click the Internet Explorer icon.

Internet Explorer is started. Don't worry if Explorer displays a "page not found" message. This message will not occur after you specify the configuration script address.

2 On the Tools menu, click Internet Options.

The Internet Options dialog box is displayed.

3 Click the Connections tab.

The Connections tab provides options for connecting to the Internet.

4 Click the LAN Settings button.

The Local Area Network (LAN) Settings dialog box appears as shown on the following page.

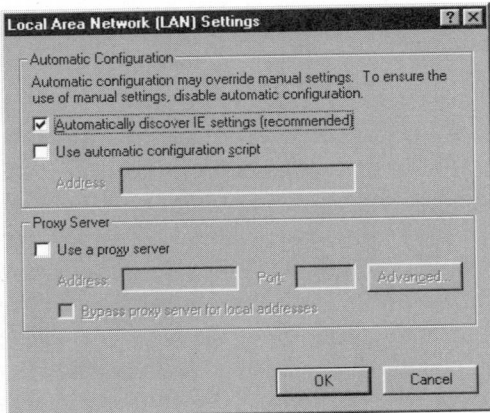

5 Click the Use Automatic Configuration Script check box.

The Address text box is no longer gray, indicating that you can now specify the address where the script resides.

6 Type the address or filename supplied to you by your network administrator, and then click OK.

The Internet Options dialog box is redisplayed.

7 Click OK.

The Internet Options dialog box closes.

8 Quit Internet Explorer, and then restart it.

The configuration script settings will now be used whenever you start Internet Explorer.

B

If You're New to Windows

If you are new to Microsoft Windows, this appendix will show you the basics you need to get started. You'll get an overview of Windows features, and you'll learn how to use online Help to answer your questions and find out more about using the Windows operating systems.

If You're New to Windows

Windows is an easy-to-use computer environment that helps you handle the daily work that you perform with your computer. You can use Windows 95, Windows 98, or Windows NT to run Internet Explorer—the explanations in this appendix are included for all of these operating systems.

The way you use Windows 95, Windows 98, Windows NT, and programs designed for these operating systems is similar. The programs look much alike, and you use similar menus to tell them what to do. In this section, you'll learn how to operate the basic program.

Start Windows

Starting Windows is as easy as turning on your computer.

❶   If your computer isn't on, turn it on now.

❷   If you are using Windows NT, press Ctrl+Alt+Del to display a dialog box asking for your user name and password. If you are using Windows 95 or Windows 98, you will see this dialog box if your computer is connected to a network.

❸   Type your user name and password in the appropriate boxes, and click OK.

   If you don't know your user name or password, contact your system administrator for assistance.

Close

4 If you see the Welcome dialog box, click the Close button.
Your screen should look similar to the following illustration.

My Computer   Desktop

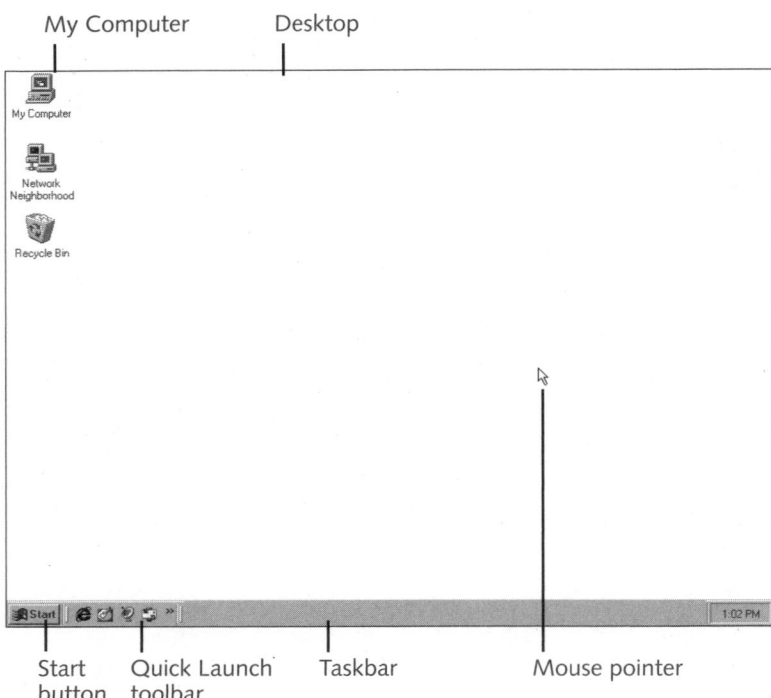

Start   Quick Launch'   Taskbar   Mouse pointer
button   toolbar

Using the Mouse

Although you can use the keyboard for most actions, many actions are easier to
do using a *mouse*. The mouse controls a pointer on the screen, as shown in the
above illustration. You move the pointer by sliding the mouse over a flat sur-
face in the direction you want the pointer to move. If you run out of room to
move the mouse, lift it up and then put it down in another location.

important

In this book, we assume that your mouse is set up so that the left button is the
primary button and the right button is the secondary button. If your mouse is
configured the opposite way, for left-handed use, use the right button when we
tell you to use the left, and vice versa.

You'll use five basic mouse actions throughout this book.

When you are directed to	Do this
Point to an item	Move the mouse to place the pointer over the item.
Click an item	Point to the item on your screen, and quickly press and release the left mouse button.
Right-click an item	Point to the item on your screen, and then quickly press and release the right mouse button. Clicking the right mouse button often displays a shortcut menu with a list of command choices that apply to that item.
Double-click an item	Point to the item, and then quickly press and release the left mouse button twice.
Drag an item	Point to an item, and then hold down the left mouse button as you move the pointer. Once the item is moved to the appropriate location, release the left mouse button.

Using Window Controls

All programs designed for Windows have common elements that you use to scroll, size, move, and close a window.

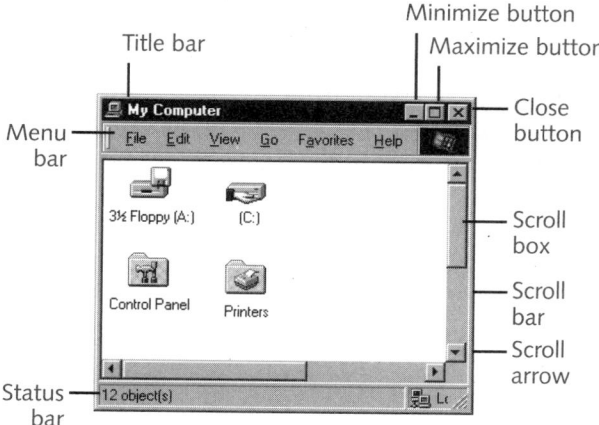

To	Do this	Button
Move, or *scroll*, vertically or horizontally through the contents of a window that extends beyond the screen	Click a scroll bar or scroll arrow, or drag the scroll box. The previous illustration identifies these screen elements.	
Enlarge a window to fill the screen	Click the Maximize button, or double-click the window title bar.	
Restore a window to its previous size	Click the Restore button, or double-click the window title bar. When a window is maximized, the Maximize button changes to the Restore button.	
Reduce a window to a button on the Windows taskbar	Click the Minimize button. To display a minimized window, click its button on the Windows taskbar.	
Move a window	Drag the window title bar.	
Close a window	Click the Close button.	

Using Menus

Just like a restaurant menu, a program menu provides a list of options from which you can choose. On program menus, these options are called *commands*. To select a menu or a menu command, click the item you want.

tip

You can also use the keyboard to make menu selections. Press the Alt key to activate the menu bar, press the key that corresponds to the highlighted or underlined letter of the menu name, and then press the key that corresponds to the highlighted or underlined letter of the command name.

In the following exercise, you'll open and make selections from a menu.

Open and make selections from a menu

1 On the desktop, double-click the My Computer icon.

The My Computer window opens.

You can also press Alt+E to open the Edit menu.

2 In the My Computer window, on the menu bar, click Edit.

The Edit menu appears. Some commands are disabled; this means they aren't available.

Your screen should look similar to the following illustration.

Command is not available

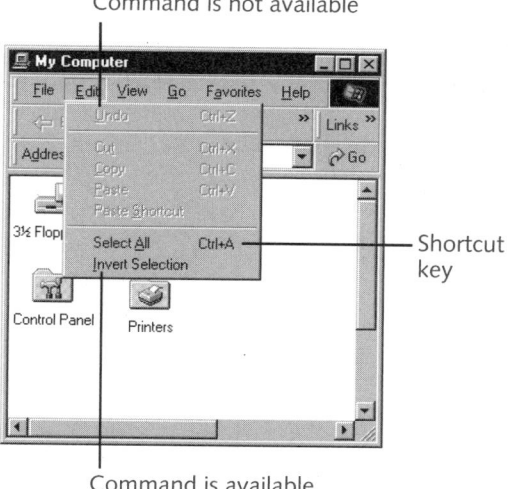

Shortcut key

Command is available

❸   Click Edit again to close the menu.

❹   On the menu bar, click View to open the View menu.

❺   On the View menu, click Status Bar if there isn't a check mark beside it. Then click View again.

Your screen should look similar to the following illustration.

A check mark means that multiple items within a group can be simultaneously selected. A bullet means that only one item can be selected.

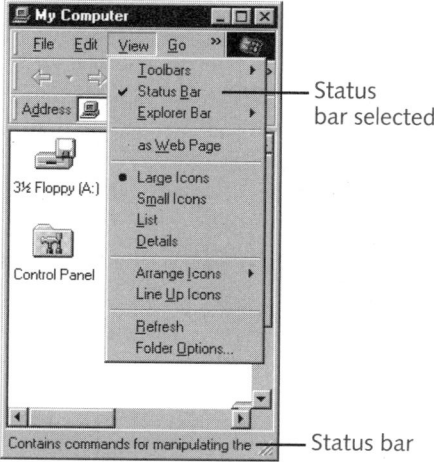

Status bar selected

Status bar

❻   On the View menu, click Status Bar again.

The menu closes, and the status bar is no longer displayed.

Your screen should look similar to the following illustration.

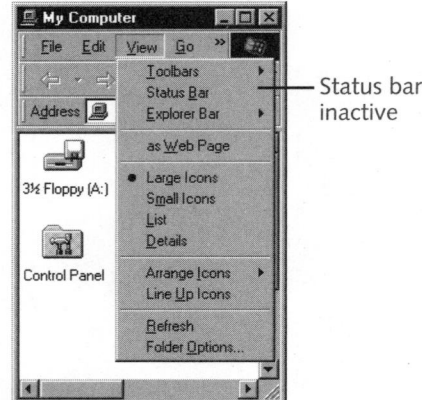

Status bar
inactive

*A right-point-
ing arrow
appearing
after a com-
mand name
means that
additional
commands are
available.*

7 On the View menu, click Status Bar again.

The status bar is displayed.

8 On the View menu, point to Arrange Icons.

A submenu listing additional menu choices appears.

9 Click By Drive Letter.

The icons representing the drives on your computer are arranged alphabetically by drive letter.

10 In the upper-right corner of the My Computer window, click the Close button
to close the window.

Close

tip

If you do a lot of typing, you might want to learn the key combinations for commands you use frequently. Pressing the key combination is a quick way to activate a command. If a key combination is available for a command, it is listed to
the right of the command name on the menu. For example, on the Edit menu,
Ctrl+C is listed as the key combination for the Copy command.

Using Dialog Boxes

When you choose a command name that is followed by an ellipsis (...), a dialog box appears so that you can provide more information about how the command should be carried out. Dialog boxes have standard features, as shown in the following illustration.

Tab   Text box

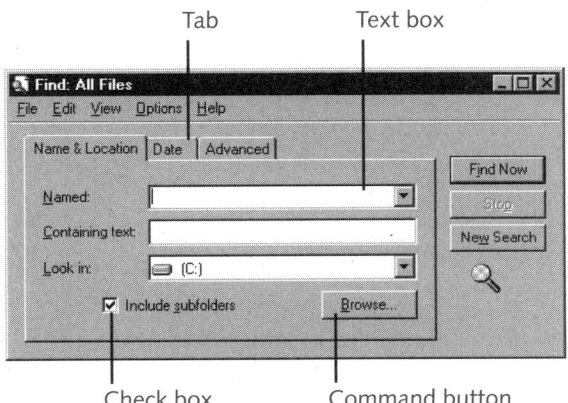

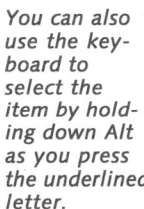

You can also use the keyboard to select the item by holding down Alt as you press the underlined letter.

Check box   Command button

To enter text in a text box, click inside the box and begin typing. Or you can press the Tab key to move around the dialog box.

Display the Taskbar Properties dialog box

Some dialog boxes provide several categories of options displayed on separate tabs. In this exercise, you customize the list of programs that appears on your Start menu.

❶ On the Windows taskbar, click the Start button.

The Start menu appears.

❷ On the Start menu, point to Settings. In Windows 95 and NT, click Taskbar. In Windows 98, click Taskbar & Start Menu.

The Taskbar Properties dialog box appears.

Click the top of an obscured tab to make it visible.

❸ In the Taskbar Properties dialog box, click the Start Menu Programs tab to make it active.

❹ Click the Taskbar Options tab, and then select the Show Small Icons In Start Menu check box.

When a check box is selected, it displays a check mark.

Click here ———

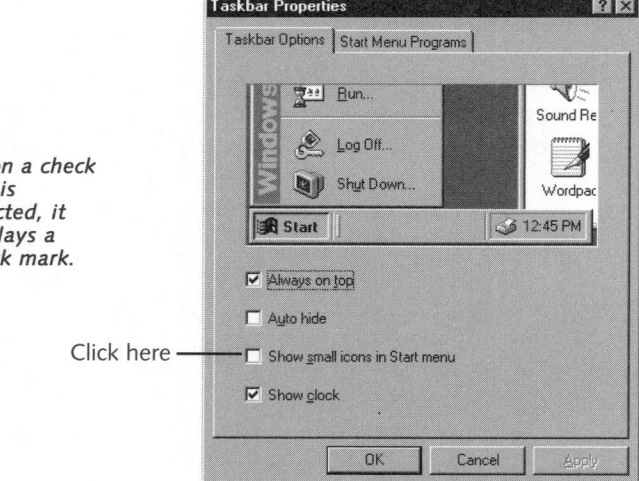

⑤   Clear the check box, and then select it again; be sure to watch how the display in the dialog box changes.

Clearing a check box will turn off the option, and selecting a check box will turn on the option.

⑥   Click the Cancel button.

The dialog box closes without changing any settings.

Getting Help with Windows

When you're at work and you have a question, you might ask a coworker or consult a reference book. To find out more about functions and features in Windows, you can use the Help system. Using Windows Help is one of the quickest, most efficient ways to find your answer. You can access Windows Help from the Start menu. For Help specific to a program, such as Internet Explorer, each Windows program also includes its own Help system.

After the Help window opens, you can choose one of three ways to best research your question. To find instructions about broad categories, you can look on the Contents tab. Or you can search the Help index to find information about specific topics. Finally, you can look on the last tab (in Windows 95 and Windows NT, the Find tab; in Windows 98, the Search tab) to search the Help files based on keywords that you provide. The Help topics are short and concise, so you can get the exact information you need quickly. There are also shortcut icons in many Help topics that you can use to directly go to or to perform the task you want or to list Related Topics.

In Windows 98, on the Help toolbar, click Web Help to automatically connect to Microsoft's Support Online Web site. Once connected, you can expand your search to include the Microsoft Knowledge Base, Troubleshooting Wizards, Newsgroups, and downloadable files. Just follow the directions on the screen.

Viewing Help Contents

The Contents tab is organized like a book's table of contents. As you choose top-level topics, called *chapters*, you see a list of more detailed subtopics from which to choose.

Find Help about general categories

Suppose you want to see what documents you've chosen to print. In this exercise, you look up Windows Help instructions for finding out this information.

Windows 95 and NT

1. On the Windows taskbar, click Start, and then click Help.

   The Help Topics window appears.

2. If necessary, click the Contents tab to make it active.

3. Double-click How To.

   The icon changes to an open book, and a set of subtopics appears.

4. Double-click Print.

   More subtopics appear.

5. Double-click Viewing Documents Waiting To Be Printed.

   A Help window appears.

6. In Windows 95, to see a definition of *print queue,* click the underlined words.

   A pop-up window containing the definition of the term appears.

7. Click anywhere outside that window to close it.

8. In both Windows 95 and Windows NT, read the information about viewing documents in the print queue, and then close Help.

Windows 98

1. On the Windows taskbar, click Start, and then click Help.

   The Windows Help window appears.

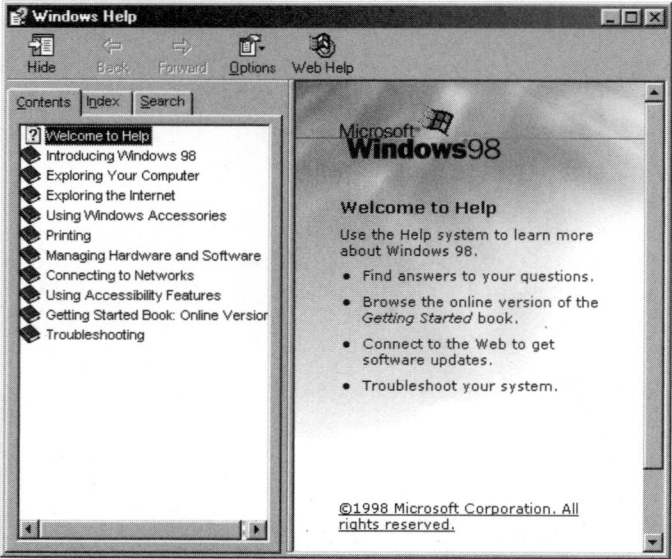

2️⃣ If necessary, click the Contents tab to make it active.

3️⃣ Click Printing.

The icon changes to an open book, and a set of subtopics appears.

4️⃣ Click View A List Of Documents Waiting To Be Printed.

The topic appears in the right frame of the Windows Help window.

5️⃣ To see a definition of *print queue,* in the right frame, click the underlined words.

A pop-up window containing the definition of the term appears.

6️⃣ Click anywhere outside that window to close it.

7️⃣ Read the information about viewing documents in the print queue, and then close Windows Help.

Finding Help About Specific Topics

The two remaining tabs in the Windows Help window allow you to find specific Help topics. The Index tab is organized like a book's index. Keywords for topics are organized alphabetically. You can either type the keyword you want to find or scroll through the list of keywords. You can then select from one or more topic choices.

On the Find or Search tab, you can also enter a keyword. The main difference between these two tabs is that you get a list of all Help topics in which that keyword appears, not just the topics that begin with that word.

Find specific Help topics by using the Help index

In this exercise, you use the Help index to learn how to print help topics.

Windows 95

1 On the Windows taskbar, click Start, and then click Help.
The Help Topics window appears.

2 Click the Index tab to make it active.

3 In the text box, type **printing**
A list of printing-related topics appears.

4 In that list, click Help Information, Printing A Copy Of, and click Display.
The Windows Help window appears.

5 Read the information, and then close Windows Help.

Windows NT

1 On the Windows taskbar, click Start, and then click Help.
The Windows NT Help window appears.

2 Click the Index tab to make it active.

3 In the text box, type **printing**
A list of printing-related topics appears.

4 In that list, click Help Topics, and then click Display.
The Windows NT Help window appears.

5 Read the Help topic, and then close Windows Help.

Windows 98

1 On the Windows taskbar, click Start, and then click Help.
The Windows Help window appears.

2 Click the Index tab to make it active.

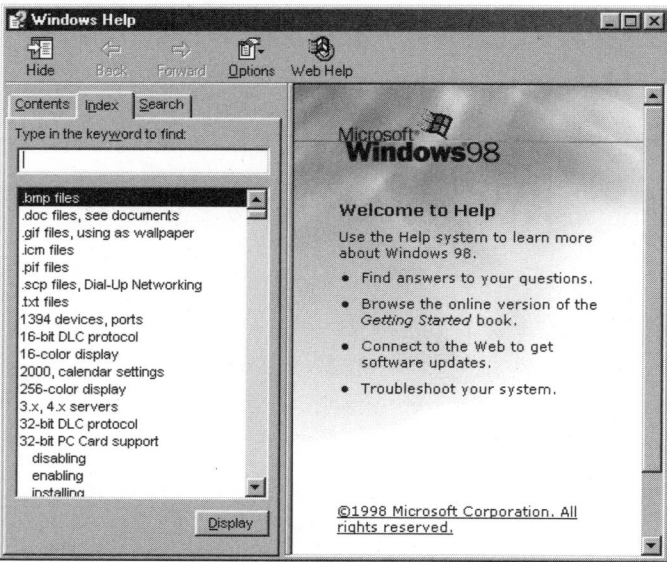

❸   In the Type In The Keywords To Find box, type **printing**

A list of printing-related topics appears.

❹   In that list, click Help Topics, and then click Display.

The topic is displayed in the frame on the right side of the Help window.

❺   Click the underlined word, *frame*.

A pop-up window containing an explanation of the term appears.

❻   Click anywhere outside that window to close it.

❼   Read the information about printing Help topics, and close Windows Help.

Find specific Help topics by using the Find or Search tab

In this exercise, you use the Find or Search tab to learn how to print a document.

Windows 95

❶   On the Windows taskbar, click Start, and then click Help.

The Help window appears.

❷   Click the Find tab to make it active.

❸   If you are using Find for the first time, the Find Setup Wizard dialog box appears. Click Next, and then click Finish to complete and close the wizard.

The wizard creates a search index for your Help files. This might take a few minutes.

4 In the text box, type **print**

All printing-related topics are displayed in the third list box.

5 In the Click A Topic Then Click Display list, scroll down, click Printing A Document, and then click Display.

The Windows Help window appears.

6 Read the information about printing a document, and close Windows Help.

Windows NT

1 On the Windows taskbar, click Start, and then click Help.

The Windows NT Help window appears.

2 Click the Find tab to make it active.

3 If the Find Setup Wizard appears, click Next, and then click Finish to complete and close the wizard.

The wizard creates a search index for your Help files. This might take a few minutes.

4 In the text box, type **printing**

All printing-related topics are displayed in the third list box.

5 In the Click A Topic Then Click Display list, scroll down, click To Print A Document, and then click Display.

The Windows NT Help window appears.

6 Read the information about printing a document, and then close Windows NT Help.

Windows 98

1 On the Windows taskbar, click Start, and then click Help.

The Windows Help window appears.

2 Click the Search tab to make it active.

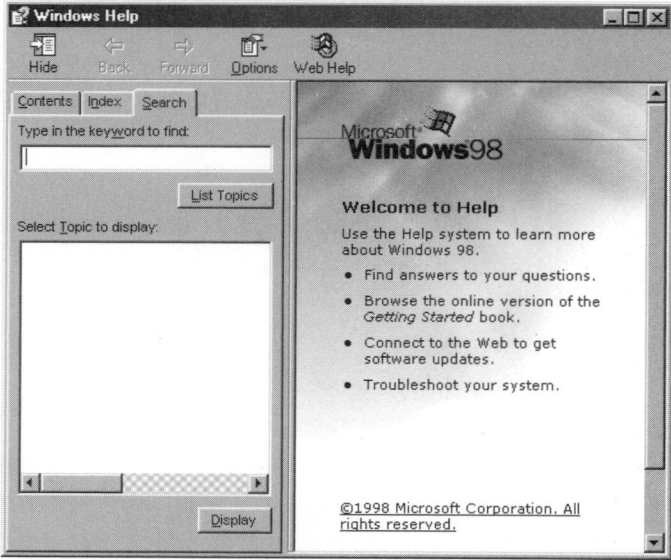

❸   In the Type In The Keyword To Find box, type **print** and click List Topics.

A list of print-related topics is displayed in the Select Topic To Display list box.

❹   In the Select Topic To Display list box, scroll down, click To Print A Document, and then click Display.

The topic is displayed in the right frame of the Windows Help window.

❺   Read the information about printing a document, and close Windows Help.

Find Help in a dialog box

Almost every dialog box includes a question mark–shaped Help button in the upper-right corner of its window. When you click this button and then click any dialog box item, a Help window appears that explains what the item is and how to use it. In this exercise, you'll get help in a dialog box.

❶   On the Windows taskbar, click Start, and then click Run.

The Run dialog box appears.

❷   Click the Help button.

The mouse pointer changes to an arrow with a question mark.

❸   Click the Open text box.

A pop-up window providing information about how to use the Open text box appears.

④ Click anywhere outside the Help window to close it.

The mouse pointer returns to its previous shape.

⑤ Close the Run dialog box.

---

tip

Windows NT and Windows 95 users can change the way the Help topics appear on the screen. In any Help topic window, click Options, point to Font, and then click a font size option to change the size of the text.

Quit Windows

Close

① If you are finished using Windows, close any open windows by clicking the Close button in each window.

② On the Windows taskbar, click Start, and then click Shut Down.

The Shut Down Windows window appears.

Windows 95

③ Be sure the Shut Down The Computer option is selected, and then click Yes.

A message indicates that it is now safe to turn off your computer.

Windows 98

③ Be sure the Shut Down option is selected, and then click OK.

A message indicates that it is now safe to turn off your computer.

---

important

To avoid loss of data or damage to your operating system, always quit Windows by using the Shut Down command on the Start menu before you turn off your computer.

Windows NT

③ Be sure the Shut Down The Computer option is selected, and then click Yes.

A message indicates that it is now safe to turn off your computer.

Index

Page numbers in italics indicate references that are illustrated.

A

ActiveX controls, 81
Address bar
    defined, 6
    helpful hints, 14
    using, 10, 72–73
    searching, 29
Address Book, 166–71, 248
Address, IP. *See* IP Addresses
animated GIFs
    defined, 125
    viewing, 128–29
attachments, e-mail
    defined, 150
    opening, 162
    using, 155–56, 162
    viewing, 162
audio. *See* multimedia; NetMeeting; Windows
    Media Player
Autosearch
    defined, 29
    using, 29, 33

B

Back button
    defined, 9
    using, 12, 72
backgrounds
    changing color of, 54–56, 58–60, 74
    printing, 16

browsers. *See also* Internet Explorer
    adding components, 98–99. *See also specific*
        component names
    defined, 4
    navigating, 9–10, 12–13
    opening, 5
    upgrading components, 98–99
browsing, 6–7
buffers, 129–30
business cards. *See* electronic business cards
buttons. *See specific button names*; toolbars
    adding, 61
    customizing, 18
    removing, 62

C

cache. *See also* Temporary Internet Files folder
    clearing, 197
    defined, 46
channels, 34
Chat window. *See also* NetMeeting
    closing, 227
    defined, 226
    opening, 227
    printing messages, 228
    receiving messages, 227, 250
    saving, 228
    sending messages, 227, 250
    sending private messages, 227
code, country, 7
collaborating, 235–36, 240–41, 250
components
    adding, 98–99
    defined, 81
    list of, 98
conferencing. *See* NetMeeting
configuring
    Content Advisor, 87, 88, 90–91, 140
    History folder settings, 45
    multimedia settings, 133–36
    Temporary Internet Files folder, 47–48

Content Advisor
    defined, 86–87
    disabling, 92
    enabling, 87, 89
    configuring, 87, 88, 90–91, 140
    password, 89, 91
copyrights, 18
country code, 7
credit card security. *See* **Microsoft Wallet**
customizing
    background colors, 54–56, 58–59
    buttons, 18
    display, 57
    layout of Outlook Express, 147–148
    link underlines, 68–69
    Search Assistant, 32
    text, 55–58
    toolbar, 60–63
    view, 54–57, 60

D

desktop
    adding to Favorites, 36
    shortcut, 14–15
    Web Style feature, 4
digital certificates, 93
digital IDs, 175–79
domain name,
    defined, 6
    second-level, 6
    top-level, 6–7
downloading
    defined, 9
    helpful hints, 13

E

electronic business cards
    adding, 172-173
    creating, 172
electronic mail. *See* e-mail

e-mail. *See also* **Outlook Express**
    Address Book, 166–71, 248
    addresses, defined, 148–49
    attachments, 150, 155–56, 162
    blocked senders, 159–60
    creating messages, 148–49, 152–53
    customizing layout, 147–48
    digital IDs, 175–79
    directory services, 173–75
    electronic business cards, 172–73
    forwarding, 163–65
    HTML, 149
    MSN Hotmail, 150
    opening, 160–61
    plain text, 149
    printing messages, 165–66
    receiving messages, 156–59
    replying to messages, 163–64
    sending messages, 149–52, 248
    signature, 150, 154–55, 248
    stationery, 149, 153–54
    storing messages, 157
e-mail directory services. *See also* **Outlook**
    Express
    defined, 173
    Find People, 174
embedded files, 21
encoded content, 92
encrypted content
    defined, 93
    digital IDs, 175

F

FAQ, 199
Favorites list
    accessing from Windows, 38
    adding desktop to, 36, 72
    adding entries, 34–36, 72, 141
    creating folders, 39
    defined, 34
    deleting, 43

Favorites list, *continued*
   deleting offline content, 118–19
   exercises, 72
   filling folders, 40–42
   managing, 38–43
   marking for offline viewing, 105–6
   naming links, 43
   renaming links, 42
   synchronizing, 111–15, 141
   using Favorites bar, 37–38
   using Favorites menu, 38
filenames, 7
File Transfer Protocol. *See* FTP; protocols
find. *See also* Search Assistant; searching
   command, defined, 10
   Find People, 174
   ILS directory, 214, 221
   information, 73
   IP address, 216, 218–19
   text, 14
folders
   history, 43–46, 74
   path, 7
Forward button
   defined, 9
   using, 12, 72
frames
   defined, 11
   printing, 17, 19–20
   saving, 22
Frequently Asked Questions. *See* FAQ
FTP
   defined, 8, 237
   sending, 238
   using, 237

G

GIF, 126
Graphic Interchange Format, 126
gopher, 8

graphics
   animated, 125, 128–29
   file formats, 124–26
   illustrations, 124
   photographs, 125, 127–28
   view properties, 126–27

H

help. *See* Personal Support Center
History button, 44
History folder
   clearing, 46, 74
   configuring settings, 45
   defined, 43
   viewing, 44–45, 74
Home button
   defined, 10
   using, 13
home pages
   defined, 7, 10
   returning to, 13
   specifying, 52–53
hover
   color, changing, 67–68, 74
   defined, 65–66
   underlining, 68
   using, 67
HTML
   defined, 21
   e-mail, 149
HTTP, 6, 8
HTTPS, 8, 85
hyperlinks
   customizing link underlines, 68–69
   changing color, 65–67, 74
   defined, 6, 64
   displaying, 53–54
   hover colors, 65–68
   printing, 17, 19–20
   using, 11, 72

Hypertext Markup Language. *See* HTML
Hypertext Transfer Protocol. *See* HTTP; protocols
Hypertext Transfer Protocol, Secure, 8, 85

I

identities, 200
illustrations. *See* graphics
ILS directory
  defined, 214–15
  SpeedDial, 221
Internet, 4
Internet Explorer
  adding components, 98–99
  features, 9, 10, 11,
  introduction, 4
  offline, 116–17
  protocol, 8
  starting, 4–5
  status bar, 53–54
  upgrading components, 98–99
Internet Locator Service directory. *See* ILS directory
intranet
  defined, 80
IP addresses,
  defined, 215
  finding, 216, 218–219

J

Joint Photographic Experts Group, 126
JPEG, 126

K

keywords, 28

L

LAN, 5, 216
links. *See* hyperlinks

Links toolbar
  adding, 64–65
  removing, 64–65
local area network. *See* LAN
logging on, 214

M

messages
  Chat, 226–28, 250
  e-mail, 148–49, 152–53
  newsgroup, 191–93, 194, 200–2, 205–7
  posting, 199, 202, 249
  printing, 165–66, 203, 228
  saving, 228
Microsoft Wallet. *See also* Content Advisor
  credit card information, 94–97, 140
  defined, 92–93
  encryption, 92
  installing, 93
  password, 92
  personal information, 93–94
MSN Hotmail, 150
multimedia. *See also* graphics; Windows Media Player
  activating selected elements, 135
  conferencing, 212. *See also* NetMeeting
  configuring, 133–36
  deactivating, 134
  default settings, 136
  defined, 123
  sounds, 130–32, 140
  Shockwave, 137, 140
  video, 132–36

N

navigating, 6–7, 9–12
NetMeeting. *See also* Chat window; Whiteboard
  audio, 221–23, 225, 250
  collaborating, 235–36, 240–41, 250

NetMeeting, *continued*
  defined, 211
  FTP, 237–38
  ILS directory, 214–15
  IP addresses, 215–16, 218–19, 250
  local area network (LAN), 216
  opening, 212–14
  options, 216–17
  placing a call, 215, 218–21
  preview video, 224
  sharing applications, 235–36, 239
  sharing files, 235–36
  SpeedDial list, 221
  video, 219, 221–25, 250
newsgroups. *See also* **newsreader**
  accessing offline, 196–98
  classifications, 186
  defined, 183–85
  finding, 187–90
  subscribing, 186, 187, 190–91, 196, 249
  unsubscribing, 191
newsreader. *See also* **newsgroups; Outlook**
    Express
  defined, 183–85
  deleting messages, 205–7
  Local File Clean Up, 206–7
  opening message in new window, 194
  Outlook Express, 183–84
  posting messages, 199, 202, 249
  printing posts, 203
  replying, 200–2
  threads, 191–92, 194–96
  viewing messages, 191–93
news server, 184
Next button, 28

O

offline, working. *See* **working offline**
online support. *See* **Personal Support Center**

Outlook Express. *See also* **e-mail; newsreader**
  compact folders, 205
  creating identities, 200
  defined, 145
  empty folders, 204–5
  Local File Clean Up, 206–7
  opening, 147
  setting default, 146

P

personal information, security. *See* **Microsoft**
    Wallet
Personal Support Center
  accessing, 241–42
  defined, 241
  searching, 243
pictures. *See* **graphics**
photographs. *See* **graphics**
Play button, 131
PNG, 126
Portable Network Graphics. *See* **PNG**
posts, 184, 185
  posting messages, 199, 202, 249
  printing, 203
  replying to, 200–2
  viewing, 191–93
preferences, 86–88
printing
  backgrounds, 16
  button, 15, 17
  Chat messages, 228
  color, 16
  e-mail messages, 165–66
  entire Web page, 15–16, 72
  frames, 17, 19–20
  hyperlinks, 17
  linked documents, 19–20
  newsgroup messages, 203
  options, 15, 17

printing, *continued*
  selected items, 15, 18–19
  table of links, 20
  Whiteboard, 233–34
Print button, 15, 17
progressive loading, 126
protocols
  defined, 6
  file, 8
  gopher, 8
  FTP, 8, 237–38
  HTTP, 8
  HTTPS, 8, 85
  telnet, 8
  WAIS, 8

R

Refresh button
  defined, 9
  using, 13
remote users, 215
rule lines, 124

S

saving
  as archive file, 21–23
  entire Web page, 21–22
  HTML file, 21, 23
  options, 21
  text only, 21–23
  viewing saved pages, 21, 24
scanning, 125
Search Assistant
  customizing settings, 32
  displaying, 29–30
  opening, 28
  using, 29–33

Search button, 28
search engine
  defined, 28
  selecting, 31–32
  using, 29, 73
searching. *See also* **Search Assistant**
  using Address bar, 28–29
  using Autosearch, 29, 33
  using Search button, 28
security. *See also* **Content Advisor; Microsoft Wallet**
  credit card information, 94–97, 140
  digital IDs, 175–78
  personal information, 93–94
security levels. *See also* **Microsoft Wallet; security zones**
  defined, 82
  selecting, 83–84
  settings, 81–82
security zones. *See also* **Microsoft Wallet; security levels**
  adding, 85–86
  classifying, 80
  defined, 80, 82
  managing, 84–86
  removing, 85–86
  viewing, 83
server, 6
sharing, 235
Shockwave, 137, 140
shortcuts, desktop, 14–15. *See also* **Favorites list**
signature, e-mail
  creating, 154–55, 248
  defined, 150
snail mail, 148
sound. *See* **multimedia; Windows Media Player**
spam, 199
SpeedDial lists, 221

stationery, 149
status bar
    defined, 53–54
    displaying, 54, 74
    hiding, 54, 74
    location, 53
Stop button
    defined, 9
    using, 12
streaming, 130
subject words. *See* keywords
subscribing, 187
support, online. *See* Personal Support Center
synchronizing
    creating schedule for, 111–14
    defined, 104, 107, 110
    existing schedule, 114–15
    newsgroups, 196–98
    using, 108–9

T

telnet, 8
Temporary Internet Files folder
    caching, 46
    configuring settings, 47–48
    deleting files, 48, 74
    updating, 47
text
    color, 56, 58–60, 74
    e-mail, 149
    finding, 10, 14
    size, 55, 57–58
threads
    collapsing, 195–96
    defined, 191–92
    disabling, 194
    expanding, 195–96
toolbars. *See also* Links toolbar
    adding buttons to, 61–62, 74
    changing button positions, 63
    customizing, 60

toolbars, *continued*
    displaying icons, 62
    displaying text labels, 63
    hiding text labels, 63
    moving buttons, 63
    removing buttons, 61–62
    Whiteboard buttons, 230
transparency, 126

U

Uniform Resource Locator. *See* URL
URL
    defined, 6–7
    navigating, 9
Usenet, 184
user assistance. *See* Personal Support Center

V

vCards. *See* e-mail; electronic business cards
views
    alternating, 60
    color, 58–60
    customizing, 54–57, 60
    review, 72, 73–74
    saved pages, 21, 24
    text size, 57
video. *See* multimedia; NetMeeting; Windows
        Media Player

W

WAIS, 8
Web pages, 4
Web sites, 4
Web Style feature, 4
Whiteboard. *See also* NetMeeting
    defined, 212
    locking, 233
    printing, 233–34
    saving, 234

Whiteboard, *continued*
    toolbar buttons, *230*
    using, 229, 231–32, 250
Wide Area Information Server, 8
Windows Media Player
    defined, 129
    multimedia formats, 130
    sound files, 130–32
    streaming, 130
    video files, 132–36

World Wide Web, 3–4
working offline
    defined, 103
    deleting offline content, 118–19
    marking Web sites, 104–6
    newsgroups, 196–98
    synchronizing files, 108–9, 141
    viewing, 115, 117
www, 3–4

ActiveEducation & Microsoft Press

Microsoft Internet Explorer 5 Step by Step has been created by the professional trainers and writers at ActiveEducation, Inc., to the exacting standards you've come to expect from Microsoft Press. Together, we are pleased to present this self-paced training guide, which you can use individually or as part of a class.

ActiveEducation creates top-quality information technology training content that teaches essential computer skills for today's workplace. ActiveEducation courses are designed to provide the most effective training available and to help people become more productive computer users. Each ActiveEducation course, including this Step by Step book, undergoes rigorous quality control, instructional design, and technical review procedures to ensure that the course is instructionally and technically superior in content and approach. ActiveEducation (*www.activeeducation.com*) courses are available in book form and on the Internet.

Microsoft Press is the book publishing division of Microsoft Corporation, the leading publisher of information about Microsoft products and services. Microsoft Press is dedicated to providing the highest quality computer books and multimedia training and reference tools that make using Microsoft software easier, more enjoyable, and more productive.

About the Author

Mary Millhollon has over 15 years of computer experience and has more than 10 years of publishing experience. Her most recent publications include *Microsoft Internet Explorer 4 FrontRunner* (Coriolis Group Books) and *Using Microsoft Publisher 98* (ActiveEducation). Within the past year and a half, Mary has also written books about HTML (beginner and advanced) and Outlook.

Due to work and obsession, Mary spends quite a bit of time on the Internet, and she's a strong supporter of communication (especially e-mail). Therefore, if you have specific questions or comments regarding this book or any other Internet-related topic, feel free to e-mail Mary at the following address:

mcmail@primenet.com

MICROSOFT LICENSE AGREEMENT
Book Companion CD

IMPORTANT—READ CAREFULLY: This Microsoft End-User License Agreement ("EULA") is a legal agreement between you (either an individual or an entity) and Microsoft Corporation for the Microsoft product identified above, which includes computer software and may include associated media, printed materials, and "online" or electronic documentation ("SOFTWARE PRODUCT"). Any component included within the SOFTWARE PRODUCT that is accompanied by a separate End-User License Agreement shall be governed by such agreement and not the terms set forth below. By installing, copying, or otherwise using the SOFTWARE PRODUCT, you agree to be bound by the terms of this EULA. If you do not agree to the terms of this EULA, you are not authorized to install, copy, or otherwise use the SOFTWARE PRODUCT; you may, however, return the SOFTWARE PRODUCT, along with all printed materials and other items that form a part of the Microsoft product that includes the SOFTWARE PRODUCT, to the place you obtained them for a full refund.

SOFTWARE PRODUCT LICENSE

The SOFTWARE PRODUCT is protected by United States copyright laws and international copyright treaties, as well as other intellectual property laws and treaties. The SOFTWARE PRODUCT is licensed, not sold.

1. **GRANT OF LICENSE.** This EULA grants you the following rights:

   a. **Software Product.** You may install and use one copy of the SOFTWARE PRODUCT on a single computer. The primary user of the computer on which the SOFTWARE PRODUCT is installed may make a second copy for his or her exclusive use on a portable computer.

   b. **Storage/Network Use.** You may also store or install a copy of the SOFTWARE PRODUCT on a storage device, such as a network server, used only to install or run the SOFTWARE PRODUCT on your other computers over an internal network; however, you must acquire and dedicate a license for each separate computer on which the SOFTWARE PRODUCT is installed or run from the storage device. A license for the SOFTWARE PRODUCT may not be shared or used concurrently on different computers.

   c. **License Pak.** If you have acquired this EULA in a Microsoft License Pak, you may make the number of additional copies of the computer software portion of the SOFTWARE PRODUCT authorized on the printed copy of this EULA, and you may use each copy in the manner specified above. You are also entitled to make a corresponding number of secondary copies for portable computer use as specified above.

   d. **Sample Code.** Solely with respect to portions, if any, of the SOFTWARE PRODUCT that are identified within the SOFTWARE PRODUCT as sample code (the "SAMPLE CODE"):

      i. **Use and Modification.** Microsoft grants you the right to use and modify the source code version of the SAMPLE CODE, *provided* you comply with subsection (d)(iii) below. You may not distribute the SAMPLE CODE, or any modified version of the SAMPLE CODE, in source code form.

      ii. **Redistributable Files.** Provided you comply with subsection (d)(iii) below, Microsoft grants you a nonexclusive, royalty-free right to reproduce and distribute the object code version of the SAMPLE CODE and of any modified SAMPLE CODE, other than SAMPLE CODE, or any modified version thereof, designated as not redistributable in the Readme file that forms a part of the SOFTWARE PRODUCT (the "Non-Redistributable Sample Code"). All SAMPLE CODE other than the Non-Redistributable Sample Code is collectively referred to as the "REDISTRIBUTABLES."

      iii. **Redistribution Requirements.** If you redistribute the REDISTRIBUTABLES, you agree to: (i) distribute the REDISTRIBUTABLES in object code form only in conjunction with and as a part of your software application product; (ii) not use Microsoft's name, logo, or trademarks to market your software application product; (iii) include a valid copyright notice on your software application product; (iv) indemnify, hold harmless, and defend Microsoft from and against any claims or lawsuits, including attorney's fees, that arise or result from the use or distribution of your software application product; and (v) not permit further distribution of the REDISTRIBUTABLES by your end user. Contact Microsoft for the applicable royalties due and other licensing terms for all other uses and/or distribution of the REDISTRIBUTABLES.

2. **DESCRIPTION OF OTHER RIGHTS AND LIMITATIONS.**

   - **Limitations on Reverse Engineering, Decompilation, and Disassembly.** You may not reverse engineer, decompile, or disassemble the SOFTWARE PRODUCT, except and only to the extent that such activity is expressly permitted by applicable law notwithstanding this limitation.

   - **Separation of Components.** The SOFTWARE PRODUCT is licensed as a single product. Its component parts may not be separated for use on more than one computer.

   - **Rental.** You may not rent, lease, or lend the SOFTWARE PRODUCT.

   - **Support Services.** Microsoft may, but is not obligated to, provide you with support services related to the SOFTWARE PRODUCT ("Support Services"). Use of Support Services is governed by the Microsoft policies and programs described in the user manual, in "online" documentation, and/or other Microsoft-provided materials. Any supplemental software code provided to you as part of the Support Services shall be considered part of the SOFTWARE PRODUCT and subject to the terms and conditions of this EULA. With respect to technical information you provide to Microsoft as part of the Support Services, Microsoft may use such information for its business purposes, including for product support and development. Microsoft will not utilize such technical information in a form that personally identifies you.

- **Software Transfer.** You may permanently transfer all of your rights under this EULA, provided you retain no copies, you transfer all of the SOFTWARE PRODUCT (including all component parts, the media and printed materials, any upgrades, this EULA, and, if applicable, the Certificate of Authenticity), **and** the recipient agrees to the terms of this EULA.

- **Termination.** Without prejudice to any other rights, Microsoft may terminate this EULA if you fail to comply with the terms and conditions of this EULA. In such event, you must destroy all copies of the SOFTWARE PRODUCT and all of its component parts.

3. **COPYRIGHT.** All title and copyrights in and to the SOFTWARE PRODUCT (including but not limited to any images, photographs, animations, video, audio, music, text, SAMPLE CODE, REDISTRIBUTABLES, and "applets" incorporated into the SOFTWARE PRODUCT) and any copies of the SOFTWARE PRODUCT are owned by Microsoft or its suppliers. The SOFTWARE PRODUCT is protected by copyright laws and international treaty provisions. Therefore, you must treat the SOFTWARE PRODUCT like any other copyrighted material **except** that you may install the SOFTWARE PRODUCT on a single computer provided you keep the original solely for backup or archival purposes. You may not copy the printed materials accompanying the SOFTWARE PRODUCT.

4. **U.S. GOVERNMENT RESTRICTED RIGHTS.** The SOFTWARE PRODUCT and documentation are provided with RESTRICTED RIGHTS. Use, duplication, or disclosure by the Government is subject to restrictions as set forth in subparagraph (c)(1)(ii) of the Rights in Technical Data and Computer Software clause at DFARS 252.227-7013 or subparagraphs (c)(1) and (2) of the Commercial Computer Software—Restricted Rights at 48 CFR 52.227-19, as applicable. Manufacturer is Microsoft Corporation/One Microsoft Way/Redmond, WA 98052-6399.

5. **EXPORT RESTRICTIONS.** You agree that you will not export or re-export the SOFTWARE PRODUCT, any part thereof, or any process or service that is the direct product of the SOFTWARE PRODUCT (the foregoing collectively referred to as the "Restricted Components"), to any country, person, entity, or end user subject to U.S. export restrictions. You specifically agree not to export or re-export any of the Restricted Components (i) to any country to which the U.S. has embargoed or restricted the export of goods or services, which currently include, but are not necessarily limited to, Cuba, Iran, Iraq, Libya, North Korea, Sudan, and Syria, or to any national of any such country, wherever located, who intends to transmit or transport the Restricted Components back to such country; (ii) to any end user who you know or have reason to know will utilize the Restricted Components in the design, development, or production of nuclear, chemical, or biological weapons; or (iii) to any end user who has been prohibited from participating in U.S. export transactions by any federal agency of the U.S. government. You warrant and represent that neither the BXA nor any other U.S. federal agency has suspended, revoked, or denied your export privileges.

DISCLAIMER OF WARRANTY

NO WARRANTIES OR CONDITIONS. MICROSOFT EXPRESSLY DISCLAIMS ANY WARRANTY OR CONDITION FOR THE SOFTWARE PRODUCT. THE SOFTWARE PRODUCT AND ANY RELATED DOCUMENTATION ARE PROVIDED "AS IS" WITHOUT WARRANTY OR CONDITION OF ANY KIND, EITHER EXPRESS OR IMPLIED, INCLUDING, WITHOUT LIMITATION, THE IMPLIED WARRANTIES OF MERCHANTABILITY, FITNESS FOR A PARTICULAR PURPOSE, OR NONINFRINGEMENT. THE ENTIRE RISK ARISING OUT OF USE OR PERFORMANCE OF THE SOFTWARE PRODUCT REMAINS WITH YOU.

LIMITATION OF LIABILITY. TO THE MAXIMUM EXTENT PERMITTED BY APPLICABLE LAW, IN NO EVENT SHALL MICROSOFT OR ITS SUPPLIERS BE LIABLE FOR ANY SPECIAL, INCIDENTAL, INDIRECT, OR CONSEQUENTIAL DAMAGES WHATSOEVER (INCLUDING, WITHOUT LIMITATION, DAMAGES FOR LOSS OF BUSINESS PROFITS, BUSINESS INTERRUPTION, LOSS OF BUSINESS INFORMATION, OR ANY OTHER PECUNIARY LOSS) ARISING OUT OF THE USE OF OR INABILITY TO USE THE SOFTWARE PRODUCT OR THE PROVISION OF OR FAILURE TO PROVIDE SUPPORT SERVICES, EVEN IF MICROSOFT HAS BEEN ADVISED OF THE POSSIBILITY OF SUCH DAMAGES. IN ANY CASE, MICROSOFT'S ENTIRE LIABILITY UNDER ANY PROVISION OF THIS EULA SHALL BE LIMITED TO THE GREATER OF THE AMOUNT ACTUALLY PAID BY YOU FOR THE SOFTWARE PRODUCT OR US$5.00; PROVIDED, HOWEVER, IF YOU HAVE ENTERED INTO A MICROSOFT SUPPORT SERVICES AGREEMENT, MICROSOFT'S ENTIRE LIABILITY REGARDING SUPPORT SERVICES SHALL BE GOVERNED BY THE TERMS OF THAT AGREEMENT. BECAUSE SOME STATES AND JURISDICTIONS DO NOT ALLOW THE EXCLUSION OR LIMITATION OF LIABILITY, THE ABOVE LIMITATION MAY NOT APPLY TO YOU.

MISCELLANEOUS

This EULA is governed by the laws of the State of Washington USA, except and only to the extent that applicable law mandates governing law of a different jurisdiction.

Should you have any questions concerning this EULA, or if you desire to contact Microsoft for any reason, please contact the Microsoft subsidiary serving your country, or write: Microsoft Sales Information Center/One Microsoft Way/Redmond, WA 98052-6399.

Microsoft®
Internet Explorer 5
Step by Step CD-ROM

The enclosed CD-ROM contains ready-to-use practice files that complement the lessons in this book as well as the Internet Explorer 5 software. To use the CD, you'll need either the Windows 95, Windows 98, or the Windows NT version 4 operating system.

Before you begin the Step by Step lessons, read the "Using the Microsoft Internet Explorer 5 Step by Step CD-ROM" section of this book. There you'll find detailed information about the contents of the CD and easy instructions telling you how to install the files on your computer's hard disk.

Please take a few moments to read the License Agreement on the previous pages before using the enclosed CD.

Register Today!

Return this
Microsoft® Internet Explorer 5 Step by Step
registration card today

Microsoft®*Press*

mspress.microsoft.com

1-57231-968-2

Microsoft® Internet Explorer 5 Step by Step

FIRST NAME	MIDDLE INITIAL	LAST NAME

INSTITUTION OR COMPANY NAME

ADDRESS

CITY	STATE	ZIP

	( )
E-MAIL ADDRESS	PHONE NUMBER

U.S. and Canada addresses only. Fill in information above and mail postage-free.
Please mail only the bottom half of this page.

For information about Microsoft Press®
products, visit our Web site at
mspress.microsoft.com

Microsoft ® Press

Register Today!

Return this
Microsoft® Internet Explorer 5 Step by Step
registration card today

Microsoft·Press
mspress.microsoft.com

OWNER REGISTRATION CARD

1-57231-968-2

Microsoft® Internet Explorer 5 Step by Step

FIRST NAME   MIDDLE INITIAL   LAST NAME

INSTITUTION OR COMPANY NAME

ADDRESS

CITY   STATE   ZIP

(   )

E-MAIL ADDRESS   PHONE NUMBER

U.S. and Canada addresses only. Fill in information above and mail postage-free.
Please mail only the bottom half of this page.

For information about Microsoft Press®
products, visit our Web site at
mspress.microsoft.com

Microsoft®*Press*